MAKING A LIVING IN CRAFTS

MAKING A LIVING IN CRAFTS

DONALD A. CLARK

LARK BOOKS

A Division of Sterling Publishing Co., Inc.
New York

PATTI QUINN HILL. *Ancient Myths,* 17" x 13"
Cotton, archival paper, acrylic & metallic paint
PHOTO BY ARTIST

Frontispiece gallery image courtesy Brookfield Craft School

Opposite top: **MARCIA LAGING CUMMINGS,**
Follow the Yellow Brick Road. 9" x 8". Seed beads, bugles,
assorted beads. PHOTO BY ROGER BRUHN

Opposite bottom:
PHOTO BY JOHN WIDMAN

Editor: **RONNI LUNDY**

Art Director: **DANA IRWIN**

Cover Designer: **BARBARA ZARETSKY**

Assistant Editor: **SUSAN KEIFFER**

Associate Art Director: **SHANNON YOKELEY**

Assistant Art Director: **LANCE WILLE**

Art Production Assistant: **JEFF HAMILTON**

Editorial Assistance: **DELORES GOSNELL**

Editorial Intern: **DAVID SQUIRES**

Library of Congress Cataloging-in-Publication Data

Clark, Donald A., 1944-
  Making a living in crafts : everything you need to know to build your
business / Donald A. Clark.-- 1st ed.
      p. cm.
  Includes index.
  ISBN 1-57990-650-8 (hardcover)
  1. Handicraft--Vocational guidance. I. Title.
TT149.C58 2005
745.5'068--dc22

                                                          2005017769

10 9 8 7 6 5 4 3 2 1

First Edition

Published by Lark Books, A Division of
Sterling Publishing Co., Inc.
387 Park Avenue South, New York, N.Y. 10016

Text © 2006, Donald A. Clark
Photography © 2006, Lark Books unless otherwise specified
Illustrations © 2006, Lark Books unless otherwise specified

Distributed in Canada by Sterling Publishing,
c/o Canadian Manda Group, 165 Dufferin Street
Toronto, Ontario, Canada M6K 3H6

Distributed in the U.K. by Guild of Master Craftsman Publications Ltd., Castle Place,
166 High Street, Lewes, East Sussex, England BN7 1XU
Tel: (+ 44) 1273 477374, Fax: (+ 44) 1273 478606, e-mail: pubs@thegmcgroup.com,
Web: www.gmcpublications.com

Distributed in Australia by Capricorn Link (Australia) Pty Ltd.,
P.O. Box 704, Windsor, NSW 2756 Australia

The written instructions, photographs, designs, patterns, and projects in this volume are
intended for the personal use of the reader and may be reproduced for that purpose only.
Any other use, especially commercial use, is forbidden under law without written
permission of the copyright holder.

Every effort has been made to ensure that all the information in this book is accurate. However,
due to differing conditions, tools, and individual skills, the publisher cannot be responsible for any
injuries, losses, and other damages that may result from the use of the information in this book.

If you have questions or comments about this book, please contact:
Lark Books
67 Broadway
Asheville, NC 28801
(828) 253-0467

Manufactured in China

ISBN 13: 978-1-57990-650-4
ISBN 10: 1-57990-650-8

For information about custom editions, special sales, premium and corporate purchases, please
contact Sterling Special Sales Department at 800-805-5489 or specialsales@sterlingpub.com.

CONTENTS

INTRODUCTION

It all began on a quiet day in Lenox, Massachusetts, sometime in the summer of 2002. The daily shipment of new work had arrived at Ferrin Gallery, where I am a partner. There was something unusual and alarming about one of the packages. The loud rattling that came from it when the deliveryman set it down told me there was trouble ahead. The return address indicated the box had come from a new artist who was a recent graduate of a highly respected four-year art school. We had quickly sold this artist's small sculpture (the only piece we had) at a national fair and were anxious to present more of her work to our audience. Curiosity compelled me to immediately open that box, first, to find the source of the rattle, and second, to see the pieces sent for the next show.

It all began with the loud rattling...

The author, right, discusses a piece of woodfired stoneware with the artist, Michael McCarthy.
PHOTO BY CARINA KELLY

Well, pieces are just what I did find, lots of them, some small ones, and some big, each a part of what once must have been two very beautiful clay sculptures. The only other materials in the box were packing peanuts. Without the aid of tissue paper, newsprint, or bubblewrap, cardboard dividers, and inner boxes, these works didn't have a chance.

I was saddened by the loss of these beautiful objects and braced myself for the phone call to the artist. In the course of our conversation I learned that in the required curriculum of the school she had attended, there had been no practical classes about running a business (including the fundamentals of shipping fragile objects). As I repacked the box to take it to the dumpster (clearly, no insurance claim would be honored on this one), I was reminded that there are many kinds of skills required for successfully making a living in crafts. These skills run a broad gamut, from deciding where to live and work, to knowing how to pack your product to get it safely to market. They include the age-old act of one-on-one communication as well as high-tech information-age savvy. They require knowledge of production schedules as well as tax schedules.

As a shop owner, I often find myself answering questions for craftspeople about various facets of the business. "What can you sell this for?" is perhaps the most common. However, there are numerous other questions about marketing, including: decisions about printed materials, choosing fairs, placing display ads, and where to sell work. Then there are the production questions, including what items to make based on what's selling, or when to begin production. Sometimes the questions are even larger. Craftspeople just starting out may wonder where to live in order to maximize their potential success, and experienced artists at a new juncture in their career have many questions about changing or expanding their working situation.

There are colleges, classes, and workshops devoted to teaching crafts, and there are books that deal with marketing or office management skills. But there are few sources that deal with the full range of the complex issues that make up a successful life in crafts. And those that do exist seem to originate from the premise that the world of crafts will never change. In fact, it has changed dramatically in the last few years due to expanding technology coupled with increased access to the worldwide marketplace, and those changes require new information and fresh perspectives.

Thinking of this, I saw a place for a book that addressed the many questions a craftsperson will encounter over the span of his or her career. I saw a need for a book that explored the recent major changes in technology, the typical consumer's shopping habits and the effect these changes are having, and will continue to have, on our field. I have spent my life in the crafts world, and I have a life-

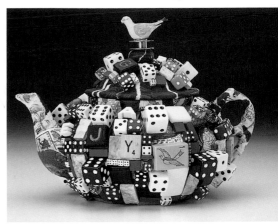

DONALD CLARK
Bird Tea
Assemblage on ceramic pot
7" x 9" x 6½"
PHOTO BY
MICHAEL COHEN

7

I decided to create a handbook for a life in crafts.

DONALD CLARK
Nature Tea #1
Assemblage on ceramic pot
6"x 8" x 6½"
PHOTO BY
MICHAEL COHEN

CRISTIN
MITSU SHIGA
Nebula Brooch
Sterling silver, enamel
and field grass
2⅛" x 2½" x ¾"
PHOTO BY
COURTNEY FRISSE

time of experience and information to share. So I decided to create just such a book, a handbook for a life in crafts.

I've drawn on the knowledge and skills I have acquired in each of the various crafts-related jobs I have worked over the past 35 years. In addition, I've developed a knowledgeable network of colleagues in many aspects of the crafts world, and I have tapped their intelligence and experience in writing this book. Sixteen conversations with crafts professionals in a broad range of fields are included, offering informed perspectives on the many facets of our profession. The result is a volume of time-tested, pertinent information about making a living in crafts from those who have actually done so. It is, in a sense, a network of wise and experienced colleagues gathered to share their wisdom with you as you make your living in crafts.

PERSPECTIVES FROM MY LIFE IN CRAFTS

I was born in the early 1940s, totally unaware of the important crafts-related events that were then taking place, events that began the diverse modern crafts movement we have today. My parents are working class

folks who had little information about the arts or things handmade and no money to bring them into my life. Nonetheless, from an early age, I was very interested in beautiful things. Then a miracle happened in junior high school: In the course of the eighth-grade arts rotation, I ended up in the classroom of Clara Skinner Guy. Clara, a friend until her death many years later, was an artist, and soon I knew I wanted to be an artist just like her. Through her introduction to the world of art and the artists who she knew, I realized that I wanted to go to art school, to work in my studio, and to use my creative skills to present my point of view through the objects I made.

When it was time to make real career choices, the ideas held by my practical-minded parents prevailed. Instead of following an art curriculum, I studied art education at the University of Bridgeport. For 15 years I taught; first, elementary art and then first and second grades. (It turned out that kids were much more interesting to me than art supplies.) Along the way I had the opportunity to teach traditional crafts classes at the college level.

Teaching allowed me to do my own work in the summer and during vacations. I was, and continue to be, fascinated by the process of assemblage and designed a line of products that used this approach. I built a totally unworkable booth (failure is a great teacher) and was one of the early exhibitors at the ACC shows in Rhinebeck and Baltimore. This let me satisfy my need to make things and at the same time support my family.

In the early 1980s, everything flipped. I left teaching and my family. I moved to western Massachusetts and, with a partner, opened a retail shop. I loved retail, but didn't love what I was selling. I soon sold my share of the shop and subsequently worked a number of jobs, including one as a traveling salesman representing a large giftware company. These experiences taught me about both retail and wholesale selling. In addition to selling in my territory, I was responsible for working in the company's booth at various wholesale gift shows, including setting up and taking down the booth. This gave me even more experience with both the mechanics and subtleties of selling at a show.

In 1989 I became a partner in both Pinch Pottery and Ferrin Gallery, where I continue. In this position I handle display for both a retail shop and a gallery. I buy merchandise for the shop and help select artists to be represented by the gallery. Each new show or shipment of goods needs to be unpacked and I am a part of this process. Work needs to be returned to artists after each show, and I often do this. A gallery prints a lot of materials, so I have a good working knowledge of publishing and publicity. I work actively in our two locations with our customers, learning about their very different motivations and needs. I have a job I love and one that has allowed me to see a cross-section of our field intimately. I have learned a lot about manufacturing and selling handmade items, and this book is my way of sharing this valuable information with others who, like me, desire to have a life making and selling beautiful work.

BUSINESS MATTERS

Art curricula do not typically address the business of art. There are good arguments for this. Students are in school to strengthen the creative abilities that will carry them through their productive lives, and a student's creative vocabulary should be developed without constraints. It is feared a business sense might compromise the students' aesthetics to conform to the demands of the marketplace. But, based on my belief that the sale of a work of art *completes* the creative process, I would argue that understanding the business of art is essential to a student's development, and certainly essential to professional survival.

The need for such practical knowledge isn't just the concern of the beginning artist. Throughout a successful craftsperson's career, questions will arise again and again about how to best approach the work and the business. Change is not only *inevitable* in our profession, it is *essential* to success. Sometimes it will come from the artist's need to expand creatively; sometimes from a need for the business to expand or adapt; and sometimes it will be provoked by innovations within the larger world of crafts.

> **Change is not only inevitable in our profession, it is essential to success.**

My intention is to provide useful information for people at all levels of development in the crafts field. In addition to the specific nuts-and-bolts sort of information this book provides, it is also my intent to offer suggestions for ways of thinking about your product, your business, and your craft that will continue to be valuable even as the world of crafts around you evolves in the 21st century. My ultimate hope is that here you will find the tools and information to help you enjoy a life in crafts as fulfilling as mine.

9

Interior of Ferrin Gallery, Lenox. MA. Artwork from left to right by Randall Diehl, Sergei Isupov, and Nanny Vonnegut. PHOTO COURTESY FERRIN GALLERY

BUILDING GOOD FOUNDATIONS

The minute you begin to think about making a living in crafts, it will seem there's a decision to be made at every turn. Established artists also find that even though they are well into their careers, circumstances may require a reassessment of such basic issues as where to live, what to make, and when and how to make it. Resolving these issues thoughtfully will build a solid foundation for your business.

Each decision you make will have an impact on those that follow.

In order to learn your craft, you may have gone through a formal program at a university or an art school, served an apprenticeship, or taught yourself by attending classes and workshops. Using your skills, craftsmanship, and creativity, you either have developed a product or have an idea for developing one, and you plan to start a business

The same attributes that you tapped to perfect your craft will help you succeed in business: creativity, passion, willingness to learn and hard work.
PHOTO COURTESY OREGON
COLLEGE OF ART AND CRAFT

to produce and sell it. Now what? You know you're an artist and that you will need to become a businessperson. The very same personal attributes you've used to get to this point in your craft will help you succeed in business: creativity, a passion for your craft, a willingness to learn, and hard work.

Figuring out what you're going to produce, what you're going to do with your product, and how to do it are among the first challenges. Then there's the issue of whether you're going to work from home or find an affordable workspace. Can you do the work yourself, or will you need to think about hiring employees? What else will you need in addition to your studio, materials, and tools? Each of these decisions will have an impact on the others, so it is important to consider them carefully and in the overall context of your life in crafts. These are questions you will want to resolve even before you think about the legal issues of setting up a business.

TO BE OR NOT TO BE?

This is the question: Will you make production items for shops and to sell yourself at fairs, or will you make one-of-a-kind pieces for galleries? It's a decision that will influence most of the other choices you make about your work and life, from the size of your studio to whether you work alone or with assistants. And while some successful craftspeople manage to do both production and one-of-a-kind work, most find they are more adept at one or the other ways of working and marketing their work. It will be helpful to determine which you are early on.

● Production Work

At its simplest, production work means developing items that you will make again and again, with or without variations. To be successful, you must create items with retail strength, which means the designs will be strongly

influenced by current consumer preferences. To be a successful production craftsperson, you must be willing to give up a good deal of latitude in terms of your artistic expression. In exchange, you will gain a more predictable marketing plan and production schedule.

To be successful at production, you must learn to find the joy in repetitive work. Joni Conrad Neutra founded and operated Madrid Earthenware in Madrid, New Mexico, from 1974 to 1992. Her successful production line of tableware grew naturally out of her artistic passion. She says, "The process of throwing so compelled me that I loved being constantly at the wheel. It was logical for me to become a production potter because that's where my passion was."

To be a successful production craftsperson, you must learn to find the joy in repetitive work.
PHOTO BY DAVID H. RAMSEY

11

A young potter explores the intricacies of throwing at Oregon College of Art and Craft.
PHOTO COURTESY OREGON COLLEGE OF ART AND CRAFT

There are many ways to find interest in production work. Jeweler Roberta Williamson (see page 24) says, "Maybe doing it over and over becomes boring, but I'm a counter. I like to count things, to see things lined up on the work bench."

You also will have to be strongly interested in marketing and selling your work, since the majority of production items are sold by the maker, either wholesale or retail. You will need to attend wholesale shows, and you also may show your work at retail fairs. You may decide to open a retail outlet of your own. Aggressive marketing is essential for the production craftsperson, and it will take you away from both your studio and family life. The marketing of your work will be as important as the creation of it. This is an important consideration.

Some successful production craftspeople have been able to minimize the amount of time spent away from cre-

Delight with texture and color inspires many production weavers to spend long hours at the loom.

ative work by hiring others to manage a storefront or keep the books. But even if you can find competent help in these realms, you will still need to be actively involved in the marketing of your work. A great part of the appeal of handmade crafts is the personal connection to the maker.

● One of a Kind Work

If constant creative stimulation and latitude of expression are very important to you, you may choose to focus on creating and selling one-of-a-kind items. You'll seldom repeat a piece, although you may work in a series as you explore an idea or respond to a self-imposed intellectual challenge.

One-of-a-kind work allows you to pursue your ideas, but the successful craftsperson in this field will need to have an abundance of them. You will need to be a person who enjoys the challenge of solving the problems that are a part of the creation of each new piece. In an interview for the Smithsonian archives, internationally acclaimed fiber artist Walter Nottingham described those challenges by saying, "There are two ways a craftsman can work. A craftsman can make an object by developing a technique and learning as much as he or she can about the technique, and then use that technique to make an object. But there's another way an artist can work, and many do. A craftsman can take an idea of an object and then create a technique to make that object." A high comfort level with exploring new territory is essential for the craftsperson interested in making one-of-kind work.

If you choose to create one-of-a-kind pieces, your work schedule may be erratic, particularly when compared to that of the production craftsperson. You may find yourself putting in long hours as you create a new piece or series of pieces. This intense work cycle could be followed by days, or maybe weeks, away from the studio while you recharge and prepare for the next work cycle.

MARKET RESEARCH
FOR PRODUCTION CRAFTS

If you plan to build a wholesale line, it is never too early to begin serious market research. In fact, the designs you devise for your production line should be strongly influenced by the demands of the marketplace. Careful attention to what you like to make and a strong clear focus on why you entered this field is essential as well. But to be successful today, production craftspeople need to be aware of the workings of the broader wholesale marketplace.

So how do you access the marketplace and determine the place of your product in it? I find it helpful to read home decorating, do-it-yourself, and fashion magazines and study relevant catalogs. You might want to tune in to HGTV or other mainstream cable shows on home, garden, and style. Craftspeople who make jewelry and wearable art can learn about coming trends by observing what stars are wearing on award shows and the major soaps. But the information you can gather by visiting one of the large wholesale craft, gift, or fashion-related shows is priceless.

in large factories, both in the United States and abroad. You can learn a great deal here since these are the products that are competing with yours for consumer dollars.

Large wholesale shows provide you with the opportunity to observe the current and potential trends that are driving the market and will drive it in the future. For example, if you spot a number of booths offering larger than normal mugs, make a note. If you see a

Wholesale shows provide invaluable marketing info, but any craft fair is an opportunity to learn something new about how to present your work.
PHOTO BY JOHN WIDMAN

To be successful today, production craftspeople need to be aware of the workings of the broader wholesale marketplace.

Wholesale Education

The wholesale show is a showcase for the new products that manufacturers hope to sell by convincing the wholesale buyers that the public will buy them at retail price. Unless a show is solely dedicated to representing handmade items, you'll be viewing goods typically made

color reoccurring throughout the show, make another note. The fiber artist might note the types of yarns and fabric being used. Watch for items that incorporate an overall conceptual theme. For instance, the number of companies offering upscale high-end items for pets, especially dogs, is rapidly expanding.

There are wholesale shows in all regions of the country. You can register as a guest for a fee on the day you plan to attend, or you can contact the promoter's office in advance and get a pass as a potential exhibitor.

Consider going to the show on its last full day when there are fewer buyers. Be sure to bring a notepad. Get a show catalog when you check in. Make note of the way the show is laid out—related products are often grouped together—make a plan for how you will see the show, and go to work.

about the lighting, the floors, how shelving is installed, and where they locate their show storage and office. Make note of visuals used to draw you into a booth and the props used to enhance the perceived value of the products offered. Notice the traffic flow into, around, and out of booths. You also might look at and collect printed materials.

Jill Pearson, a jewelry designer working in Los Angeles has a clear and practical approach to product development. "I often begin the design process by reviewing what has sold in the past and then apply those ideas to the pieces that will be the core of the new collection.

"The businessperson in me evaluates several factors: a) what has sold well in the past; b) what is happening in the marketplace in regard to fashion trends (i.e. color, length, size); c) what margins can be achieved; d) what

With a clear understanding of the marketplace you can educate your public about the value of handmade items

Be sure to look at prices, not only of other handcrafted work, but also of the mass-produced goods similar to your product. It's not that you can, or necessarily want to compete with mass-produced goods, but these are the items your customers will be comparing to your work. With a clear understanding of the broader marketplace you'll be better prepared to educate your buying public about the cost factors affecting the manufacture of handmade items in the United States and the value of purchasing them.

Although it's not the primary reason for your visit, spend some time looking at display techniques. The major wholesalers spend tens of thousands of dollars designing and building their booths. Learn from their successes and failures. You will want to make notes

materials are already in my inventory; and e) whether or not I have the manufacturing ability/capacity to meet the potential production needs.

"The designer in me contemplates things on a different level with different concerns. The questions these ideas pose cannot be quantified by statistics. 'Do I like it? Have I ever seen anything like it before? How does the piece make me feel?' These concerns do not revolve around cost, sales potential, or trends. To me, this is when I truly feel like I am designing. In the end, the development process is successful if my customers like it. Someone once told me that a 'Design isn't any good unless someone buys it.' I don't know if that's completely true, but if I can't sell it, then I'm in the wrong business."

If you are successful and receive several commissions in a short time frame, you may find yourself pushing your creative energies to the limit.

Similarly, your earnings also will come in bursts and droughts. Many one-of-a-kind craftspeople find it necessary to have a "day job" to pay the bills on a regular basis. One excellent solution is to find a teaching position that allows you a studio and some time to do your own work, plus keeps you active in your field.

The objects you make most likely will be consigned to galleries. You will have to build this market, first by searching for an appropriate gallery or galleries. (More information on this is in Opening the Gallery Door, page 106) Once you have found the proper representative(s) for your work, you will need to become an excellent communicator with them. Time at home will be spent writing about your work, why you do it, and what it means to you. You will need to make phone calls, send images, and often travel to keep your connection to the gallery viable. The romantic image of the one-of-a-kind craftsperson suggests that all you need do is follow your muse and then buyers will flock to purchase your visionary object. The truth of the matter is that you and your gallery will have to work hard and work together to build a market for your work.

FINDING YOUR PLACE

There are many personal and professional considerations that will have an impact on your decision about where to live and work. Everyone has particular needs, and you should determine what really matters to you. It can be helpful to write down what you want and need from the place where you live, with no judgment at first about what is of the most importance. (The list of a writer friend has both "a community of fellow artists for stimulation and advice" and "access to a good lap pool.")

Once you have made your list, you can then prioritize

your needs. When you consider possible places to live and work, you can consult this list to see how many of your criteria are actually met. Few places will satisfy all of your needs, but you will be able to judge more clearly if you are willing to do without certain things for the sake of others, and you will be able to make plans to compensate for what the place may lack. For example, an isolated rural setting may be ideal for your desire to have large blocks of uninterrupted creative time, but it's not going to meet your need for a network of other craftspeople in your field with whom you can share information. To compensate, you can join a professional organization with a strong Internet site that includes chat rooms for you to talk with your peers.

Take time to compare the benefits of living in an urban area with those of the country, and be careful not to romanticize either. A city can offer lots of convenience

Fork Mountain Road Studio, near the Tennessee/North Carolina border is nestled in an inspiring rural location.
PHOTO BY
DAVID H. RAMSEY

Ray Pierotti, designer of artistic window and wall coverings and freestanding screens, has the best of both worlds. His barn studio in rural Shellman, GA is for large pieces while his Atlanta studio space is for design and smaller work.

and stimulation, but that is useful only if you can afford to take advantage of it, and not be distracted from your work by too much going on. The countryside offers pastoral tranquility and great blocks of uninterrupted time for working, but you may find yourself spending a lot of time driving to town for supplies, entertainment, and such mundane tasks as shipping your work. It is important to think about these things in relation to who you are and how you like to spend your time.

● Cost and Quality

In addition to climate and geographic considerations, there are two other important issues to consider when deciding where to live. These are the cost-of-living and the quality of life in the potential location.

The cost-of-living numbers can be obtained by contacting the extension service of an area university, or by going to www.google.com and asking for the information for the area you are considering. There are two websites that are filled with information about the nationwide housing market. A listing of real estate being offered for sale can be found at www.realtor.com. This is a multiple listing site with information about thousands of properties. At www.domania.com you can find the actual prices paid for housing in the area you are researching.

A fellow craftsperson living in the area can be your best source of information about the quality of life there, both personal and professional. You also can go to the website of the local newspaper and read random issues chosen from the last year or so to get a sense of the place. Read the ads as well, and make sure to read the letters to the editor; they will give you a feel for the things residents value and have on their minds.

● A Creative Community

Is there a creative community in the area you are considering? Whether you're just starting out or are relocating, this may be an important consideration when deciding where you want to establish your business. Because

Russian-born, Chicago-based fabric artist Nina Krasikoff uses the rooftop porch of her urban studio to test how her clothing will move.

Communities with a vibrant art scene can provide you with plenty of creative stimulation. PHOTO BY JOHN WIDMAN

seem like an issue that's years away. However, even if you work alone now, it would be good to know that you could find help if you needed and wanted it. A nearby art or crafts school can be a source of skilled apprentices, or a local high school art department may be a source of students who could work part time. If it's possible, talk to a craftsperson in the area about this issue, or to another small employer about the availability of workers, the rate of turnover, and the expectations of the local job market.

At Ben Owen Pottery in Seagrove, NC, the sales gallery and working studio are combined.
PHOTO BY
DAVID H. RAMSEY

craftspeople typically work alone, it's of great importance to be able to interact with other like-minded people. There is practical information that you get from being part of a creative community, such as: Where did you get this material? Who did your web design? How do you make that? And then there's the stimulation of other creative thinkers that will help keep your creativity alive.

Communities with a strong arts scene can provide you with a ready-made market for your work and plenty of creative stimulation. They are usually aesthetically attractive places to live as well, but unfortunately, this can drive real estate prices sky high. You will have to decide if the higher price you pay to live in such an area is worth it. Or you may be able to find more reasonably priced spaces in an area near such a town, allowing you to access the benefits you derive from an art community without the high prices of actually living and working there. If you choose to live in a very remote area, be aware that travel, shipping materials in, or getting goods out can become a problem.

When planning where to live, you also may want to consider the availability of a trainable work force. When you're just starting out in business this may

ESTABLISHING YOUR WORKSPACE

Planning and setting up your studio is another opportunity to make lots of decisions. Studios are as varied as the creative people who need them and the media they use. Even so, there are some general concepts that apply to all workspaces.

The most important issue for any manufacturer—and craftspeople fall into this category—is the availability of affordable workspace. Some of us can work anywhere and under any conditions; others need to feel a stronger ownership of their workplace.

● Sharing Space

At the beginning of your career you may find it necessary to share a studio. Later, some artists choose to stay in a shared studio situation for the creative stimulation, as well as for the financial advantages. In a *FIBERARTS* magazine story on studios, Polish quiltmaker Bozena Wojtaszek explained why she continues sharing studio space with a colleague, even though the room they work in is very small. She said, "I share my space with another artist, my friend, who is a cross-stitcher. The

whole room is about 12 square meters. What makes it great for me? It's bright and friendly (sort of cozy). The small space puts some discipline on me: At some point I have to finish work in progress to make space for new projects. But the main factor is atmosphere. (My friend and I) are both working with fabric and threads, though in different areas. This is very stimulating—we never compete but always share our creative thoughts."

Sharing a studio early in your career can be an opportunity to find out if it appeals to you. You could join an established studio when one of the residents leaves, or you and a friend or friends could find a space and set up your studio together from scratch.

Joining an established studio can be financially advantageous since the basic bones of the place are already there. Generally, you only need to provide your own tools, pay for your work area, and you're ready to go. You also may benefit from working alongside colleagues with more experience. On the downside, you're moving into an already established community—even if it only involves one other person—and patterns of use and behavior have been established without your input. This means you'll need to be able to "fit in" to the existing situation rather than tailor-making the studio to suit you.

Starting a shared studio may cost more money and take time away from your work, but you and your studio mates can plan the space to exactly match your production needs, and create a workspace that pleases you aesthetically. The shared creative spirit of starting a studio with peers also may provide energy that spills over into your work.

● Home or Away?

If you decide to establish your own studio alone, you have to determine whether you're going to work at home or in a space away. In many areas of the country,

Metalsmith Mark Brown and quiltmaker Susan Boss of Boss/Brown Artists share studio space and ideas in Easthampton, MA.
PHOTOS BY CAROL LOLLIS

large former factory buildings are being converted into multi-use studio/small manufacturing spaces. These conversions result in spaces that are perfect for the craftsperson. As with a shared studio, you will find yourself in a workspace with other artistic people, but you will have control over your personal studio space and how you choose to use it. Some tenants of facilities such as this come together to form buying co-operatives for acquiring materials more economically, or may purchase expensive equipment jointly to be shared. An extra benefit to such places as these are seasonal "open studio" tours that establish the building or area as a source for both retail and wholesale buyers.

On the other hand, working at home may appeal to you for a variety of reasons—anything from family obligations to pure personal comfort. In addition, it's almost always less expensive to work in a space you already own or rent than to buy or rent another space. A home-based studio saves time—not to mention money—in transportation, and can provide more flexibility in regard to working hours. Many craftspeople find it appealing to alternate between work and home responsibilities in a day. But if you are more likely to be distracted by the life in your home, it might be best for you to commute to work, have a place just for work, and a schedule for when you will work.

Textile artist Jennifer Morrow Wilson of Little Deer Isle, Maine, reflected on the impact of her home life on her work, saying, "When my daughter was younger, it seemed like my creative work consisted mainly of rearranging my studio space. In fact, at one point, I considered documenting the process and exhibiting the photos as my work...I felt if I could just come up with the right arrangement, I could be more productive. What was really lacking in my studio life was time, not space, and as my daughter grew and I had more time—things fell into place for my own work to became a larger part of my life again."

Sharing space may also allow you to share the costs of more expensive equipment with fellow artists.
PHOTO COURTESY PENLAND SCHOOL OF CRAFTS

● Designing Your Studio

Whether you're setting up a home studio, or buying or renting a separate space, you will most likely need to alter that space to fit the production needs of your particular craft. The actual designing of your studio should be great fun.

Take the time to create the perfect workplace for you. Design it to match your lifestyle and your craft. One of the most important studio-design considerations is light, but the type of light you utilize should meet the needs of your craft. The natural light essential for the craftsperson working with color may not be important to the blacksmith. The extensive and expensive exhaust systems necessary for the woodworker may mean nothing to the weaver.

However, there are design elements that are common to every craftsperson's studio. Most important of all is to consider how you will be in the space. Do the many processes used in creating your work require you to move around? If not, you'll need to consider the ways you can change postures or take a break from repetitive movement. Plan a studio that will allow you to do some of your work sitting and some of it standing, allowing

LESSONS
FROM THE MASTERS

I have always been drawn to the work at home concept, and this has worked well for me thanks to the indestructible work ethic passed on to me from my parents. If you are strongly motivated and disciplined in your approach to your work, this can be a good choice for you, as well. However, if you're going to have your studio at home, I would advise you to be as Monet, not as Picasso. Monet created a very beautiful garden that separated where he lived from where he worked. Monet went to work, then came home from work to be with his family. Picasso, on the other hand, lived and worked in the same space within the same structure. Eventually his work life and his creations overran his large Mediterranean villa. In the words of Gertrude Stein, who knew him well, Picasso "is one who is working, one who is always working."

different muscle groups to rest and work. Make sure the stools and chairs in your studio are constructed for the use you plan to put them to, and that they're designed to protect your back. Always be sure your work surfaces are at the right heights, whether you sit or stand.

Plan for efficient and safe tool storage—you want to easily reach a needed tool. And always try to buy the best tools, even if you need to acquire them over time because of additional cost. Good tools do the job right, last longer, and using them is a pleasure.

LIVING A CRAFTS LIFE

Most of you have chosen to go into a craft business because you want a creative life that you control. Being in charge of your life's direction means that motivation and self-discipline are essential. You're the boss, and there are no imposed work hours. If you work too little, you won't have the goods to sell. If you work too much, you won't have a personal life. It's up to you to establish the work rhythm you need to lead a balanced life.

To discover your personal work rhythm, you may consider first serving an apprenticeship. An apprentice may be paid a small salary as well as be given workspace in the studio and perhaps access to material. Usually the work schedule allows the apprentice time each week to develop his or her own work under the watchful eye of a master. It can be time well spent honing your craft, as well as learning the ins-and-outs of a craft business. Michael McCarthy, who spent two years as an apprentice to master potter Mark Shapiro, has this to say about apprenticeships: "It is a full spectrum education; you learn about the lifestyle, as well as the craft, by going to work in someone's studio over a long period of time. This is best for the dedicated, confident, and committed person since you have to go to work every day, whether you're inspired or not. It gets you past any romantic notions you may have about the work."

If you can't, or choose not to be an apprentice, it's still a good idea to test the waters to discover the best ways for you to make a living in crafts. This is also useful if you are considering making a change in your already established career. When starting out, or trying a new method, don't over-commit yourself. You may want to start out slowly, going to only a few shows a year to see if this is what you really want to do and to test your line in the marketplace. You may think that it will suit you better to sell directly from a gallery at your studio, but before making that leap, try working in an established gallery part-time to see what this actually requires.

When you can't actually "try on" an aspect of work you may be considering, this is when it's time to consult your colleagues. Don't simply ask if they like having a gallery in the studio, or traveling to shows, but ask why they prefer one form of working or selling over another. Take into account the differences in your personalities and values when evaluating if their preference is akin to yours.

Working as an apprentice can teach you about the lifestyle as well as giving you the craft. Albuquerque jeweler Susan Skinner is pictured here with long-time assistant Erin Dengler.
PHOTO BY MARGOT GEIST

KNOW
THE CODE

Before you lease a space that needs alterations or even contemplate modifying any existing spaces, knowing the building code is a must. You may not want to contact an inspector until you know what you want, so don't initiate a specific inquiry prematurely. But you do need to know the local zoning laws and how they apply to what you plan to do.

Are you, for instance, even allowed to have a home studio in your neighborhood? If you're adding or extending a room, or putting in plumbing, or upgrading your wiring, what do you need to do to get a building permit? Do you know of any ease-ment restrictions? Some places prohibit the use of gas kilns in residential neighborhoods and make it nearly impossible to have a wood kiln; it also may be difficult to get permission for a glass furnace. (Many of these issues can be avoided by putting your studio in an industrial building.)

To find out what your local code says, visit the build-ing inspection office and ask for a copy of the munici-pal code restrictions. If you discover that something you want to do is prohibited by code in your area, you may be able to apply for and obtain a variance, but be sure to do so before you invest in any remodeling or equipment that is prohibited.

Ceramic sculptor Deborah Fritts created a spacious studio by modifying the carport of her suburban Atlanta home.
PHOTO BY DAVID H. RAMSEY

● Building a Network

One of the most useful tools for making a living in crafts is a broad network of helpful contacts. Your student years have already brought you into contact with fellow crafts-people, students, and teachers. It's always great fun to be in touch with other creative people who share your craft. What better way to figure out if this is the life for you than to talk to others who are living it? Developing a supportive network of other crafts professionals, including the press and suppliers, is a very valuable tool for building a business.

You'll find that the craft community is wide and welcoming. Your network will be the people with whom you share information about materials, new processes, good and bad gallery and shop owners, grants and fellowships, and opportunities to show your work. They may be people associated with craft schools, universities, or local art organizations.

Annual gallery walks/open house events are one perk to setting up your studio in an old factory area with other artists. PHOTO BY STEVE MANN

Being an effective networker doesn't mean you have to go everywhere and know everyone, but it does mean getting to places where other craftspeople gather so you can listen, ask questions, and share information. You can join a guild, subscribe to a trade magazine, or join in on Internet bulletin boards or forums. The latter is an exciting tool. We are the first generation to have access to a huge network without having to actually meet anyone in person or leave our homes. Be sure to use your new best friend, the Internet, as a source for answers to any questions you can imagine asking. (In addition, the Internet is a great resource for finding supplies.)

23

This opening reception at Bookworks Gallery in Asheville is a full cultural experience with a lecture and a performance by a band featuring the exhibiting printmakers.
PHOTOS BY JOHN WIDMAN

Perspective from a Life in Crafts
David and Roberta Williamson

(inset) **ROBERTA**
AND **DAVID**
WILLIAMSON
A Precious Gift
3" x 3" x ½"
Brooch of sterling silver,
tin, mother of pearl,
goldstone
INSET PHOTO BY
JAMES BEARDS
PORTRAIT COURTESY
MARY ENGELBREIT'S
HOME COMPANION

Roberta and David Williamson have been a professional craft producing team since 1982. The duo produces award-winning jewelry designs that are intricate, exquisite and whimsical. Living now in Berea, Ohio, where David is a professor of art at Baldwin-Wallace College, they met at Northern Illinois University in Dekalb where both were taking art classes. In this interview, they talk about their work process and their evolution as production jewelers.

You're both trained in ceramics, in addition to jewelry. When did you begin to make only jewelry?

Roberta: I started taking jewelry classes in college, and then Dave jumped in. We loved trying new techniques, so we taught each other. That was perfect because we could experiment with things together, and processes fascinated us. We'd go to the ceramics studio and do that work together, and then we were taking jewelry classes together, too. Then little by little we began to specialize. We were trying to be practical, knowing that it probably would be better if we each specialized in a [different] area. Eventually Dave got his master's in ceramics, and I got mine in jewelry at Virginia Commonwealth University.

So Dave was a potter, and I was a jeweler. But little by little, I lured him in. There were certain things I didn't want to do, like solder when I was pregnant. I kept saying, "Oh, Dave, would you help with this?" More and more he became part of the jewelry studio. The loneliness was definitely a factor for my wanting Dave in the studio.

David: I think of the practicality. When we would go to art fairs, trying to juggle a ceramics booth and a jewelry booth just got to be too much.

I think of you as artists who are running a business that has grown and evolved, and you have developed the skills necessary to be successful.

Roberta: Yes, I think that we could see that there was a lot of potential in the jewelry area. It just seemed like what we were doing was really clicking with people. We did do art fairs in undergraduate school, but it really clicked when we were in graduate school. Since we didn't have any money, it was a necessity to figure out how to have an income to pay for food and every-

thing else, so we started doing art shows. We got in so much trouble in graduate school. It was horrible! The teachers thought we were really selling out by selling our work at an art fair.

David: I think they thought it would interfere with the development of our creativity [if we were designing by] thinking for the market and trying to make things that would have an appeal to the average customer, and even letting selling enter into the design aspects or creative part of what we were doing. They felt that you should just make it and not worry about the consequences of selling or not selling. But I think that goes against the craft tradition of making things that will be appreciated and possibly used by people of all different income levels who have an appreciation of craft.

Roberta: We would do these little art shows that we just loved doing, because we would get feedback from people, and it was exciting because we made enough

ROBERTA AND DAVID WILLIAMSON
White Dots
3½" x 1¾" x ½"
Brooch of sterling silver, antique dice, painted tin, mother-of-pearl

ROBERTA AND DAVID WILLIAMSON
I could hear a gentle stir
3" x 2¼" x ½" each
Sterling silver, crystal, antique paper, citrine, mother-of-pearl, wood, tin, antique pin, bark, buttons, glass
PHOTOS BY JAMES BEARDS

The Williamsons create "display environments" for their work, and this series of brooches is displayed in an antique butterfly specimen box.

ROBERTA
AND DAVID
WILLIAMSON
*When I Was a
Ladybug Child*
4" x 2¼" x ½"
Brooch of sterling silver,
crystal, paper, tin,
rutilated quartz, peridot
PHOTO BY JAMES BEARDS

money to buy food for a few months. What was wonderful was that the faculty then started coming to look at these shows we were doing, and then they started doing them too!

The feedback that we'd get (from browsers at the shows) would really help us to develop our way of thinking, like realizing we did need to do production things. Customers would say a bigger, one-of-a-kind, piece was too expensive, but they really liked the work. We would think, well, we can't afford our work either. That's really what's driven the production work, so that people who might not be able to purchase a big piece could buy things, too, and enjoy them.

We've always felt that production work took equal weight with our other work because it was really important to do things that people could appreciate and want to own. The one-of-a-kind pieces were important for our creativity. However, the production work is also a real creative challenge: to do something in quantity, keeping the price down, but still create something people would love to own.

It sounds to me like you start thinking about pricing a piece when you're drawing it.

Roberta: Right. From the very beginning, as people told us, "Oh, I like that, but I can't afford it," we just began thinking that way. It's just out of necessity, so that we could sell things. As we're working, and the piece isn't even done, I'll say, "Well, Dave, do you think $600 is too much?" And then, he'll go, "No, it should be $800." We're discussing it the whole time we're making it.

It's also about ego. We've always been more about pricing so the work will sell so that we don't feel bad. You go home without selling anything, and you think, "What's wrong with me? Why doesn't anybody like my work?" But it could have everything to do with what it costs. If you're going to put yourself out there to sell, you have to think about the price right from the beginning; otherwise you could be just feeling really bummed.

Another little thing I've learned: you have to offer things that are cheaper so people will [initially] engage with your work. Eventually they will build up to buy more expensive pieces.

And then when you get to the shows you have a fabulous booth. Are your booth displays always different?

Roberta: We try to make them different each time because, for me, that's the fun. I love the jewelry work, but I love the displays even more. So we really begin thinking about that even while we're doing the work. Typically, we have our shelf sizes cut out and laid on our living room floor, and we're making things and installing them as we make them. So the display, just like the pricing, is happening from day one. There's no throwing it together at the end.

David: We're putting this little production together, and the drama takes place from the first day as it begins to develop. I think it's really exciting to see this thing grow from these empty pieces of paper sitting on the living room floor to actually putting the pieces in (their display shelves).

How do you work together?

David: We go over the pieces again and again, and there's no ego involved. We've always said what's most important is that the work be as strong as it could be, and so you have to let the ego go.

Roberta: The craftsmanship is so important to us that we're very critical of it. We pass each piece back and forth as we're working on it. I do a lot of the sawing, because I've done it for so many years, and I'm so efficient at it. I also do most of the sanding and preparing, and then I'll hand it to Dave for, say, a soldering technique. He'll hand it back to me for clean up. I'll hand it back to him for the next soldering step. We sit at a table across from each other, and every piece goes back and forth, so we're continually critiquing one another. Every single piece is equally inspected and worked on by both of us.

We're so lucky to have one another, because I think when you're an artist working on your own, it's hard because of the isolation and the uncertainty. And I think it's so fortunate when you can have someone to bounce things off of and a partner, not only in life but also in your work.

David: I'm thinking about the honesty and the effort that goes into design, and the way we pass the work back and forth. It's really just the way things work for us: We're in it together. From the moment we get up in the morning, we begin to think about and plan the day and our work schedule. During the fall work cycle, when you've got beautiful days and are working seven days a week, it's an integration of eating, laundry, taking care of the yard, and the studio work. This is why we try to plan to make time for all the different things that happen, so that we don't leave our life on the doorstep. I think it takes some real cooperation to make everything function, not just the studio work but our life also.

Roberta: This is something that I always felt from the beginning: You don't need an elaborate studio; you don't need incredible equipment; and you don't have to wait for that moment when everything seems perfect, because it will never be perfect. You just have to jump in and make do. When we didn't have tools or money to buy silver, we just made stuff out of twigs. You find a way to make the work without excuses. You just jump in and make it, and if you work at those ideas, no matter what materials, and what equipment you have, you can make incredible things that people will love. Don't be afraid. Just start working and learning, being open to learning and making work that is rewarding to you. The business part will follow.

Perspective from a Life in Crafts
Beth Mueller

BETH MUELLER
Clockwise from top

Platter
23", ceramic
PHOTO BY BOBBY HANSON

Happy Vase
7" high, cast earthenware
PHOTO BY GLENN MOODY

*Cows After
A Hard Day*
5' high, ceramic
PHOTO TOM HODGE

Circus Teapot
10" high, ceramic
PHOTO BY
MICHAEL BELENKY

Candelabra
14" high, ceramic
PHOTO BY
MICHAEL BELENKY

Beth Mueller is a successful studio potter working in northern Vermont. She sells her work through wholesale shows, primarily the New York Gift Show. She talked to us about the life of a production craftsperson.

What led you to become a production potter?

Beth: I studied art in college, and I made one-of-a-kind objects like you are encouraged to do. Yet I have always loved functional objects. I grew up in southern Indiana, in a very rural community. We had simple beautiful things—farm crocks and quilts—and now my work is an honest reflection of the simple things I love.

In the beginning I did everything the hardest way I possibly could. I made all my own glazes and threw all my own pottery on a manual kick wheel. Everything was completely handmade. There is a small part of me that admires sculptural pieces. I would try to do them and got some satisfaction, but when I got right down to it, it just wasn't me.

I think you are drawn to things that you find lovely and that's what you can put your heart and passion into making. However, the marketplace always tempers my choices. I have to make a living. If I were making things that I thought were beautiful and no one else did, I'd have to change a bit.

Were there considerations, other than the financial ones, that influenced your decision to enter the wholesale market in a serious way?

Beth: I did retail shows for quite a while. When I was in my twenties it was really fun to travel around and meet new people, but after a while it got to be wearing. I wanted to be home. Now I do two wholesale shows that are the serious part of what I do. Every once in a while I do a retail show, but that's not the focus of the business.

Your pieces are cast. Do you have helpers in the studio?

Beth: Originally I was doing absolutely everything. Then the demand got too big for me to handle. First I incorporated my husband into the business, and then we brought in a guy to do the packing because it was pretty easy to train someone to do that, and then we brought in two more people to do certain parts. I still do all the painting. I'm now at a point where I can't delegate anything else unless I change everything I do.

How do you develop new product?

Beth: It's pretty organic: I get ideas for imagery all year, and I make notes and sketches. We make a clay model and then a mold. If I get an idea that I think is great, I'll just stop and do it; that's what makes it interesting for me. My husband is very good at mold-making so it's not a big deal. I don't have a set time to do product development, but I do set aside time to make new samples.

What do you think attracts buyers to your product?

Beth: People need something to latch onto. What I'm doing is not that hard to understand. They see "Friend" on one of my bottles and think, "I need a gift for a friend; I'm going to get that, and I think it will make them happy." I think we can get caught up in making what we feel is beautiful just out of our own desire to create. There has to be a market, unless you want to line them up in your house. We have to make something that connects with the rest of the community and fills a need.

What's your approach to accounts that are past due?

Beth: We always call and check credit references, but as careful as we are, we still occasionally have an account that doesn't pay. What am I going to do? I just keep going. What I have working for me is that my work sells quickly, and we won't ship additional product until we get paid.

You have 150 to 200 accounts. How would you describe the growth process of your business?

Beth: For me it grew organically. In the beginning I would get a $300 order and think, "Oh yeah, I'm going to be busy for a whole month." I grew as the demand grew and I figured out how to do it. Because of the way my work is made, growth is limited since I am doing the painting on each piece.

You and your work were featured in *Country Home* magazine; how did you feel about that?

Beth: When I was in art school I would never have thought that would happen. Why would a magazine be interested in what I do unless it was *American Craft*? That's my part of the world. It's interesting to find how much everything seems to be crossing over and mixing up. It's not so narrow.

WRITING A PLAN

A Any new venture promises exciting and almost unlimited opportunity. You will want to keep that enthusiasm as you pursue your dream, but you also will want to get it right. Getting it right means becoming familiar with good economic practices and planning your business accordingly. Many talented people never realize the dream of making a living from their craft because they aren't prepared to handle the issues involved with running a small business. You don't need to let this happen to you. This chapter will provide the information you need to get started on a solid business path, and will direct you to places and organizations that can help you along the way.

Getting it right means learning good economic practices.

Running a small business well requires commitment, planning, and good organization.

PHOTO BY JOHN WIDMAN

YOUR BUSINESS PLAN

The business plan is one of the most important tools you can provide for your business. It will help you focus and prompt you to analyze your ideas by forcing you to define your business and products. It's also an essential tool for any craftsperson planning to seek a bank loan.

Once you have established your business, you'll find the plan will be an essential management tool. You'll refer to it when you're checking your progress, to see if you're meeting your goals. It also will help you stay focused on your business budget. Each time you begin to develop a new product, your business plan will be your guide. Does the new item fit the plan? It also will help you decide if you have the money to develop the new product and whether you'll be able to make a profit from it. And finally, the business plan is the key that opens the door to borrowing money from banks, government agencies, and private investors.

Anytime you approach a lending institution for a business loan, they'll ask to see your business plan. It's not only a means of communication when going for a bank loan; it can help you when you approach any funding agency. Your chances for an artist's grant will increase substantially when you present a business plan as part your application. Private lenders, even family and friends, will feel more confident about lending you money if you present them with a well-written plan.

Lenders see many business plans in the course of a year. A disorganized or sloppy business plan will speak volumes about your ability to start and run a business. Your job is to take your ideas and goals and put them in a format that's easy for lenders to read and understand. Fortunately, there is a standard format that outlines the information you need to include.

● Writing the Plan

A typical business plan has four parts, beginning with a cover sheet that has your business name (see "Making a Name for Yourself" on page 36) and logo, if you have one. Then there's a table of contents, followed by the plan itself, which is a narrative backed up by appropriate charts. The well-crafted business plan ends with any necessary support materials, including leases, tax returns, resumes, etc.

If the process intimidates you, begin writing your business plan much as you would sketch a new design. Jot down ideas. Write out how you see the business today, then five or ten years from now. Set down what you want out of the business. How much profit do you want to make each year? What will your income help you do? Where will you work, and what equipment do you need?

At this stage, don't censor yourself. Write it all out, put it aside for a day or two, then go back and refine it. Keep working on this verbal sketch until you feel it fairly presents your business and what you want for yourself and your business in the future. This will become your core information. Now, using this refined sketch follow the guidelines below to expand and format the information you already have.

● *General Description*

First, you need to set forth a general description of your business. If you're in the planning stages, state just that. If your business is already functioning, discuss its current situation, including products, employees, and financial strength. Include your projected timeline for beginning the business or implementing the proposed changes. Discuss how you got going with this business and lay out your short- and long-term goals.

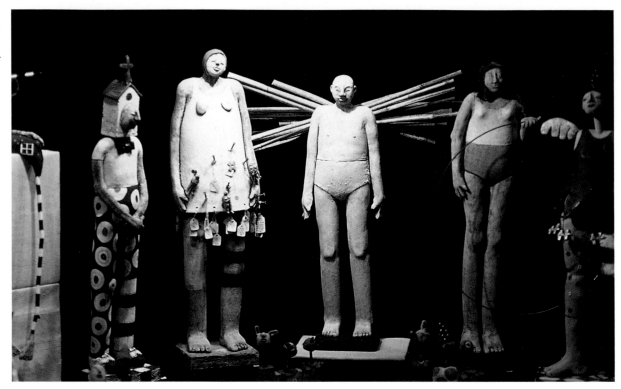

Craft fair display of various art dolls by Nancy Kubale-Wicker of Rutherfordton, NC.

● *Introduce Yourself*

You'll want to devote adequate space to clearly establishing who you are, including your education, skill level with the materials you use, and related work experience. The goal of this is to reassure yourself and to convince others that you can run this business. Spend time formulating a clear and strong statement of your craft philosophy, including the connection between it and your business. If you're going to present your business plan to a bank, be sure to include references to your involvement in your community, including clubs, volunteer work, committees or board work, etc. Banks like to support people who support their community.

This section also should include at least three thoughtful personal references. These are not about the business side of you; they're about you as a human being. They can come from a friend, a religious leader, a person from a team you play on, a fellow student, or any other person who knows you well and can describe your attributes.

● *Detailed Description*

This section describes your business in detail. Begin with a discussion of the products you make, including information on how you decide to include items in your line. Present any market research you did to support salability of your product. In this section, it's important to address the competition you'll face in selling your products. Discuss whether it's from other craftspeople or larger manufacturers, either here or offshore. Use any documentation that supports your findings. Follow this with your plan for counteracting the effects of this competition. This could mean better designs, better control of production costs, and, of course, better marketing.

Your marketing plans should go in this section. Present your selling plan, including the types of shows you will attend, both wholesale and retail. Do you intend to work with a sales representative or offer your products on the Internet? Include information about your potential customers: who they are, their core characteristics, and why you believe they need and will purchase your products. End this section with a simple explanation of the processes you use, as well as the machinery and materials needed to produce your products.

● *Location*

You'll need to explain where you will locate your business. You want to document the availability of potential employees and materials. This is the section where you'll describe the space you'll use for your production and its costs. Spell out the attributes that make the space suitable for your business. For instance, does it have a freight elevator and receiving and shipping facilities? If you're altering an existing space and have sketched plans or blueprints, include them.

● *Projected Business Costs and Personal Finances*

At this point, it's time to turn your attention to financial matters. You will need to account for three major areas of expenditures:

● Your fixed expenses, including rent or mortgage payments, insurance, office supplies, loan payments, phone, and any payroll that is not related to production, such as a bookkeeper or an accountant.

● Your production costs, including materials, production-related payroll, and utilities.

● Your marketing costs. These range from show entry fees to photography-related expenses. They also include the cost of advertisements and travel, hotel, and food expenses related to doing shows.

When you balance this information against your anticipated income, you come up with a very simple profit-and-loss profile. This is all you need at this point. This relationship of expenses to income will determine whether you are, or will be, able to run your business profitably. Finish this section with any documentation of your financial strength by including income-tax forms and bank statements.

● *Funding*

The last component of the business plan deals with the amount of money you'll need to begin or continue production. Begin by identifying your start-up costs for studio space, manufacturing equipment, materials, and office supplies. Document the funds you have in hand from accumulated profits and previous investments in your business. Then discuss where the additional needed funds will come from. Legitimate sources include your family or spouse, private investors, and, of course, the bank.

Good photography can make or break your career.

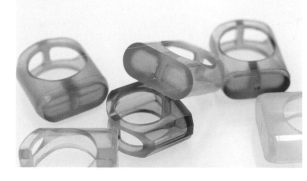

MIKIKO MINEWAKI
Lighters
1" x 1" x ⅓"
Rings of disposable lighters
PHOTO BY MIKIKO MINEWAKI

33

LOUISE FISCHER COZZI
Sophie Necklace
1½" x 16½" x 3³⁄₃₂"
Polymer clay, paint, pencil, leafing pen, telephone wire
PHOTO BY GEORGE POST

AASE HAUGAARD
Bowls
Left: 5⅛" x 5½";
Right: 5⅛" x 6 ¹⁄₁₆"
wood, terra sigilata slip

GOOD THINGS TO KNOW

THE CRAFT ORGANIZATION DIRECTOR'S ASSOCIATION

The Craft Organization Director's Association (CODA) is an association that supports the work of crafts administration professionals of state, regional, and national crafts-related organizations. In a groundbreaking survey done in 2001, CODA was able to verify that the making and selling of handcrafted objects has significant value to the economy and that craft is worthy of investment and support. The findings of the Craft Industry Economic Impact Survey include the following facts:

● There are over 100,000 craftspeople working in the United States.

● Gross sales average, per craftsperson, is $76,025.

● The impact of craft sales is $12.3 to $13.8 billion per year on the economy, about one-third the volume of shoes purchased in the USA.

● Median household income of craftspeople is $50,000 per year.

● Direct retail accounts for 52.9 percent of annual sales, with just over 50 percent sold at craft fairs.

● The average craftsperson derives 27 percent of annual sales from wholesale and 11.2 percent from consignment to galleries.

The survey also found that the median age of people who make their living in crafts is 49; that 79 percent of them work in a studio located on or in their residential property; that 78 percent are members of a crafts organization; that 64 percent work alone; 18 percent work with a partner or family member; and 16 percent work with paid employees.

CODA hopes the survey will provide evidence to government and business leaders that the crafts industry is not only thriving, but actually spawns cultural tourism and overall community progress. The organization fur-

ther hopes that this data will inspire state and local leaders to provide assistance to working artisans, and will encourage the promotion and advancement of this portion of our country's entrepreneurship.

For more information about CODA and details about ordering the 70-page survey report, go to www.craftassoc.com.

SMALL BUSINESS ADMINISTRATION

The United States Small Business Administration is a powerful resource tool for the craftsperson wanting to become a business owner. For nearly 50 years SBA has been offering technical and financial assistance in starting up a business, assistance in managing a business, and recovery assistance in the event of a disaster. There is also information and training designed specifically for women.

SBA can teach you what a business plan is, and how to write and use it. It can teach you how to raise capital, borrow money, and how to manage the financial operations of a business. The SBA can also train you in the basics of marketing your craft, using such tools as trade shows, eMarketing, signage, and ads.

A free small business startup guide is at www.sba.gov/starting_business/startup/guide. This is a three-page detailed roadmap with everything you need to know. The site includes several links to other supporting resources, including a calendar of training seminars for each of the 50 states.

SERVICE CORPS OF RETIRED EXECUTIVES

The Service Corps of Retired Executives (SCORE) is a non-profit organization that uses the experience and knowledge of retired businesspeople to provide free assistance to new or inexperienced small businesspeople. The organization consists of over 10,000 volunteers and 389 chapters across the United States. Since its inception in 1964, SCORE has provided over six million small-business entrepreneurs with professional resources and information, one-on-one business counseling, workshops, and, most recently, a website (www.score.org).

SCORE's user-friendly website provides a number of resources, including a business "tool box," testimonials from recipients of SCORE's assistance, a listing of chapters in the United States, important business news, and a learning center containing various categories of information about small-business practice.

Free and confidential SCORE counseling services also are available through Ask SCORE, an online communications tool that allows you to ask specific business questions, such as how to develop a business plan, and to receive answers via e-mail. Counselors are assigned who are qualified to assist in specific areas, with assistance sometimes given at a SCORE office, or even at your business location. Go to www.score.org for more information.

ASSOCIATION FOR ENTERPRISE OPPORTUNITY

Businesses with five or fewer employees, that require no more than $35,000 in start-up capital, and that have difficulty accessing traditional commercial banking loans are exactly the kind of businesses the micro-enterprise development industry wants to help. The Association for Enterprise Opportunity (AEO) represents nearly 500 of these micro-enterprise programs in the United States.

Some of the core services offered include business training and technical assistance, access to credit, and consultation services. From start-up, to funding, to expanding, the AEO programs are favorable to crafts artists. The association stays in contact with its members through its website, newsletters, and listserv.

AEO believes small business are integral to the national economy and focuses on traditionally underserved populations facing barriers because of race, gender, ethnicity, income, job market fluctuations, and location. More information can be found at www.microenterpriseworks.org.

35

Felter Beth Beede at work in her Northampton, Mass. studio.

RAE DUNN
Mr. Wong
10" x 8" x 2"
Stoneware, oxides
and engobe
PHOTO BY
CHARLES INGRAM

● Making a Name for Yourself

Your name will identify your business and be one of your most important marketing tools. Over the years you'll invest money and time developing name recognition for your product; therefore, it's important to think through the ramifications of the business name you choose. If you're making one-of-a-kind objects this is less of an issue since you will likely use your own name. It can be good to use your name for a production business as well. People like to know and buy from the maker. However, what if you decide to sell your business, or take on a partner? Bill Smith Weaving is no longer an appropriate name when Joan Murphy joins as a partner, or buys the business. On the other hand, you don't want to confuse loyal customers with a drastic name change. Consequently, having a name for your business that is not owner/artist-specific can be a boon in changing circumstances.

When choosing a name for your business other than your own, it's important to avoid being too vague or too specific. I believe it's also important to keep a name short and simple. The best names give some clue to the nature of the business, for instance, Fireborn Pottery and Blackthorn Forge. However, keep in mind that your successful business will grow and change, and you will have to adapt the name, or compensate, to reflect that change. For example, The Clay Pot in Brooklyn began as a pottery shop, but now has one of the largest collections of handmade wedding bands in the East. The original name reveals nothing of this major product line, and the owners had to advertise extensively to get the word out about their wedding-band business.

In another instance, three women potters began a business in 1979 and called it Pinch Pottery. Several years ago the remaining partner and I enlarged the store's product mix. We felt we were limiting our customer base because shoppers who were not looking for pottery passed by. So we eliminated "Pottery" from the name and renamed the business P!NCH. This name change kept the positive associations of loyal customers to the original business, but has resulted in a much broader customer base and a stronger business.

Once you're on the track of a name for your business, it's important to make sure your choice is "clear," meaning it's not being used by anyone else. You can do a search for registered names in two places. You can contact the U.S. Patent and Trademark Office at www.USPTO.gov, or you can contact the Secretary of State in the home state of your business. Once you have confirmed that your chosen name is clear, it's important to register it with your Secretary of State's office. This procedure varies from state to state so you will want to contact your local office for the specific details.

Perspective from a Life in Crafts
Bonnie Laing-Malcolmson

Bonnie Laing-Malcolmson has been the president of Oregon College of Art & Craft, Portland, since 2000. Previous to joining OCAC she was the executive director of Paris Gibson Square Museum of Art, Great Falls, Montana. She has also served on numerous professional boards and committees and continues to make craft and artwork. She talked to us about the role of the college in teaching how to make fine crafts, and how to make a living at it.

Tell us about Oregon College of Art and Craft.

Bonnie: I think Oregon College of Art and Craft is somewhat different from some of the other crafts colleges and schools or workshop situations around the United States in that we combine both a degree program and a really extensive, far-reaching studio school program. Our mission is to promote excellence in crafts and ensure continuity of contemporary craft for perpetuity. In addition to the students in our degree programs we had 1,200 adult students last year who took classes and workshops. Some are very serious, practicing professional artisans who are coming to work with the top people we bring here, and some of them are people who are just getting their feet wet. We have had people who have taken numerous classes in our Studio School; our non-degree, non-credit program.

The Bachelor of Fine Arts degree program is designed to be sequential so that students are really working through different ways of learning how to use materials. Artists/craftspeople have carefully designed the classes so that the student grows both in skill and concept. We have a crafts history class, along with classes on how to use materials well. We also discuss how ideas influence design and form. To make strong craft work, you have to combine the technical and the conceptual. We think it's important that craftspeople have a world view and that they can write well. It's especially important that they understand other cultures because so much craft comes to us from indigenous peoples in other parts of the world. Craft is rooted in culture, and it's the way cultures express themselves.

We also want students in our BFA program to be exposed to more than one medium, so students choose an area of concentration, and they work in one or more secondary areas. And we also have marketing and production classes in all our programs.

What kind of marketing classes are you offering?

Bonnie: First of all, you get professional working craftspeople as instructors who, from the very get-go, talk about professional practices. They show by example studio practice, and exhibit practice, and what artists/craftspeople do. Students in their third year are required to take a professional practices class that includes basic law for artists, copyrighting, and many other business concerns. It includes information about bookkeeping, doing your taxes, and how to get a business license if you want to start your own business. We talk about bank loans and the different ways to get started. We talk about putting your work together to present it to galleries and museums, and how you enter craft shows and fairs. We bring in a series of visiting lecturers who are experts in each area. We also have a class that we call "production design," and in that class students talk about and put together a body of work that has a theme. They have to produce a certain number of objects that are all related and to do a kind of mini-business plan. They design business cards, logos, and stationery. They put everything together so that they have a production package. The students also have to write an artist's statement as part of that class.

Practical matters, such as pricing work and packing it for shipping, are often neglected in traditional art curricula. Do you address these issues at OCAC?

Bonnie: We really know about that. We bring in gallery people and then our gallery and gift-shop manager, and his preparers do a couple of sessions on packing and shipping and what you can use and what you shouldn't use. It's very detailed. You have to pay attention all the time, and you must be professional about every aspect of what you do. If your work is going to be beautiful and finished, then the way you package it has to be beautiful, finished, and safe. We talk about those kinds of things. And I think that it's important that people learn all of that. It's certainly different than it was 20 or 30 years ago in art education. Faculty are thinking about what students will do when they get out, and trying to give them a head start. What you want to be, and how much money you can make at it are things we try to discuss realistically.

Isn't it also important to talk about how to do it most efficiently?

Bonnie: We do in the production-design class, we definitely talk to students about things like that; for example, we say, "okay, how long does it take you to make this? If you make a prototype, can you produce the rest of them? It might take you two weeks to make a prototype, but then once you have the prototype perfected, can you then cast the rest of them and make 150 more in two days?" Those are the kinds of things we talk about, as well as, "Is this going to work?" A lot of the critiquing that happens gets people to think again about problem-solving. And in production, it's a different kind of problem-solving than it is in making unique objects. You have to think of the whole thing. In the production class, in the very beginning we think about the object, about what the object looks like, about how it's going to be packaged, how people are going to like the packaging, and what is going to seduce them into buying this thing.

How do you see the role of institutions such as yours in bringing an appreciation for American handmade objects to a broader segment of the population?

Bonnie: That's a good question. We try to reach as many local people as we can. We have a pretty active exhibit program where we show mainly crafts, and more than 20,000 people a year visit our gallery. And then our students graduate from here and sell their work around the United States and the world. We also advertise nationally. And we also have a very intensive children's program that serves over a thousand children a year. It brings them on campus, and we try to support it with almost 20 percent scholarship funding. Our summer camp brings in around 800 children, and then we have another couple hundred or so who take teen and children's classes during the school year. It exposes young people to a craft environment. It lets them get their little fingers wrapped around making things with metal, clay, wood, fiber, and paper very early on. And while our children's camp is going, our regular workshops and studio school are going on, so they're also walking past top professionals from the world who they see making things around them. They're also in an environment where there is fine craft everywhere, and that is really great. Since the people who are teaching are primarily students from our degree program, it provides them their first teaching experience, and let's them see whether or not that's something they're really interested in. It certainly introduces the children's parents to crafts they might not have been exposed to in the past.

What kinds of students do you seek, and what are the characteristics of a successful OCAC student?

Bonnie: Having a strong work ethic is important for any studio artist. Successful students will be extremely dedicated and want to work with their hands. It helps if they also are interested in learning as much as they can about the world and the humanities and the social sciences. Having a very strong work ethic is important for any studio artist . My ideal student would be open and optimistic with an attitude that

says, "I'm going to work really hard at this; I'm going to have fun doing it; I'm going to try to do it the very best way I can; and then I'm going to go on."

What do you think is the future of the crafts field?

Bonnie: I tend to be optimistic. I think today there are more sales venues and more people who are educated enough to understand that handmade objects are special and unique. I think there's the ability to have real growth in the crafts field. I see more and more interplay between the craftsperson and the public. I certainly see that interplay around the college with people who are on our board of trustees, and with people who come to see us, and in the reception that we get when we go out into businesses and show them what we do. We do a presentation with slides, and sometimes, actual objects, and people are really blown away.

But I'm concerned that from kindergarten through high school there is not enough craft education, and I think that's a real problem. It's a lot less expensive and easier to pull together crayons, pencils, and paper than it is to have potter's wheels, looms, metal equipment, and woodworking tools, but we have a deficit in craft education in the K12 schools in the United States. Some students never got to touch clay when they were in school, not once, and that's too bad, and that may be why our average age here in our degree program is 27. When you see the quilts of Gee's Bend and you know that the people made these things in the beginning, and probably still, in abject poverty, but they sang and sewed and made things that are as beautiful as a Mark Rothko. That's amazing. Making things builds community; that's the way the world should be. Making things with your hands makes you happy.

Making things with your hands makes you happy, what a perfect ending thought.

MAKING IT LEGAL

Your business has a location, a name, and a business plan. Now you need to attend to legal matters. These will not only keep you out of trouble, many of the records you will need to keep for tax purposes can also help you run your business in a smart and efficient fashion. But first, you must decide the legal structure that will best serve you and it.

LEGAL STRUCTURES

The legal structure of your business determines how you will report and pay your taxes. There are three major structures: sole proprietorship, partnership, and incorporation, and there are three forms of incorporating.

Good financial records also help you run your business in a smart and efficient fashion.

Determining which is best for your business is a major decision, and it is a good idea to discuss this with your accountant or attorney. What follows are general descriptions of the choices that you have.

● Sole Proprietorship

Among small craft businesses, the most commonly used of the three major legal structures is the sole proprietorship. This structure is for a business owned by one person, or a husband and wife who have not incorporated their business. With a sole proprietorship, you pay quarterly taxes and self-employment tax for Social Security and Medicare. The income or loss generated by the business is reported in Schedule C of your individual tax return.

The major benefit of a sole proprietorship is that you do not have to pay the costs of incorporation, the annual corporate fee, or file annual corporate reports. The major drawback is that taxes are reported on your individual return and may be paid at a higher rate than that paid by a corporation. Further, your personal assets have no legal shield, meaning they are not protected from creditors seeking payment for debts incurred by your business.

● Partnership

Multiple business owners who have not incorporated can form a partnership. Owners of a partnership must file Form 1065, which documents the partnership's return of income. Partners are not employees and are not given W-2 Forms. In addition, they must issue a K-1 Form stating the percentage of ownership for each partner. This form is then filed with the individual's tax return.

Each partner pays taxes on his or her distribution share even if the money stays in the business. Conversely, each may claim their share of any losses the business may incur. As with the sole proprietorship, the partners must pay quarterly taxes and self-employment tax for Social Security and Medicare. The clearest advantage of a partnership is that it provides a legal business structure for two or more unrelated people that will protect each of their interests without the formality of incorporation. The biggest disadvantage is that each partner is responsible for the total debt the business may incur.

● Corporation

Many people choose to incorporate their businesses because of the broad protections corporations can provide. When you incorporate, you're creating a separate legal entity that takes on a legal life of its own as a result of the Articles of Incorporation you will file with the state in which your business is incorporated. By adding this layer of legal distance between you and your business, you're protecting your personal assets from other entities that will interact with your corporation. However, there's a price to pay.

There are incorporation fees and more complex laws for reporting taxes. There must be an annual meeting, and minutes must be kept. Since incorporation is the most formal and complicated legal business structures you will definitely want to seek the assistance of an attorney if you decide to incorporate. An attorney will provide information about the types of corporations, help you choose the form of incorporation that best serves your needs, and guide you through filing the necessary papers in the home state of your business.

● C Corporation

This is the most common form of incorporation. The C Corporation has the greatest tax-reporting responsibility since the Internal Revenue Service sees it as its own entity for tax purposes. A tax return must be filed for the C Corporation, which pays the lowest tax rate on retained profits. The structure of a C Corporation makes you an employee, just as if you worked for any other corporation. You will report the income you draw from the business on your own individual tax returns. The expenses for most employee benefits are fully deductible when filing the corporation's taxes. Since you are an employee, you will only pay the employee's portion of Social Security and Medicare taxes, while the corporation pays the rest.

● S Corporation

The major difference between a C and an S Corporation is that an S Corporation is not seen as a separate entity for tax purposes. Owners must claim any income the business generates on their personal tax forms. This is called the flow-through method. The legal status of a C Corporation, which provides reduced personal financial obligations, results in most people choosing to form a C Corporation or perhaps a Limited Liability Company.

● *Limited Liability Company (LLC)*

The owners of a Limited Liability Company, or LLC, can choose the method for reporting income for tax purposes. They may choose the flow-through method described for the S Corporation, and report income on their personal returns and file Form 1065 just as in a partnership. In addition, owners file a K-1 Form. An LLC operating this way has no federal tax liability but may have to file in its home state. Alternately, the owners may choose the entity taxation method. Under this plan, just as with the C Corporation, the IRS sees your business as a separate taxpayer.

FILE IT!

A basic fact of business life is this: You are accountable for taxes, and that means you must keep good files.

A beginning filing system should include separate folders for each payable account you have, for example, each material supplier, all utilities, advertising-related expenses, and rent or mortgage expenses.

In addition, you will need to document your income. You can do this with careful record keeping of all deposits made into the business account. In addition, it is useful to note two items on your copy of each invoice for goods shipped: the number of the check used to pay it; and the date the check was deposited into your business account.

There are several excellent software programs available that can help you set up a simple bookkeeping system to track your income, accounts payable, inventory, and payroll. However, even though you may do all your bookkeeping on your computer, you must always have hard-copy receipts to prove any expenditure.

Careful consideration of your short- and long-term business goals should inform your decision about how to incorporate. The advice of a good small business attorney and/or an accountant can be invaluable when making this decision.

TAX IDENTIFICATION NUMBER

An essential part of completing your legal structure is getting a tax identification number. It has two purposes. First, it's much like a Social Security number for your business, and you will use it as identification on all tax-related documents. Second, a tax identification number entitles you to buy materials at wholesale prices and not pay sales tax, since sales tax will be assessed when you sell the finished product. The office handling tax collection in the home state of your business issues these numbers.

INSURANCE

It's advisable to insure your office equipment, tools, materials, and any completed product stored in your studio. You'll also want to consider coverage for your booth, furniture, and products while traveling to and from shows as well as while they're at a show. If there's any chance your product could hurt someone (and in our current legal state of mind there probably is), product-liability insurance is a consideration. Most of this coverage is available in a blanket policy designed to protect small businesses. Talk to your colleagues, however, to see if there are specific insurance needs for your type of work, and for recommendations for a reputable insurance agent who has worked with businesses such as yours.

You certainly want to provide health insurance for yourself and your family, and you may want, or even be required by law, to offer health insurance to your employees. Health insurance is increasingly expensive and difficult to obtain. The cost continues to spiral out of control, and making the right decision can be quite complicated. Because you're a small business with few, if any, employees, other than yourself, the costs are even higher and the product more difficult to get.

Typically, small business owners find it necessary to join some sort of organization that offers a group plan to its members—this means paying a membership fee, but it may be well worth it. By doing a quick Internet search using the keywords "insurance for self-employed crafts-people," I was able to access several different websites that offered helpful insurance information directed at small craft businesses. In some states, the local Chambers of Commerce are considered a legal group for this purpose and can facilitate lower monthly premiums. It's worth checking with your local Chamber.

HIRING HELP

Deciding whether to hire employees is always a dilemma. Besides determining if your business can afford the additional cost, you have to ask yourself if you're ready to be a boss. Look at your production routine. Just because there's more work than you can do, it may not be time to hire help. Perhaps you can plan better or purchase equipment that will make your work more efficient. There may be parts of the process you can outsource. It might actually make sense to turn down orders to keep your business small and manageable, particularly if you are not comfortable being the boss or sharing your workspace and regimenting your work routine.

If you do decide to hire, you'll need to factor the costs into your budget, including the employee's hourly wage, the employer's (your) contribution to Social Security and Medicare, the cost of additional tools, and possible costs for health insurance, vacation time, and sick days. As part of the process of deciding to get help, it's impor-

tant to know how much additional production will be necessary to pay each new employee. If you determine you have enough extra work to pay a major part of a new salary, you can probably sell a bit more product and safely move ahead.

● Employees

The most common type of help is an employee. In theory an employee does what you tell him and does it your way. This person files a W-4 Form with you, and you deduct income taxes and the employee's share of Social Security and Medicare from her paycheck. You pay the employer's portion of these taxes and provide the employee with a W-2 Form stating the amount paid and the deductions taken during the year. This form must be given to the employee by January 31 of each year. You also may choose to offer other benefits, negotiated at the time of hiring, that may require payroll deduction. The employment code also requires a new employee to provide evidence that she is allowed to work in the United States; this could be a Social Security number, a green card, or a U.S. passport. You must report this information to your state employment office.

Just because there's more work than you can do, it may not be time to hire help.

● Independent Contractors

The other kind of helper is the independent contractor, who works much like a freelancer. Independent contractors work for themselves and sell you their services by the hour for an agreed-upon hourly fee, or by the project for a specified sum. Typically they use their own tools and work in their own space. You set the deadline for having the work finished and back to you.

When working with an independent contractor, it's essential that both of you know exactly what you'll get from the other. Note the word "contractor" in the title. This implies a contract between the two of you. While a verbal agreement can be legally binding, an unwritten agreement can be misunderstood easily by one or both parties. A written contract doesn't have to be formal, but can be a simple letter outlining the specifics of the job and salary and signed by both parties. A simple but good contract will specify what you will pay for the satisfactory completion of the work, give a clear description of the work required, a deadline for completion of the work, and an explanation of what compensation, if any, will be paid the contractor if the completed work is not satisfactory.

With an independent contractor, you pay nothing toward any taxes and provide no benefits. However, you must provide the contractor a 1099 Form by January 31 of each year stating the amount you paid him the previous year. You will include a copy of all 1099s you issue with your taxes. The independent contractor pays all of the taxes related to this income, including quarterly tax payments based on estimated annual income.

Be warned: If independent contractors work in your space, use your tools, and work a regular schedule, you have established that they are employees and the IRS requires that they be treated as such. In other words, under these conditions an independent contractor becomes, in fact, your employee, and you are required to pay taxes for him or her accordingly.

PLANNING AFTER START-UP

In the early stages of putting your business together, you made a business plan that helped you determine how to make a living from your craft. Now that you have passed that hurdle, it is time to formulate a financial plan that will ensure that you are keeping accurate records of your expenses and income. Ongoing financial records are essential for tax purposes, but this also will help you be sure that your financial reality is on track with your income projections. Note that you will make adjustments as you go along.

● Financial Aid

Your financial plan will include a number of helpful tools. For expenses, you'll want one spreadsheet to monitor production costs, including materials, another to track overhead expenses, and another for marketing expenses. These costs are described fully in the chapter, "The Pricing Game," page 50. Another spreadsheet will monitor income and where it came from; for example, sales or teaching.

The expense sheets should be set up to give you monthly numbers that can be available by the first week of the following month. Careful monitoring of the costs of materials will reward you with more profitability on your product. You always will want to get three comparison prices on each component of your product. It is important to research new sources on a regular basis. Talk to your major suppliers about ways to cut costs, such as buying in quantity or taking advantage of seasonal price swings. In addition to price, however, you will want to consider reliability, quality of the materials, and past service history. Regularly scheduled inventories of the materials you have on hand will allow you to buy appropriately, avoiding any unwanted overstock, or being without an item when you need it.

● Accounting for It

There are two accounting methods for recording and reporting the financial activities of your business. The first, and most commonly chosen, is the cash method. With the cash method, you report income in the year that you get it, and you deduct expenses in the year that you pay them. With the second, the accrual method, you report income in the tax year it is earned, even if payment is received in another year. The IRS doesn't care which method you choose as long as you stay with the plan you have chosen. If you decide you want to change, you must ask permission from the IRS to prevent any double-dipping on expenses.

A good bookkeeper will help you avoid financial complications. A professional bookkeeper is the first help I would seek, regardless of how small the business. The bookkeeper will keep track of all accounts receivable and accounts payable, will handle payroll, and will prepare reports for your accountant to file tax returns. As part of the accounts receivable work, she will provide an accounting of the money you are owed, who owes it, and how long it has been outstanding. The bookkeeper also will prepare a list of accounts to whom you owe, noting how long the account has been outstanding and allowing you to determine who should be paid when.

● Tax Matters

Your tax responsibilities will vary depending on whether you have employees, if you are incorporated, and where your business is located. A good accountant is essential to determining what you must pay at the federal, state, and local levels.

In most states, there are sales taxes to collect and pay. You must collect the appropriate sales tax on any item you sell in the state where you sell it, and pay those taxes to that state. (If you sell to an out-of-state buyer and ship the goods, most states do not collect sales tax on such, but check with the state treasurer's office to be sure.) You are required to collect and account for sales tax in the host state of any show or fair. It is your responsibility to get an ID number for any state in which you do business, and to follow their guidelines for collecting sales tax. Most show producers have this information available for their exhibitors. Lately, as states have been struggling

CRAFT
EMERGENCY RELIEF FUND

The Craft Emergency Relief Fund (CERF) was founded in 1985 in order to provide financial and educational support to craft artists in the United States. The goal of CERF is to foster and maintain the careers of crafters, as well as protect the cultural and economic benefits that crafters bring to communities in the U.S. The services provided by CERF include emergency relief, business development assistance, and advice on safety and insurance.

CERF founders were inspired to create the organization after observing great generosity in the craft community. Craft-fair exhibitors often "pass the hat" to collect funds for fellow crafters in need of emergency aid. Founding CERF as a non-profit organization was an attempt to direct, build upon, and encourage this natural desire among crafters to help one another.

Since it began making loans in 1987, CERF has provided assistance to hundreds of craft artists by lending over $500,000 in direct funds and over $250,000 in services, including waived craft-show fees and discounted or donated equipment and supplies.

A recent survey conducted for CERF found that 30 percent of the respondents had no fire or product liability insurance and that 18 percent had no health insurance. Cornelia Carey, executive director of CERF, noted that of the craftspeople applying for assistance from CERF, 60 percent do not have a blanket policy that includes disaster or product liability coverage, and 31 percent have no health insurance. CERF is currently trying to remove barriers by helping craftspeople understand the importance of being insured and by helping the insurance industry understand the needs of the working craftsperson. You can get more information about CERF at www.craftemergency.org.

with federal budget cuts, they have become aggressive about collecting this money, no matter how small the amount might be. The rules for filing vary from state to state, so be sure you have the right information for each.

● More Help

You may wish to engage a payroll service if you have employees other than yourself. You will report each employee's hours, and this service will issue paychecks drawn from your account. In addition, they will prepare all the forms needed for paying all state and federal taxes related to employees, and will prepare W-2 Forms in January.

You may want to establish a line of credit. This is a loan that is not a loan until you draw on it. The bank, or lending institution, authorizes you for a certain amount and issues checks to you that you may use at any time for any amount (sometimes there is a minimum) up to the maximum you are allowed. Interest only begins to accrue when you write a check, and you only owe what you actually use. In other words, if you are authorized for $25,000, but only write checks totaling $5,000, that $5000 is the amount that accrues interest. Even if you don't like the idea of borrowing, a line of credit is a good thing to have for unexpected crunches or opportunities. Say your best client suddenly wants to triple their annual order, and you are short of cash for materials. Your line of credit can get you over the hump and into the profit zone.

You will want to plan for retirement. Nearly everyone is eligible for an IRA or a 401k of some sort, and your accountant is your best source for helping you decide what plan works for you and your situation. For information, you also can visit www.401khelpcenter.com online. As your business grows and prospers, you may want to consider offering some sort of retirement options for long-term employees. This is the sort of perk

that will help prevent too frequent turnovers, even if they pay part of the deposit themselves.

● Go with the Flow

The information generated by your bookkeeper should be used to generate another form to track monthly cash flow. Begin by entering the cash on hand at the beginning of the month. To this number, add your anticipated income for the month based on product that was invoiced last month and which will presumably be paid this month. Then subtract your overhead costs. Next, subtract your estimated production costs based on the items you plan to make in the month at hand, and any marketing costs expected in that month. The number before you is your bottom line, the report on the financial status of your business for the month.

Your bottom line has to be a positive number if you are going to make money. If it is a negative number, it is time to look for places to cut expenses. Perhaps you can eliminate a planned ad, or delay printing a mailing or find a way to print it at less cost. If you know the cash shortfall is temporary, you could take less income for yourself in this month. However, it is not a good idea to continually lend your business money in the form of reduced compensation. Likewise, it can be tempting to cut the hours of your employee(s) a bit for the month and work longer hours yourself. But if your employees can't depend on working regular hours, they will soon be looking for another job.

One way to help ensure that your bottom line is positive is to be aggressive about being paid in a timely manner. Delinquent 30-day accounts should receive a letter when the amount is 45 days out; a first phone call at 55 days; and a second phone call at 65 days. At 90 days, you should send a certified letter demanding payment within five days. Notify the account that you will send the bill to a collection agency if it's not paid by the date specified.

Perspective from a Life in Crafts
Wendy Rosen

Wendy Rosen is the founder of The Rosen Group, the leading craft show producer in America, and the author of Crafting as a Business. *I asked her to tell us about intellectual property in the new global marketplace, and this is what she wrote:*

Time and again, I hear artists say, "I won't sue someone who steals my design; I'll just design something new. I'll head in a new direction."

This is probably the most dangerous position to take when your business assets are at stake. Good design and new creative ideas truly are the most valuable assets any artist has. In fact, equipment, talent, and acquired skill all follow in importance after an artist's ability to craft a strong, yet unique, design.

Find that concept doubtful? Simply look at the number of successful artists at any wholesale craft show: You will find that the top selling pieces have been around for a decade and are often the backbone of the business. Creating new best sellers is not easy. Great ideas and solid designs are rare, and chances are you can't come up with a new best seller overnight. It can sometimes take eight or 10 years to hit your next hot concept.

This foundation of a successful craft business—distinctive, good design—is also what makes artists the target of international crime. It's true! Glass blowers and potters all across the country are being observed by large retail chains, foreign manufacturers, and their design scouts, because of their ability to quickly adapt to market trends, to come up with fresh designs, and their understanding of local and regional tastes.

Scouting For Originality

Unfortunately, artists are not often approached by scouts and asked to sell their designs to the companies the scouts work for. More frequently, design scouts legitimately enter a trade show, where they can observe, photograph, or take notes on interesting designs to be copied. Or they may buy a piece of work only to turn around and ship it overseas for reproduction. These scouts do their research at some of the largest international trade shows, targeting small companies, which are least likely to legally protect their design rights if they are under threat.

47

Because entering these large international trade shows is so easy and because the number of small family businesses is so plentiful, there is little to prevent authentic designs from literally walking out the door. Design scouts have, unfortunately, become so good at their jobs that they can quickly walk by a booth, assess the marginal designs, hone in on the best-selling items, and leave the booth with a catalog or photo of exactly what they plan to recreate and resell for less. With cell-phone cameras it couldn't be easier.

One more piece of discouraging news: Even once successfully prosecuted, design scouts and knock-off companies experience minimal penalty. If a big-box retailer begins carrying a knock-off craft replica and is required by a judge to stop carrying the item, frequently these "seconds" will be sold to another chain store outside of their area. This means your replica art object can hop from the U.S. to Canada to Europe, all in the blink of an eye and without putting a dent in anyone's business other than the artist's.

Thus, some of your favorite mega-chain stores have organizational structures and business strategies that encourage and support the idea of stealing designs and ideas. In fact, some of these companies have even changed the job title of "Product Designers" to "Product Scouts." This new job title often doesn't appear on business cards.

Preventing Knock-Offs

Eliminating the risk of design infringement is impossible. However, there are many simple steps artists can take to limit the likelihood of their designs being stolen for overseas reproduction.

First, create delicate designs that can't be easily replicated in a mold. Sometimes, details do make all the difference.

Second, copyright your surface designs, especially those that are "drawing like."

Third, use great hangtags that clearly state "Handmade in America" or "Proudly Made in North Carolina, USA." Referencing where your work is made can be a point of pride, a sales feature, or a way of differentiating your authentic handmade item from the cheap replica made in Asia.

Fourth, make the purchase more personal. Tell consumers about yourself, include a photo of the artist in the studio, or even an image of your family or your pets. Foreign knock-off companies are looking to make money quickly, not duplicate your whole story.

Fifth, combine your skills and work across two mediums. The likelihood of your work being knocked off goes down when the amount of equipment and skill required to create your work goes up.

Sixth, do only tradeshows where show management is willing to support design integrity. Do your show research beforehand. You will likely find that while most show management companies won't remove copies from the show floor, provide you with defense advice, or punish exhibitors who are obvious and recurrent "counterfeiters," there are some that do. Seek these shows out!

Seventh, encourage your professional membership groups and trade show managers to create arbitration committees so that you don't have to sue to get knock-offs of your work off shelves, or off the show floor.

Eighth, keep the business cards of each and every person you give a catalog or postcard to. Write the date and show or city where you exchanged the card for a brochure. Design scouts are rarely shy, and they assume you will be too busy to document the meeting and contact information.

Ninth, ask wholesale show managers to keep your brochures on file so that they can quickly identify exhibitor applications that include knock-offs. Expect more than just sales from your trade shows.

Knocked-off... Now What?

If you have had your original designs stolen by a foreign company, there are several steps you should take immediately:

1 Call a lawyer and purchase a "Cease and Desist" letter. Don't let the attorney act for you without your approval and an estimate of time and cost for every action, letter, form and call. (They'll tell you that they don't work that way, but most will.)

2 Design infringement cases can run into fees of $100,000 or more if you aren't in control. If you do receive a bill that is higher than expected you can hire a professional to audit the bills. Keeping costs in line is the difference between satisfaction and disaster. Art studios can easily fall into bankruptcy from high legal bills alone.

3 The Department of Commerce's Intellectual Property Division suggests that you register your designs with Customs in addition to your regular copyright registration with the Library of Congress. Once knocked-off you can submit a simple letter of complaint which Customs will use to create a "Customs Block," allowing the government to seize the knock-offs at the port of entry. Registered designs receive top priority. Don't be shy about contacting the Intellectual Property Division of the U.S. Customs office at 202-572-8710.

Ensuring the Future of Craft

Most counterfeiting and consumer deception come from the simple act of removing a paper sticker that states "Made In China" (or elsewhere). It happens at retail fairs and in small gift shops, where owners and employees often don't know that they are committing a criminal offense.

Since 2002, the Rosen Group has been researching and lobbying members of Congress to enforce the full intention of the Trade Act of 1930 which requires "Country of Origin Labeling in a permanent and indelible manner."

Business competition, whether at retail fairs, trade shows, or local boutiques should be honest and fair, not deceptive. Retail store shelves should be filled with a variety of products, not deceptive copies with fraudulent promotional hangtags and labels that prevent consumers from making an informed decision.

As China's manufacturing strength grows, Congress becomes more and more interested in helping small businesses, like craft producers, to address these issues. Artists, gallery owners, and others who support this issue are encouraged to write their senators and congressional representatives. Remind them that every time a consumer is duped we lose some of the value, integrity, and authenticity of American crafts that artists and retailers have worked so hard to achieve.

To aid in this effort, the Rosen Group branched out to found the American Made Alliance in 2005. A trade association intended to present legislative topics of interest to the arts community, the American Made Alliance also seeks to bring Washington up to speed with issues affecting the arts entrepreneurs. You can find out more, add your name to the list of community supporters, find sample letters, or read personal stories submitted by artists and galleries at www.americanmadealliance.org.

THE PRICING GAME

Determining the right price for your product is one of the trickiest, but ultimately most important, parts of running a successful crafts business. Consider it a serious round of "The Price Is Right" without Bob Barker there to help you. Unfortunately, many production craftspeople wait until their product is finished to decide how to price it—this is a sure way to lose the pricing game. If you want to win, you have to consider pricing during every step of development, whether you're making an individual piece or creating a whole line. There are actually two pricing games, the more complicated, but rational, one is for the production craftsperson selling at shows or stores. The process for the one-of-a-kind artist working with galleries is more intuitive.

THE RULES OF THE GAME

We'll begin with four rules designed to help you win the production pricing game. These rules are also helpful guidelines for the one-of-a-kind craftsperson to consider.

● Rule 1: Know the Price Before Going to Market

As the owner of a store that sells crafts items, I'm repeatedly asked to help determine the price for an item based on what I think I can sell it for. I always turn this back to the craftsperson, asking what it needs to sell for to earn the maker a profit. All too often, when the crafter begins to look at what it costs to produce the item at this late stage, she discovers she has spent so much time, or invested so much in materials, that there's no way the item

You have to consider pricing during every step of the development.

could sell for enough to cover expenses, let alone make a profit. There's little customer interest in $100 mugs or $/5 placemats. While salability is ultimately the deciding factor in the viability of an item, the time to consider this factor isn't when it's being presented to the buyer, but much, much earlier in the process.

● Rule 2: Do Your Product Research

Pricing considerations need to begin even before the first sketches are made, and it's essential to work this problem starting from the consumer's standpoint. All product development must begin with accurate assessments of the consumer's perceived value of the item being designed.

You'll want to do plenty of product research before you begin the design process. First, make an index card for each new item you're considering for your line. Allow room on the card for the item name, production and decorating descriptions, prices, and the source of the data. Then go shopping with your index cards in hand. To collect data on items similar to the one you are making, visit craft shops, department and specialty stores, and the better discount stores. Don't forget to look on the Internet! Note the lowest price and the highest price you can find and try to determine what's influencing them. For instance, are precious materials, time-consuming techniques, or the fame of the maker contributing to a higher price point? Are lower prices dictated because an item is of poorer quality or is less attractive? Armed with this information, you can return to the studio and begin the other end of the process: designing and producing your item so it can compete in the marketplace. Remember that you don't have to meet or better the lowest prices you have found if you can offer more value in a way that can be clearly understood and appealing to your customer. You must be confident that you can produce an item at a price the consumer will find attractive, both aesthetically and price-wise, or you will not be able to run a profitable business.

Can you produce the item for reasonable cost? New Orleans jeweler Thomas Mann at work.
PHOTO COURTESY THOMAS MANN

● Rule 3: Base Your Retail Prices on Your Costs

This one is quite simple: The only accurate way to determine profitable retail prices is to base them on accurate costs. Therefore, all pricing considerations must begin with the careful accounting of all production costs, including, not only materials, but the time you have spent on production of the piece, as well. There's more specific information on how to determine your costs in "Setting Your Price" (next page).

It's essential to first consider price from the consumer's standpoint.
PHOTO BY JOHN WIDMAN

● Rule 4: Avoid Pricing Too Low

Be aware that it can be counterproductive for you to take less than a suitable retail markup for your work. Underselling yourself, so to speak, can be a very costly game to play. There may be strong initial interest in your product if it's less expensive than that of your peers, but you will lose money in the end if you need to produce a quantity of items that you've priced too low. (Also be aware that underselling other craftspeople won't win you many friends in the craft community.)

A more complicated problem is the perception you create with customers if your price is too low. Discriminating shoppers tend to believe that you get what you pay for. If your price is notably low compared to the market, your potential buyer may suspect that the item is therefore of poorer quality than comparable, higher priced work. Pricing right for the market avoids this sort of misperception.

SETTING YOUR PRICE

Now that you know the rules of production pricing, how do you begin? First, create a Simple Costs sheet for each item you're developing (see page 179). This sheet should be designed to accommodate two categories of information. You need an area to list the materials involved in making a single item and its cost. Then you need an area where you can record work time and calculate its cost. Since many items require more than one work session, be sure to allow enough space to enter multiple work times. You should plan to bill this time at your hourly rate even if an employee will eventually do this work. (You bill at your rate in anticipation of perhaps doing the work yourself. It's

also how you make money on the items produced by employees.) Multiply the number of hours worked by the hourly rate to get the total amount billed for each task.

When you have done this process a number of times, and have developed a clear sense of the market, as you look at the projected costs on the worksheet, you may begin refining the process to reduce them. Is gold going to be too expensive for the market you have observed? Then consider making jewelry in silver or copper. Does this process require too many hours? Then look for a different means of production that is less labor intensive.

Once you have these costs determined, enter the figures on the Pricing Sheet (page 178) in the appropriate places.

● Overhead and Marketing Costs

Many craftspeople make the mistake of thinking that material and time are the only factors to be considered in cost. They are not. You will need to determine your overhead and marketing costs as well.

Determine your overhead costs by using an Overhead Inventory sheet (page 177). Fill in each line in the expense column with one of your overhead expenses. Overhead expenses are the costs of running your business, and they include monthly rent, or mortgage payments and property taxes; health and business insurance; debt and loan payments (both interest and principal); utilities; office supplies; membership dues for professional organizations and subscriptions to publications that have

to do with your work; and the payroll for any employees not directly involved in the production, such as a bookkeeper.

Next create a Marketing Costs Inventory (page 176) following the same formula as for the Overhead Inventory. Marketing costs include booth rentals; travel expenses; graphic design; photography and printing costs; advertising expenses; credit card processing costs; provisions for bad debts; and the cost of the labor needed to do the marketing.

Since expenses can vary from business to business, you will want to go through your checkbook to be sure you find all the expense categories that pertain to your business. Add categories to the charts as necessary. If you are an established business, you will find much of this information in your federal tax returns.

You will note that both charts are divided so you can record a monthly number and then determine the annual total. Some categories, such as insurance, booth rentals and dues, will not have monthly numbers. So you may wonder why you're not just entering the annual total for each expense. If you create the charts with monthly itemization, this will help you see the ebb and flow of expenses throughout the year and plan accordingly. For the purpose of pricing, however, you will want the annual total, and this is the number you enter on the Pricing Sheet, (page 178) along with the total costs of materials and labors from the Simple Costs worksheet (page 179).

Next you will need to estimate how many of the item you plan to make in a year. Look at the information on the worksheet establishing how much time it takes to produce a single item and project how many of them you could actually produce in a year's production time. If you intend to make other items in the year, subtract that time from your potential production time. Also remember that you will not spend all of your work time in production. You will need to allot work time for marketing, product development, and bookkeeping. Taking all of this into account, come up with a "ballpark" figure of how many items you could physically produce.

Monthly rent for your studio space is part of your overhead cost.
PHOTO COURTESY
THOMAS MANN

53

If you create the charts with monthly itemization, this will help you see the ebb and flow of expenses throughout the year.

Then, using this figure as the outside limit of what you *could* do, determine how many of the items you actually *want* and *need* to make for the market. This is very difficult, particularly when you are starting out, since you don't know how the item will be received at market. This is a time when consulting your network of more experienced colleagues can provide you with valuable guidelines.

Once you have determined how many items you need to produce, and how many hours that will take, you need to determine what percentage of your total production time

Be sure to determine a reasonable cost for the time you spend making work.

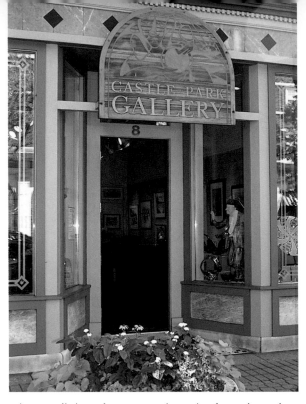

this represents. Will this item take half of your year's total production time to manufacture? A quarter? Enter that percentage in the appropriate places on the Pricing Sheet (page 178) and use it to calculate what sum equals this percentage of your Overhead Costs and Marketing Costs, the costs applicable to producing this item annually.

Then multiply the material and labor costs for producing a single item by the number you intend to produce and enter these annual totals on the pricing sheet. Add the annual totals for all four categories of costs to get the total annual cost of the production line. Divide this total by the number of items to be made to determine the actual cost of making a single item. This is your baseline for setting your price.

Now you need to decide how much to add to these costs as profit. This is the most subjective of all the numbers generated so far, but you have your market research to help you here. Retailers generally mark up two to two-and-a-half times the wholesale price. Double the cost of producing your single item and see if this figure is in line with the price points of comparable items you've observed in the marketplace. If it's less, then you can raise the price of your item to more closely match that of the competition. If it's higher than the prevailing market, you will have to determine if you can convince the buyer, through presentation or marketing materials, that your item is actually worth more than those it is competing with; or you will need to go back to your design and find a way to cut costs in either materials or labor.

In the beginning there is apt to be a good deal of adjusting as you determine how to make your product profitably. This may seem like a lot of work at first. But once you have developed the overhead and marketing numbers, you can use them again and again until your expenses change more than marginally. This will considerably reduce the time needed for calculations as you develop later products. And it is absolutely essential that you deter-

mine a realistic and accurate price point for each product that you make in order to succeed in the crafts business. Keep in mind that one of the prime rewards of running a healthy business is that it will provide you with the means to grow as an artist and to continue to live the lifestyle you have chosen.

A DIFFERENT VERSION OF THE GAME

Pricing one-of-a-kind work that will be sold at shows and in galleries is quite different than pricing for a production line: It is much more subjective. The forms used above can provide you with guidelines for determining your costs, but determining the actual market potential of your work is more complex. The essential question is: "How much will the collector pay for this one?" To answer this, there are several factors to consider.

The sale price will be based on the quality of both this piece and your past work. It will be affected by the demand for your work in the past and the state of your career at the moment. In other words, your reputation (or lack of one) will have a larger impact on the price you can ask than it does for a production craftsperson, although a great reputation can certainly mean higher prices in production crafts as well.

For example, an established clay artist may have only $5,000 of fixed costs and time and materials in a piece that is in the gallery priced at $36,000. The majority of this price, then, is based on the quality of the finished object, the career status of the artist, and the desirability of the piece to the collector community.

So, what if you are just starting out? (And we all started out once, even Beatrice Wood, Jack Lenar Larson, and Ed Moltrop.) Remember, this market is all about quality and perceived value. Quality comes with experience, and perceived value is a result of being in the right shows, galleries, and collections. In the beginning, you will need to price your pieces so that you recover your costs and maybe make a bit of profit. And you will need to find the right shows, galleries and artist reps to help you increase your perceived value.

In an oral history interview for the Smithsonian archives, fabric artist Walter Nottingham told interviewer Carol Owen about his shock when he discovered that his first gallery, a prestigious one in New York, was selling his work for considerably more than the $400 per piece he was being paid. Nottingham noted ruefully that he had signed a contract with the owner for that amount, assuming the mark-up would be modest, but then added, "He was very good for my career. He did all kinds of things for me, got my work into many different major influential shows, into collections, and so forth." The gallery owner had such a reputation that collectors would buy the work of the then relatively unknown Nottingham simply on his recommendation, and for much more than they would have paid if he'd been in a lesser gallery. And in time, Nottingham was able to sell his own work at a premium price based on his name and the reputation the gallery had helped him establish.

Your best guide for pricing one-of-a-kind work will be a gallery owner or dealer who follows the market in general and can place your work in context. For shows you would like to exhibit at, you should research in advance the prices of comparable work by craftspeople at comparable career/expertise stages to yours, and set your prices accordingly. But, again, you will want to know how much it has cost you to produce the work in order to recoup your costs and make enough profit to keep producing more. And if you discover over time that the price you can command in the marketplace won't cover your production costs and provide you with income, you will want to reconsider how you make your work so you can produce it in a more reasonably profitable fashion.

Your best guide for pricing one-of-a-kind work is a smart gallery owner.

55

Pricing one-of-a-kind work is more subjective.

PHILIP DUSENBURY
A Little English
Papier maché
17" x 38"
PHOTO BY TOM STEVENS

Perspective from a Life in Crafts
Rebecca Sive

LINDA SIKORA
Lidded Jar
12½" x 9" x 9"
Porcelaineous stoneware
PHOTO BY JOHN POLAK

*Rebecca Sive has designed fund-raising and commu-
nications strategies and campaigns for Sive Group
clients for almost 20 years and founded and built two
major not-for-profit women's organizations. She is
also a collector of fine crafts, particularly ceramics.
She spoke to us about the perspective of the collector.*

LINDA SIKORA
Teapot
6 ½" x 10" x 7"
Porcelainous stoneware
PHOTO BY JOHN POLAK

How did you begin to collect?

Rebecca: I was on a special program for students interested in politics and sociology in Puerto Rico, and I bought a small vase that actually was similar to what I still like. So that's when I began to collect. But in terms of what brought me to collecting, it was that my mother took my sister and me to pottery classes when we were kids. My mother bought pottery, and it's now 50 years later and the pieces she gave me are in my home. I had this exposure to pots when I was a kid.

You have a lot of work in other media, but would you think of yourself as a clay collector?

Rebecca: I'm very interested in textiles, I'm very interested in certain kinds of prints, but I've spent the most time on the clay. I can directly tie that back to those childhood experiences. Textiles interest me because my mother taught us to sew when we were very young, and I loved to sew, and made all my clothes in high school. I actually was a good seamstress. I never became a potter, however.

Do you think the aesthetic leads to the intellectual, which leads to the purchase?

Rebecca: I think you're right. The first thing is the aesthetic reaction. You go on from there to learn about the work and try to figure out what is it about that particular aesthetic that interests you, and whether you want to pursue it as a collector. That evolves over time and is why I think it pays for artists to interact with somebody who is really looking at their work either at a craft show or in a gallery. In my case the looking is about experiencing something aesthetically, also about learning about the work and also about putting this work in the context of, "Is this something I want to own?" So all three of those things are going through my mind. It's always a question of, "If I could collect this, would I?"

Collectors have this insatiable interest in the work from an aesthetic standpoint, and from an intellectual standpoint, as well as from a purchasing standpoint.

Do the things you collect have any common attributes?

Rebecca: My husband Steve and I are intensely interested in William Morris, the arts-and-crafts movement, and in Wright and Sullivan. It was both the

It's always a question of, "If I could collect this, would I?"

aesthetic ideas that William Morris and the others had, and it was the form of the work, which was frequently based in natural forms or expressed in natural forms. I found when I had the opportunity to build my own space and to put art in it that what I was drawn to was work that was very textured, frequently narrative, colorful, and handcrafted. I do think it's the case that you see something that appeals, and then you develop an understanding of where it fits within the intellectual and aesthetic tradition, and then that gives you a base from which to learn and to study and to look. Because you can't look all day long, you then go to certain places to look. So in my case, I started going to the Lill Street Gallery a lot. I would go there once or twice a week, and I was buying pots that cost $20, $30, maybe $50, and that's how the collection started.

You've purchased the work of a number of artists in-depth. What's that about?

Rebecca: It's really important to me to live in an environment that speaks of my husband and me. I've been at this a long time. The reason I collect in-depth with certain people is because I respond to the work at such a deep level that I want it to be a part of my environment, the daily aesthetic experience I have when I walk from the bedroom to the study to the kitchen. I want to see Linda Sikora wherever I go; want to see Liz Quackenbush. I want to see Tanya Schulz, and the other people whose work I have a lot of. In other cases, where I have fewer pieces of work, the impetus to purchase is because the piece speaks to me, because it tells me a story that I want to read every day in my life, in my house. I wasn't interested in building the collection as an investment or for status. I saw building the collection as part of building an aesthetic environment in which I wanted to live.

I can't imagine what would make an artist happier than to hear that someone is choosing their work because it tells a story they want to keep reading, and that then when they like the story, they buy more chapters of it. That's a pretty great way to do it.

Rebecca: That's what I did. That's how I did it. That's been the driving force. I guess the other point is that, obviously as you have more money to spend, or as your eye is trained better, you then inevitably spend more money, which is, I think, also why it's important

Collectors have an insatiable interest in the work from an aesthetic, intellectual and purchasing standpoint.

for the artist to respond when they see somebody really paying attention to their work. Now that I have so much money invested in collecting, this is important in terms of the artist. Now that I'm spending real money, I do hope that if I take the time to write to somebody and say, "Gee, I just bought a piece of yours. I hope you'll keep me posted," I really hope

that they will. Part of it is an Emily Post thing that my parents taught me, but part of is also that if I'm a serious collector, and I'm taking it seriously enough to be in touch with you, I hope you will be in touch with me.

Well, you're the end user, and we need to take care of the end user. So what you're talking about is direct contact with the artists, but do you also work through galleries?

Rebecca: I've bought much more from galleries than I have from the artist directly. In the late 1970s I started subscribing to *American Craft*, and to *Ceramics Monthly*, and I read them like they were textbooks. I tear out pictures of the work of people that I like and keep it. I keep notebooks on the people whose work I have, so if they put me on gallery mailing lists, and I get the card that has their work on it, I keep that. More recently I have used the web as a learning tool. In addition I have learned about the dealers who carry the work that I'm interested in, so then I actively contact them, and I say, please let me know when you have so-and-so's work. I will say that some gallery owners do a much better job of that than others. By way of example, in the late 1980s, when I first saw Ann Agee's work in Ann Nathan's gallery, the woman who ran her gallery at that time saw me looking at this stuff, and then she called me when there was new work to see. And I was nobody. I was just this kid, and I was interested, and lo and behold, I spent $800. I had never done that. It's important for the artist to shop around for a gallery, and to choose the gallery whose owner will spend time with people who come in and will get slides or jpegs to collectors. If I ask for jpegs I'll (need information with) pictures. If I get no dimensions, and I don't get prices, without all the information the pictures are useless.

Are there other services you expect to receive from a gallery?

Rebecca: I do want to underscore, and this is really to help the artist, that as a collector I have spent enormous amounts of time with written material educating myself on a continuous basis for 25 years. I read the magazines, I buy catalogs, and I pick up the little exhibit brochures. My point is that artists need to take every opportunity they can to get themselves into the media in whatever way they can. I think that really assiduous collectors dig deep. They don't just read the feature articles.

Artists need to make sure that when they're being represented by a gallery, or they're in a craft show or whatever, they need to just find a way to get their name on paper. The collectors take it seriously; you see the names, then you remember the names, and then you pay attention. It's not like someone is giving you the information, you have to seek it out as the collector. So the easier the artist makes it for you by working really hard to get his or her name out there, the more likely that artist is to make sales.

It's also important for the gallery owner to take the time to make sure the collectors to whom you've sold work see anything new and vaguely related when you have it. And I think it's also true for people who are willing to take the plunge with someone who isn't a "name." I think that's important. There are certain artists in my collection whose work I can't afford to buy anymore. But I did see them early on, I was attracted to them, and often I bought several pieces. There is the occasional opportunity where the younger, relatively more modest collector will go for broke in whatever her terms of going for broke mean, and you as the gallery owner or the artist want to be positioned to take advantage of that. Which is to say, staying in touch with the person.

Collectors are obsessive people. Collectors know what they like. They find a way to purchase because to some extent it's compulsive. But they can't do it unless the opportunity is there for them, so again it's to the advantage of the artist and the gallery owner to be sufficiently sensitive to whom they're selling, that they give those people—not just the wealthiest among them, but all of them—every opportunity to spend their money. What I'm saying is that "limited" budget is something like beauty. It's in the eye of the beholder. Because sometimes those collectors will just go nuts and buy what speaks to them. So you as the artist and your gallery owner want to be positioned to take advantage of that. Once you find a collector who is clearly drawn to the story you're telling, they're in it. They're deep in. It would be good for young people who have talent to really take that notion to heart. They want to see the stuff. They want to hear from you as opposed to your thinking, "Oh, that's some rich lady who's twice as old as my mother, and how am I going to relate to her?" Or to feel that they're not sincere, or to feel, "I'm the great artist. I don't have time to do this."

I think that's communication, and whether it's from the artist to the collector or the artist's gallery to the collector, it's a very important component in this process.

LINDA SIKORA
Teapot
6 ½" x 9 ½" x 7"
Porcelainous stoneware
PHOTO BY JOHN POLAK

59

OFF TO MARKET

You've written your business plan. The legal structure of your business is in place, and you've determined how to price your work. Now it's time for you to develop specific strategies for selling your product. You might have touched on some of these strategies in your business plan, but this is the time to define your customers and go after your primary markets. This chapter will provide you with an overview of the many outlets open to you for selling your products, and will give you tips and details on how they work. More specific information on three of the most important markets will follow in these later chapters: "Thriving on the Show Circuit" (page 84), "Opening the Gallery Door" (page 106), and "Spinning the Web" (page 122). But first, you must determine who is going to buy your work.

KNOW YOUR CUSTOMER

The more you know about your product in relationship to the customer, the more you can focus on finding customers who will buy your products. If you don't already

The more you know about your buyer, the more you sell.
PHOTO BY JOHN WIDMAN

know your potential customers, you can determine a great deal about them by looking at your work and making lists of who might buy your product, either for themselves or as gifts. Do you make a product that works in the kitchen or sits on a shelf? Do you make items that appeal to kids with price tags young families can buy, or are they pricey toys that Grandma would love to give as special gifts?

If you make a product only worn by men, you'll have a different market strategy than someone making dinnerware. Items with high prices are going to be purchased by a different socio-economic group than less expensive items. Functional items attract different buyers than one-of-a-kind pieces. The aesthetics of your work also will influence who buys it. Slick contemporary pieces appeal to one type of buyer, while retro items interest another.

It's also helpful to understand who your target market is in a larger sense.

In her book, *Let Them Eat Cake: Marketing Luxury to the Masses as Well as the Classes*, Pam Danziger, founder and president of Unity Marketing in Stevens, Pennsylvania, says: "The two generations that will have the greatest impact on the consumer market over the next 20 years are the 76 million strong baby boomers...many of whom are well into their empty nest life stage, and the 71 million millennial generation, the babies of the baby boomers, born from 1977 to 1994."

This information is very important to those of us who make things. On the one hand we have the "boomers" whose earning power is now at its peak. Their families are gone, and their homes are filled with things. They don't need anything, but market research shows they're buying things they love. Furthermore, they have the resources to purchase luxury items at the high end. The boomer's babies are at the other end of the spectrum. They've recently finished their education and are dealing with college debts. Their children are young and will be financially demanding for some time. This group is looking for value rather than luxury.

Wendy Rosen has identified a source for future customers drawn from both of these groups. In a speech at the National Council on Education for the Ceramic Arts (NCECA) conference she noted, "Evening classes are filled with passionate students seeking a diversion from their boring lives of law and accounting. They've returned to school to study jewelry, ceramics, glass, and more. Are these new artists your future competitors? Perhaps a few, but most of them will be your future collectors. They will understand how much work goes into each piece. They will honor, respect, and, even more, envy your lifestyle and the choice you made to create a career in art."

SHOW TIME

So how do you get your items in front of these buyers in the most efficient way? You can open a storefront in your studio or join a local crafts cooperative gallery. One of the most exciting new venues for you might be to direct-sell products from your website. But the most popular and effective way to reach the largest number of buyers is through the craft show.

Craft fairs are traditionally the most efficient way of getting your products to your consumers. PHOTO BY JOHN WIDMAN

In the last century, wholesale and retail craft shows have developed to provide a venue for manufacturers and buyers to meet. At the wholesale show, your buyers will be store and gallery owners, representatives of large retail outlets and catalogs. At retail shows, you will be selling directly to the customer. While many shows that sell handmade crafts are still quaintly called "craft fairs"; don't let that name fool you. They are major craft markets. There are several dozen prominent craft fairs and shows around the country that attract hundreds of thousands of buyers or visitors a year—each one of them a potential customer for your product. There are also national and international gift shows, as well as specialty trade shows, that can all be potential markets for your products.

In planning your market strategy, you'll need to consider the type of show you'll attend. Is your product specialized, and, if so, is there a show devoted to that specialization? You may want to participate in shows that only feature American handmade products, not simply because you qualify, but also because you support the concept. Or, you may want to find shows that can expand your customer base. For instance, turned bowls are a craft, but also could be featured at a woodworking show or high-end kitchenware exhibit. Jewelry can sell at a general crafts show as well as at an accessories show. Try to think of your product in various contexts and then find the best show where it could be marketed.

● Retail and Wholesale

Here's a quick explanation of wholesale vs. retail: If you sell your work directly to the customer, you are selling retail. If you sell your work to a buyer who is purchasing it from you with the intention of re-selling it to a customer in a store or through a catalog or other source, you are selling wholesale. Crafts shows may be retail, wholesale or both.

Every craftsperson has a reason why they choose to sell either retail or wholesale, or both. You will have to assess the pros and cons to determine which is best for you and the way you like to work. At a retail show, you're selling mostly to the general public, and your customers have paid an admission fee to attend the show. You'll be selling your product at the same price it would sell for in a retail store. At a wholesale show you're selling to buyers who are purchasing items that they'll mark up to sell in a craft or gift shop. You'll be selling your product at a lesser price that factors in the cost of materials, overhead and time, and a profit for you. (Most of the retailers who will be buying your work will want to be able to mark up the price two to two-and-a-half times what they paid you for it.) At a wholesale show, you're taking orders for your product that will be delivered at a future date, and you won't get paid until the order is delivered.

If you sell items primarily at retail shows, you're bringing your goods directly to the customers who will use them. Most likely you will attend many shows per year to maximize your profits. You will have a business relationship with the show producer to whom you'll pay a booth fee to rent your space at the show. Your prime sales contact will be your many individual customers. You will need to make enough product in between shows to keep your booth well stocked. Feedback on your product may come in conversation with customers about what they like or don't like, but your most telling information will be what sells and what doesn't.

If you sell wholesale, your prime sales contact will be the professional buyers who come to the show looking for inventory to stock their retail outlet. You will most likely attend only a few shows a year. You will take samples of your line, but you won't hand over the items at the show, you will instead take orders and then go back to your studio to fill them. If it is a juried show (and the best ones generally are), you most likely need to submit images of your product to the producer to be evaluated before you are accepted. The wholesale buyers will give you feedback on your product based on how well it does in their store, or, if you are just starting out, how it compares to items that have done well or not for them before. While you want to trust your own artistic instincts, it can be instructive to let a buyer critique your work as to its ability to sell in the current market.

You can choose to sell at both retail and wholesale shows. In fact, selling at retail shows can be a way to support your wholesale line since you'll be getting immediate money from your retail items that can sustain you as you fill your wholesale orders. Some retail shows also promote wholesale selling and have ways of marking your booth or keying the show catalog to indicate that you also wholesale your products.

● Selling Retail

There are two major reasons to retail your own product—money and people. Retailing allows you to make all the money from your product, and you get the money right away. This income will allow you to live and to purchase the materials needed to craft more products.

If you sell items primarily at retail shows, you're bringing your goods directly to the customers who will use them.

PHOTO BY
JOHN WIDMAN

63

STUDIO
SHOWS AND SALES

The simplest, and perhaps the best way to start selling retail is to have a mini show and sale in your own studio. There is star appeal to being an artist—people love to know people like you. They want to see where you work and talk to you about what you do and why you do it. Why not invite them over for a chat and sell them something? They'll thank you for making it happen. You could have an open studio one weekend each month if you live in an area with a large-enough population to support the frequency of such an event. Otherwise, you can make it an annual or a bi-annual event.

You won't have to travel, pay booth fees, or hotel bills. The primary expense for the event is the money you'll spend on advertising to get the folks to come. You may need to rearrange your studio for the sale and perhaps provide some simple refreshments. Many studios have sales before the holidays in December. This is a time of the year when people are inclined, or compelled, to spend money buying gifts, so why not help them purchase a beautiful handmade item? However, given the right publicity, you can create a sale any time of year—in spring many people are thinking ahead to wedding or graduation gifts, and a summer sale may coincide with the tourist season in your area.

There are some practical matters to tend to, however. As at a large retail show, you will probably be expected to take charge cards. Since many of the items purchased from you may be gifts, it would be a good idea to have gift boxes on hand. Your customers won't have to solve this problem and will remember how easy it was to get a great gift at your place. The yellow pages of your phone book will lead you to local sources for packaging materials. You also can contact major national suppliers, and these can be found on the web.

Spending time at a retail show allows for social interaction both with other craftspeople and customers. This may be especially important to you if you work alone in your studio for extended periods of time. While you can share ideas about materials and the marketplace with your fellow craftspeople, you also have the opportunity to talk directly with the consumers of your products. This provides valuable direct-market research that will help you gather information about your product line.

As you talk to your customers, you can ask them specific questions about why they chose your work. As they shop, listen to their comments and observe the attention they give your product. They may offer reactions or suggestions that will lead to improvements. What items get the most notice, even if not the most sales, and why? Do customers mention items they would like that you don't make, but could? Repeat customers will share information about items they have previously purchased, which may lead to the reintroduction of a line you had stopped making.

You will need to factor your costs of going to a show into your expenses for your budget. You'll be out of the studio for travel time as well as the time you're at the show. When you're figuring out your "break-even" number—the income you need from the show to make it worth your while—be sure to include an amount for the lost production time. Travel to and from the show also will generate expenses, and there will be costs for staying away from home that include food and lodging.

Your income will fluctuate in relation to the number of shows you attend in a year, but it's a complex equation. If you attend more shows, you have more opportunities to sell, but you may not have enough product—or enough new product—to take advantage of this because going to shows cuts into your production time. It's not easy to decide how many shows you'll

Customers nowadays assume that they can charge their purchases.   PHOTO BY JOHN WIDMAN

need to do. However, you'll need to have a handle on your production capacity. To make it easier, keep a calendar that shows work time and show time so you can visualize the flow of your year. Make sure to mark out days on your calendar to account for lost production time while preparing for, attending, and recovering from a show. As you get a few shows under your belt, you'll be able to plan more accurately for how much time you need in production and how much on the show floor.

Participants in retail shows are expected to collect sales tax and to pay it to the state the show is in. This will require more bookkeeping and filing for a temporary tax ID number from the state, if it's not your home state. Customers assume they can charge their purchase or pay for them with their debit card, and to make and keep sales you'll need to accommodate both methods of payment. You'll find that as you venture into the retail-craft world, the charge machine will be an essential tool of your business. You can arrange for these accounts through your bank. The fee you'll be charged is based on a percentage of sales and usually decreases as the amount of

sales goes up. You'll also need to think through your requirements for accepting checks and how you can protect yourself from taking a bad one, and how to collect on it if you do.

It's important to have a strategy for discounts because this comes up anytime you're dealing with the public. Because keeping repeat customers and filling large orders are important, consider giving a discount in these situations. Collectors and museums expect a discount. The standard collector discount is 10 to 15 percent, and you can, of course, choose not to give it at all. But don't be surprised if the collector leaves empty-handed if you don't.

● Choosing a Retail Show

The problem isn't finding shows—there are literally hundreds of opportunities each year—the problem is finding the right shows for you and your product. You want to attend shows presenting work that at least equals the quality of yours. Showing your products with

RESEARCHING
SHOWS

Retail shows are held around the country and the calendar year. One way to research shows is to use the Internet. You'll find a comprehensive listing at www.festivalnet.com. This site offers complete details about the shows listed including contact information, fees, number of years it has existed, whether it's juried or not, and attendance numbers. There is a fee for using this site, but the information you get may well justify paying it. Craft or trade magazines also will list shows and give entrance and contact information. Many shows have their own websites with an e-mail address or phone number for a contact person who will help answer any of your questions.

goods of lesser quality will lower the public's perceived value of your work. You also need to be aware of who will be attending a particular show in order to decide if there's a good match between the customers and your product. If you're just starting out, showing in too many low-quality shows can permanently damage the upward movement of your career.

If you don't know where to begin, it's time to call on your network. Colleagues who have exhibited in the shows you're considering are your best sources of accurate information. A show producer will provide you with nuts-and-bolts information about the show, but your network will give you the inside scoop. You'll want to hear from them about the location, the quality of the work sold, the nature of the audience, and how the producer treated them. Always remember that what works for one craftsperson may not work for another, so ask your sources to be specific about why something worked—or didn't—for them. Gathering a variety of opinions on any one show is highly recommended.

● *Working with Show Producers*

There's a producer for every show. The producer may be a person or persons running a for-profit business. You want to know how they run their business since this

You want to work with people who are serious about making a marketplace for crafts. PHOTO BY JOHN WIDMAN

will affect the quality of their shows and their ability to bring in the number of quality customers you will need to do well. Request a prospectus for the show, which will give you a general overview of what you can expect. Talk to the producer to get a sense of who they are and if they have any passion for fine crafts, or are they just in this for the money—it's pretty easy to tell. You want to work with people who are serious about creating a marketplace for crafts and are willing to take the time and invest the money needed to accomplish this.

Some juried retail craft shows, where you have to submit images of your work for selection, are promoted by an organization, often a non-profit. One of the best known of these is The Philadelphia Craft Show, and, as is typical for this type of show, a volunteer committee directs it. The income from this show benefits the Philadelphia Museum of Fine Arts. These shows are of consistently high quality, juried by well-known craft professionals and are very difficult to get into.

Attendance

A show producer will be able to give you information about who attends their show and the show's attendance figures. You'll want to know if the audience is primarily local, if the show attracts crafts collectors from a broad area, or if it's a large tourist event. This information is valuable since each segment of the buying public is seek-

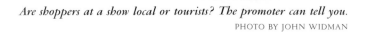
Are shoppers at a show local or tourists? The promoter can tell you.
PHOTO BY JOHN WIDMAN

ing something different. The local shopper may be looking for something for the home or, unfortunately, just looking for something to do on Sunday afternoon. Even though these attendees are actually window-shopping, their numbers count in the promoter's attendance figures.

If you find that the show attracts only a local audience, it's important to do some research about the demographics of the area. Is it an area with affluent residents? Statistically you'll do better if this is the case. If the show attracts an out-of-town audience, you will want to know if they are serious crafts buyers and collectors. Tourists are always interested in shopping—it's one of the things they do. But who are the tourists? What is their demographic? If the show is in an area that attracts affluent up-scale tourists, and if you are selling items that can be packed to travel in a suitcase easily, you are more apt to do well with this audience.

Fees

The show producer makes money by charging the public an attendance fee and by charging you, the craftsperson, a booth fee. A show producer rents raw space, finishes it with carpets and walls if necessary, and then divides it into smaller spaces called booths. The producer will rent booth space at a mark-up large enough to pay for any improvements to the raw space and to make a profit. Your booth fee is the amount you're going to pay to rent the space for your booth for the run of the show. Keep in mind that this is not a fee to rent a booth complete with custom lights, shelving, and display pieces; this is only the space where you'll set up your booth.

Fees for booth space vary according to their size and placement in the hall, and for most shows you can make both choices. Depending on the show, booth assignments are made either on a first-come-first-served basis or on a tenured system. If you know a show is first-

TAKE-HOME

If you're going to a tourist-centered show, you need to consider how your customer will get your product home. You may want to practice packaging your work in several different ways to accommodate the traveler. One helpful question to ask is, "Are you traveling by car or plane?" That way, you can accommodate airport security and baggage handlers by packing the item differently than you would for the car. Items that are oversized, extremely fragile, or for some other reason difficult to travel with are probably not going to be attractive to this shopper. However, if you offer insured shipping services that deal with this type of work, you may increase your sales.

come-first-served, apply early. A tenured system means that returning craftspeople, based on the number of years they've attended the show, are given first choice in booth selection and location.

Contracts

You will receive a contract from the producer defining your obligations and theirs. Read the contract with the understanding that it was written by the producer, and its primary function is to protect him. Check out the cancellation policy and be sure you are comfortable with it and the consequences if you have to drop out of the show. If there are provisions in the contract that seem out of the ordinary, or that you can't live with, don't sign it and assume you'll figure out a way to get around them. First see if you can negotiate the specifics and make sure that any special arrangements you and the producer agree on are noted on the contract and initialed by both of you. If the producer is unwilling to negotiate, you must be willing to abide by the contract, or you may chose not

CHOOSING
A BOOTH SPACE

Carefully consider the options offered before choosing the size of your booth. To maximize display space, you want a booth that is wider than it is deep. A booth that is 12 feet wide and 10 feet deep is better for you than one that is 10 feet wide and 12 feet deep. A corner booth will usually cost more but is preferable unless you really need wall space. Since you loose a wall with a corner you may need to figure out a way to display your product on open shelves that are viewable from inside the booth and in the aisle. Many producers will try to accommodate your request to be near friends by placing you in booths nearby, if not in the next booth. They realize the pressure of doing a show and how helpful it can be to have a friend close by. You can offer support as well as cover one another's booths during trips to the restroom or the food concession. Be sure to ask for this consideration if needed. You'll find much more on booth design in "Thriving on the Show Circuit" on page 84.

A corner booth provides a window on the world of the craft show.
PHOTO BY JOHN WIDMAN

to do the show. Also make sure the contract clearly states the goods and services you are to receive. Make sure that these agree with what you expected to get based on the prospectus for the show. If they don't, take the prospectus to the producer and ask him to adjust the contract to comply.

The money you pay as a down payment is refundable only in rare cases of severe personal tragedy. The remainder of the fee will be due on or before the first day of setup. Depending on the contract, you may be required to pay for other services provided by the producer. These could include all booth lighting or extra lights if some are provided with the booth, or a charge for electricity to your booth if you use your own lights.

If you have any doubts about any facet of the show, talk to the producers *before* you sign anything. Make sure they can provide accurate and defendable attendance numbers. Talk to people who have participated in the show. Try to find people who no longer do the show and find out why. Then turn your intuition on high and trust it. Only do a show if you feel totally positive about all its aspects including the producers, the cost, the location, the dates, and your sales projections.

● *Juried Shows*

Now that you have a fairly good idea of the shows you want to attend, you may need to get the shows to choose you. Acceptance into juried shows is based on a review of your product. The producers want a show that presents work of consistent high quality, and so do you. Obviously, more craftspeople apply to the more important juried shows, and therefore they're the most difficult to get into—as such, these are the selective high-quality shows you'll also want to get into. So how is that going to happen? Well, all it takes to get in is great product, professional quality slides, or digital images, and money.

Great Work

Because juried shows are competitive, the level of the work shown is usually of a high quality. So how can you determine whether you have "great" products? If you're just starting out, you may want to get the feel for this type of show by attending one. After viewing the products on display you'll better understand the expectations of such a show, and will know immediately if your work will qualify.

Applications

The only way a jury can consider the work of hundreds of applicants in an efficient manner is through the use of photographic images. The show promoters can't afford to house and feed a jury for an extended period of time; therefore, the jurors view and vote on the work of hundreds of craftspeople in one or two days. So what does this mean to you? It means that an absolutely great set of professionally photographed images is essential to your success in getting into shows and supporting yourself with your work. Getting the right photographer and the components of creating great images is discussed fully in "Lasting Impressions," page 142. But you should be aware at the outset that you will need images, and that you will need different types of images for different uses.

When applying to a show, it's a good idea to get in your application early. Most producers load images as they arrive at their offices. If your images are loaded early, they'll go before the jury earlier in the viewing process when eyes are clearer and minds are fresher. This gives you a decided advantage over the person whose slides come up later in the process.

Juried shows place your work among the best. Jeweler Meryl Waitz's booth at the New York International Gift Fair.

PHOTO COURTESY MERYL WAITZ

Entry Fees

You will have to pay for the privilege of being considered for a particular show. Every juried show has an entry fee in addition to the booth fee. The entry fee covers the cost of the advanced publicity designed to encourage craftspeople to submit applications, printing the actual applications, the jurying process, and any communication between the producers and applicants. This fee can range from $10 for a small regional show to $35 for a show with a national reputation. Entry fees are always non-refundable—if you change your mind or don't get into the show, the fee won't be returned to you. Once you have been accepted, you will be asked to sign a contract and to pay a down payment on your booth fee.

● Retail Stores and Artisan Co-Ops

Some craftspeople take retail to the ultimate level and open their own store. Running a retail store is a full-time job. Even overseeing the person running a store can be very time-consuming. A store is a distinctly different business that requires skills that may be very different from those you have been perfecting as a craftsperson. It means more staff to look after, rent to pay, advertising to design and pay for, as well as all the other costs of running a business. It also means you will have to increase production to fill a store with your line. And, if you are the person minding the store, your production time will be greatly compromised.

I think it's difficult, if not impossible, to make a success of a craft store that contains the product of only one maker. Most successful stores sell a variety of work, and this means that you will have to go to shows as a buyer as well as a seller. This also means more time out of the studio and a new group of business relationships to foster and maintain. Think long and hard about the hassles of running your own retail business. If you still want to, your next step is to find the best business

counselors to help you. This is where a solid network will again be invaluable.

Craftspeople often band together to form retail cooperative (co-op) galleries for their work. Each artist involved assumes a portion of the start-up costs for the retail space, including carpets, fixtures, lighting, and office supplies. Most of the work of creating a retail space is done by the artists themselves—from building artistic cabinets for display to painting the walls. They fill the space with their work, and each artist takes on a scheduled time slot for running the shop. The artists are responsible for monthly payments to the co-op to keep it running, a cost they can hopefully defray by selling their work this way. In this system, artists have an immediate outlet for their work, and, by sharing shop duties, still have time for studio production. There is more on this in "Opening the Gallery Door," page 106.

SELLING WHOLESALE

When your production capacity is large enough to allow for more sales you may want to consider one of the wholesale shows that take place around the country. These shows are seasonal and follow long-established wholesale buying patterns. There's a round of shows in winter, usually in January and February. These allow the retailer to replenish inventory after the holiday buying spree. Then in July and August there is another round of the same shows scheduled to allow the retailer to stock up for the upcoming holiday season.

The greatest difference between selling wholesale and retail is the nature of your customer and the way you will work with them. In wholesale, your customers are professional buyers from the shops and galleries that will sell your work. They're the ones you will meet at shows and with whom you'll do business. If they're also the owner of a shop, they're the ones who will contact you

You need to display the full range of items you offer for the wholesale buyer.
PHOTO BY JOHN WIDMAN

with reorders or with any complaints. Unlike retail, where you might meet thousands of customers at the shows each year, you will meet fewer buyers, but each one can potentially place large multiple orders.

When it comes to your product, you only assume as many accounts (customers) as you can service with your production output. At wholesale shows you're taking orders to be filled later. In order to do this, you'll need to know your production capacity and have an extremely organized production schedule. When you attend these shows, you should bring your production calendar with you so you can reference it when promising delivery dates to your customers. Nothing stops an account faster than a craftsperson not delivering on time.

If wholesale shows are going to be your only sales outlets, you'll need to make enough sales and new contacts at one to carry you to the next. If you're successful, you'll probably need to budget more office time for keeping

track of requests for information, making work schedules, and tending to billing and collection issues. It will probably be necessary to hire more help, at least seasonally. A series of successful wholesale shows will change your life; make sure you want your life to change.

● Choosing a Wholesale Show

You don't have many choices for American-crafts-only wholesale shows. The two biggest producers are the American Craft Council (ACC) and The Rosen Group. Each organization presents two wholesale markets a year. The ACC holds one in Baltimore and another in San Francisco; The Rosen Group holds both of its Buyer's Markets of American Crafts in Philadelphia. The ACC shows are open only to craftspeople living in the United States. The Buyer's Market now also admits craftspeople from Canada.

The ACC markets are held in conjunction with their retail shows, the wholesale schedule typically occurring over the three days preceding the retail show. The Buyer's Market of American Crafts is the only totally wholesale craft market in the United States. It's also the

A series of successful wholesale shows will change your life; make sure you want your life to change.

largest wholesale show, and it can no longer grow because it already fills the venue that houses it. Unfortunately, the scheduling of the shows can make it difficult for makers and buyers to attend both—for your sanity you're going to need to choose one.

It's a good idea to attend these shows before you apply. If you can't, talk to people who do, both as exhibitors and as buyers. Both of the producers jury their shows, and only high-quality handmade products are admitted. However, you can't assume that just because a show is of a high quality and attracts many buyers that these are the buyers for your products; you still need to know your customers. Since you want to be where your buyers are, it's important to find out which shows they attend. Talk to your existing accounts to find out where they shop. You can then make a "leap of faith" and assume that if they are at one show, the buyers from similar shops also will be there.

● *Working with the Show Producers*

The jury system for both promoters begins the same, with the prospective exhibitor submitting images for consideration. In the case of the ACC, there is one annual jury period for all their shows, so you only need apply once. The Rosen Group has a revolving jury system and looks at images on an ongoing basis.

The costs for a booth at these shows varies depending on the show date, the size of the booth, and whether you purchase a corner booth. The Rosen Group has a tenure system that assures craftspeople a booth in each show. They also allow a craftsperson to return to the same booth show after show. Another feature of The Rosen Group shows is a sabbatical year

You can't assume that just because a show attracts many buyers that they are the buyers for your products.

that allows an exhibitor to skip a show and return without reapplying. These three innovations, put in place by Wendy Rosen, are truly user-friendly and make the business of selling your work more predictable, rewarding, and nurturing.

Some handcrafted items sell well at wholesale gift shows.
PHOTO BY JOHN WIDMAN

● *The Gift Shows*

In addition to the wholesale craft shows, there's a large network of gift shows you can attend. Since early in the last century, gift shows have been the traditional product source for wholesale buyers. These shows are open to manufacturers large and small from this country as well as from anywhere in the world. The largest gift shows take place in New York, Atlanta, Los Angeles, and San Francisco, although there are shows in major cities in all regions of the country.

Large department stores, upscale gift shops, and catalogs have shown increased interest in purchasing unique handmade goods made in the United States as well as in other countries. Yet most of the buyers for those stores and catalogs do not attend the wholesale craft shows. If you think you're ready and willing to address this market, then the gift show is for you. But how will you know if you are ready for this move?

Attendees at gift shows range from mom-and-pop buyers with one small shop to buyers from the largest department store chains here and abroad. They come with very different budgets and points of view regarding product. While the producers say there's something for everyone at the gift show, you'll find, in actuality, that there are too many things for everyone. Because these shows are so large, buyers may not walk the entire show, preferring instead to concentrate on the sections that best fit their needs. So how do you decide if and where you and your handmade product can best fit within the show?

Since all gift shows group product according to concept, and also have sections based on themes, you want to find the right section for your work. Beginning about 20 years ago, many of the larger shows began adding sections designed to appeal to craftspeople and their buyers. These sections group handmade work from around the world in one area. The exhibitors in these areas are typically small manufacturers, and their products appeal to the buyer seeking unique work. These sections are best suited to goods produced by the studio craftsperson working alone or with a small staff.

You don't want to apply to a gift show until you've visited at least one of them. If you decide to apply after your visit, contact the show producer's office—you can do this online at their websites. Get a prospectus and exhibitor application. Booth fees vary depending on booth size and placement, but you can assume they will be generally higher than at craft shows; however, attendance at these shows is also significantly higher.

The jury process is different for gift shows than for craft shows. Some of the sections may be juried, but most are not. If your section is juried—aside from having a really good product—the professionalism of your promotional materials and knowledge of the marketplace are really important here. You'll no doubt be asked to provide product images, catalogs, or other printed materials, as well as any publicity materials you've generated for your product. (You'll find more on generating these materials in "Lasting Impressions" on page 142.) You'll also need to state the section of the show you're applying for. These shows are so large that each section is considered separately and may even have its own show manager. There are no entry fees for gift shows.

● Working with Sales Reps

If your production capacity exceeds your ability to make all the sales yourself, and you're ready to find additional new markets, you may want to consider a sales represen-

The sales rep you choose must have a strong interest in beautiful things.

tative, known as a *sales rep*. This person is the wholesale version of the traveling door-to-door salesman. In this case, however, they travel through a specific geographic sales territory and only call on retail establishments. For this reason, if you want to cover the country, you will need to contract with more than one rep or rep group. Many sales reps have permanent showrooms in wholesale markets where your work is featured throughout the year.

The sales rep you choose must have a strong interest in beautiful things and display some knowledge of your product category. In addition, she must have a passion for selling. It would be good to review the other lines carried and the account's list of potential reps. This will give you a sense of the other items represented and the places they call on, and if these match your expectations. You also will want to know how long they've been working their territory. Reps work on commission, and you will need to factor the 15 to 20 percent commission that they charge into your production costs.

PRODUCT
SHEETS

Whenever you sell wholesale, you'll need to have an up-to-date product sheet. You'll hand these out to prospective customers at shows, mail them to current and prospective accounts for accurate ordering, and use them to notify accounts of any price changes and/or additions or deletions to your line. If you're using sales reps, they must have product sheets to use when calling on accounts.

Your product sheet should include:

Images. These can be anything from simple line drawings to full-color sheets or brochures. Keep in mind that the extra effort to make the images look professional reflects your level of professionalism. You must key each item number to its number on your price sheet.

Product Information. The information for each product must include price, size, color, materials used, care information if applicable, as well as any restrictions on the way the product can be used.

Shipping Information. Your account needs to know how much you charge for packing and how the item will get to them so they can figure in the cost of shipping. Let them know the carrier you use, and estimate the time it will take to get to them. You may consider offering express delivery for an additional cost.

Expected Schedule of Payment. Tell your account when you expect to get paid. For most new accounts you will ask for the first payment on delivery, or COD, or request they put it on a credit card. For established accounts, payment is usually asked *Net 30*, which actually means 30 days from the time you ship the order, although few accounts will figure it this way.

The contract you will write with the sales rep will serve two purposes. First, for tax purposes it establishes a rep as an independent contractor. And second, it sets the ground rules for the business relationship. The contract should include the percent of sales to be paid as commission. Further, it must be specific about how the figure on which you will pay commission is calculated, when and how it's paid, and have provisions for handling commissions on sales that may not go through to payment. A contract also will state the territory covered and grant the rep an exclusive to sell your work in that area, with the possible exclusion of any shops you've worked with in the past, known to a sales rep as your *house accounts*. As with any contract you sign it should contain language about how it can be changed and how it can be terminated. Since this is a legal agreement, be sure to have your lawyer read this contract.

Once you have signed the contract with your sales rep you will want to train this person. I would suggest the rep spend time in your studio so she can speak knowledgeably about what you do and produce. Your rep also will need a selection of your products to show buyers who will always want to see samples of what they are buying. Think of your rep as an integral member of your production and marketing team. Keep her informed of any problems with production that might slow down deliveries of product she has sold, and keep her appraised of any new product development.

OTHER WAYS TO SELL

Aside from traditional wholesale and retail, there are other ways you can sell your products. These include consignment, direct mail, catalogs, commissions, and working with art consultants, decorators, and collectors.

● *Consignment*

If used correctly, consignment can be a very effective part of any craftsperson's marketing strategy. The CODA 2001 survey shows consignment to be the third largest method of selling crafts. Simply stated, consignment is when the maker agrees to provide the shop with work to be paid for when it is sold, and the shop agrees to display the work properly and to pay the maker in a timely manner.

For an established craftsperson, consignment can be a way of getting a larger body of work before the public than most stores can afford. Tara Silberberg of The Clay Pot in Brooklyn, New York, notes: "Consignment is part of the wave of the future for people who are trying to break into the upper end. It's important to be aggressive about offering up your work to get it in the door. I have a jeweler who two years ago sent us this entire box of wedding rings on memo, and said, put them out, let me know if you sell any. I've known your business for years, and I just want to be in your store. We put them out, and last year we sold nearly $40,000 of his work."

Often consignment is the only way a beginning craftsperson can get their product out to the public. In this case it would be wise to have a consignment-to-buy agreement. Under this plan, you would provide an initial order with consignment terms with the understanding that if it does well, the shop will purchase future shipments. Or you might consign a collection of high-end pieces when an account purchases a group of lower end pieces.

Consigning work to shops is not without its potential problems. Most obvious is the fact that your work may be tied up for an extended period of time. The craftsperson also risks not being paid in a timely manner; however, this is a risk you always take when sending out work with any terms other than prepayment. Consignment also creates more complicated record-

keeping. You will receive a list of items sold with each payment and then must check these against the master consignment forms.

Many problems can be avoided with clear communication between the craftsperson and the retailer. In an effort to clearly assign responsibilities, the parties enter into a contract. The contract will establish the financial arrangements agreed upon between the maker and the seller. The percentage to be paid the maker is stated. This can vary from 40 to 60 percent with 50 percent as

You need to be the one who determines the selling price.

the most typical, and without a doubt, the lowest return you should accept. You own the items until they are sold, and therefore you need to be the one who determines the selling price.

The contract will spell out any price reductions that can be taken. You may not want your work to be sold on sale; however, if you agree to allowing reductions on your work you certainly will not want to agree to being paid less. The discounts come out of the retailer's share. The contract will state the date that payments will be made. Since it takes time for shops to process sales sheets, checks to consigners are most often issued mid-month and cover sales made in the previous month. Consignment contracts also can address many other practical matters such as shipping, damage, and advertising and promotion.

After thinking through the consignment pros and cons, you have to decide on a case-by-case basis whether to consign your work. I suggest you only consign to well-established stores and avoid any start-up situations. You don't want to be an investor in a new business in the form of a consignment partner.

● *Direct Mail*

A well-thought-out and managed direct-mail strategy can definitely help boost your bottom line in retail and wholesale sales. Ten years ago direct mail meant stamps and the post office; today, it also means computers, websites, and the Internet. It's important to consider both approaches for reaching your targeted audience.

Developing a mailing list takes patience and diligence. Your mailing list will come from people who have already seen your product or contacted you for information about your product, or are known to have an interest in the handmade item you make. At the outset you will need to establish a database that can store and sort the names you will input. In addition to a name and address for each entry you will want to be able to include where you got it, whether it's a wholesale or retail contact, and if they've made a purchase.

Collect names any time you take your product to market. At a wholesale show collect business cards from any buyer who inquires about your work. Be sure to note on the back any information you want to remember about the interaction, especially any specific products that interested them. You also can go through the trade peri-

Postcards are a great way to share information and demonstrate your aesthetic standard.

odicals and pull names of shops and galleries you think may be appropriate for your work.

Gather information about retail buyers at retail shows or at any studio sales you may have. In both instances a preprinted Join-My-Mailing-List card would be a very useful tool. Always ask for a physical address as well as an e-mail address and plan to use both kinds of mailings since not everyone uses e-mail, and it's always good to present yourself in more than one way. You might ask the customer to indicate the way they would prefer being contacted. When you return home, enter the new names right away.

Once you've established a mailing list, you need to build time into your schedule and money into your budget to use it. You can use your mailing list to let buyers know which shows you will be attending, to contact prospective buyers, introduce new product to existing buyers, and remind lapsed buyers that you continue to be a source of wonderful items. You can use your mailing list to announce new product to retail customers, as well, and to inform them where and when you'll be showing your work. It could also be wise to offer retail customers a discount on their purchases when they show up with the card.

Informed businesspeople are using both snail mail and the Internet to sell their products. If you're not comfortable using the computer and the Internet, hire someone who is, either to teach you how to use it or to do the work for you. (You'll find more on Internet selling in "Spinning the Web" on page 122)

You also will want to have a system for removing names from your list. An easy and quite effective way to know who's interested in what you send is to ask them to indicate their continued interest on a mailback card you include with one mailing each year. In the case of e-mails, you ask recipients to respond either "yes" or "no" to continue being on your e-mail list.

● Catalogs

When you can produce large quantities of your products you may want to approach one of the many companies that sell with catalogs sent into American homes. Wholesale buyers for catalogs are very cautious and spend far more time evaluating products than their store counterparts. Due to the limited number of items they can offer and the high costs of printing and mailing, they have to be confident each item they offer will produce strong sales. You'll likely be asked to submit product to be considered at a buyer meeting. At that time, the overall attractiveness and potential salability of your product will be compared with a number of others.

If your product is chosen you typically will receive two initial orders. The first will have a ship date coinciding with the mailing of the catalog. The second order will have a later ship date and carries the understanding that if the first group did not sell, this order may be canceled. The problem this creates for your small studio may be enough to keep you out of this business. You could find you've produced a number of one of your items, only to learn they don't want them. On the other hand, your product could sell very well, and the catalog will continue to reorder and work with you on products for future editions.

● Commissions

Commissions can be interesting and challenging projects for craftspeople. Furniture, stained glass windows, woven panels, and ceramic tiles are examples of items often commissioned for specific sites. A commission may take the form of recreating an existing piece with slight changes in color or size, designing a piece with specific attributes for a specific site, or it might entail creating a piece designed by an architect or interior designer. Regardless of who designs the piece, it's important that you, the maker, manage the commission well so you can enjoy producing the work and make money.

AL LADD
Arts + Crafts Style Jewelry Box
8" x 11" x 7"
Spalted maple, jatoba, wenge, leopard wood, ebony
PHOTO BY JOHN WALLEN

Careful planning on your part will ensure you quote a price that will allow you to deliver the piece and show a profit for making it. Your existing work and costs are the best place to start this process. Since a commission is usually for a variation of something an artist already makes, you can plan based on the costs of producing an existing work. To estimate costs, start by figuring time and materials for a similar object, then adjust them to fit the new project. If the piece is to be installed on a wall, you can determine a per-square-foot cost based on the estimated time involved and the cost of materials.

After you have determined the actual costs for producing the piece, you will want to add money to cover the time you have spent and will spend in meetings with

Manage the commission well so you can enjoy producing the work and make money.

the client and any contractors involved with the project. You will want to be paid for your design time as well as for any office time necessary to get quotes and to order materials. It is also advisable to plan for travel time and expenses involved with the installation of the piece. If the commission came through a gallery you will have to include the cost of the gallery's commission in the final price. It is common practice for the percentage paid to

JO ANN
BAUMANN
*Bodacious
Beaded Beads*
9" x 8" x 1¼"
Seed beads,
assorted beads,
clear acrylic balls
PHOTO BY
LARRY SANDERS

a gallery to fluctuate up and down based on the amount of time the gallery spends on the project.

Communication is the most important element in the relationship between a client, the client's agent who might be an architect or interior designer, and you, the commissioned artist. It's essential they hear what you can and are willing to do. This will be most easily achieved if you provide a working relationship in which the clients can determine what they want and how they want to get it. When all the parties have agreed on a design, what it will cost, and the production schedule, it is important to put these decisions into a contract.

To be effective, a commission contract needs to be very precise. It will clearly state what you'll be paid and when payments will be made. You want a contract that gives you one-third of the total when it's signed. This allows you to purchase materials and pay your bills while you work on the project. You want to receive another third when the project is half finished and has been reviewed by the client. The final third is due when you deliver and/or install the piece, and the client approves it.

You will want the contract to establish dates on which you will have completed predetermined parts of the work. There should be language protecting you from delays caused by other contractors working on the site.

Working on commissions can give your career a big boost.

The client will probably want the contract to include language releasing them from any liability should the piece hurt someone; before agreeing to this be certain you have proper insurance for this situation. You also want to have insurance coverage for any damage that might be done to the site while you are installing the piece. Another issue that may come up and be included in the contract is who owns the intellectual property rights to the piece. It could be you, it could be the client or it could be owned jointly. Your lawyer can advise you on this when the contract is reviewed before you sign it.

Once you're back in your studio with a signed contract, you'll make a flow chart covering the production of the piece. This will take into account any outside factors that will determine the amount of time you can spend on the piece each week, such as other production commitments. It also should allow for any delays or problems with any outsourcing you will do. Establish the amount of work that needs to be done each week, and then rearrange your schedule if you get way ahead or fall behind.

Working on commissions can be very rewarding, both psychologically and financially, and can give your career a big boost. One of the easiest ways to destroy your client's confidence in you is to fall behind schedule. You want to finish on time even if the other elements of the project fall behind schedule, as is often the case. A carefully planned and completed commission will most likely lead to other work with either the architect, the designer, the client, or the client's friends.

Art Consultants and Decorators

Art consultants are people who are hired to choose art works for building projects, often large office buildings. You might be approached by an art consultant and asked to provide samples of your products to be considered by the client. If your product is chosen, the client may order multiple objects from you. This can be very lucrative. As with commissions, you'll want to be very clear about expectations—and if the project is really large, you'll want a contract similar to the one used for the commissioned piece. You also will want to be prepared to hold your ground on price. You might reject any situation where you are asked to offer a large discount so the art consultant or decorator can mark up the objects to make their money. It is probably best for you to work with people being paid a set fee or an hourly rate that doesn't fluctuate depending on how much the products they acquire cost.

Collectors

A collector is the most discerning buyer you can have. A collector knows the field and knows good work. I believe that some of us are born with the gene that motivates us to acquire things and become collectors. The collector has been, and continues to be, an important component in the development of our field. They're the connoisseurs who consistently encourage emerging artists as well as reward the old masters by purchasing their major pieces. Collectors are also the screeners of objects headed to museum collections. This facet of collecting will be increasingly important in the next decade. The early collectors are aging and beginning to dispose of their entire collections as they move to smaller residences. On the other hand, younger collectors are giving away selected pieces to create room in their homes, allowing them to continue collecting.

Nearly every media has a collector group that meets at designated times each year to compare notes and learn from one another as well as from the artists they invite to join them. They also like to travel and visit artists' studios and important collections, both in public institutions and in private homes. A number of them regularly donate pieces from their collections to public institutions.

The only thing a collector likes as much as finding a great piece is being given a discount when purchasing it. Galleries have traditionally given collectors a discount in acknowledgement of their importance to the field and in an effort to establish them as ongoing customers. The percentage of the discount given varies but is usually in the 10 to 15 percent range. You will be expected to offer the same courtesy discount when and if a collector purchases directly from you. You should be wary of the collector who demands a discount larger than the one given by your galleries.

Regardless of the venues you choose for selling your work, or the types of buyers you establish relationships with, bear in mind that selling your work is as important as making it. I always think that selling work is the final part of the creative process: A piece is not finished until it goes out into the world. Selling your work successfully will require creativity and the same energy level you use when going into the studio to make it.

79

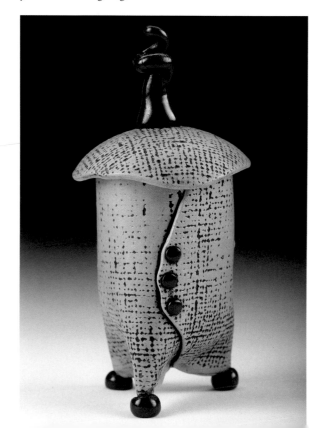

IRENE
SEMANCHUK
DEAN
3-Legged Vessel
5" x 2" diameter
Polymer clay
acrylic paint
PHOTO BY
STEWART STOKES

Perspective from a Life in Crafts
Tara Silberberg

Since receiving a BA from Sarah Lawrence College in 1990, Tara Silberberg has worked at The Clay Pot, her parents' store in Brooklyn. She has been the buyer for the past 12 years, and since 1997, a partner in the business. In addition to buying for more than 25 different categories, from candles to diamonds, she also creates all the graphics and advertisements for the company.

Tell us a little about The Clay Pot.

Tara: My parents started it in 1969. Our store is located in a very high-density neighborhood in Park Slope, Brooklyn, where we have a tremendous number of repeat customers because it is really a neighborhood store selling crafts. It started in my mother's pottery studio, and they ran it as a gallery selling high-end pottery for many years. When that started to fall off they looked for something to do with it, and got into the wedding-band business. We started out doing maybe eight orders a month, and now we're doing 10 orders a day. Jewelry is now about 75 percent of our business. I have a staff of five people in the wedding-band department. All they do is sell rings. It's pretty remarkable that this business has really flourished the way it has.

Why do you think the wedding jewelry area has flourished at The Clay Pot?

Tara: I think that we hit on two key elements in terms of marketing wedding bands. First, we offered something unusual. Even if they don't buy something unusual, our customers want to see unusual and interesting things. Only 50 percent may buy a handmade or more interesting item, but they all want an interesting shopping experience. And second, our staff provides unbelievable customer service. These two things combined are very attractive to people, especially when they're getting married, and they're looking for people to take care of things for them.

Can you talk about changes in craft marketing you have observed over the years?

Tara: The whole field has become much more of an industry, and much more businesslike compared to going to Rhinebeck in 1979 when I was traveling around in the van with the folks. I do feel it's harder and harder to market crafts, and one reason is that the imports coming in are so strong. The globalization that everyone talks about is very evident in this field. I've observed that the one area people have continued to buy at the higher end is jewelry.

Why do you think that is?

Tara: I think that a lot of it has to do with perceived value, and people seeing this item as being a designer-made piece of jewelry versus a designer-made piece of pottery. They see a necklace for $100, and they think, I'm not going to be able to find that necklace anywhere else, and I really like it and it's a designer piece, and it's interesting, and I'm going to get a lot of compliments. It's going to be part of my personal appearance. People are willing to pay more for that. At the same time, they look at a comparably priced vase, and say, "Oh, that's too much," and they don't buy it.

Is that happening with clothing and accessories too?

Tara: Yes, we sell bags now and are trying to create more of an accessories area in the store, and it's been really successful. All of the bags are selling, and perhaps 95 percent are made overseas. The crafts world here does not seem to have their thumb on the taste, or quality, or they look too handmade, and people want bags that look like a bag.

So The Clay Pot buys items made offshore?

Tara: Yes, we definitely buy things that are not made here. It really is just about the price. People just don't want to pay $15 for a set of chopsticks. They just don't. We are constantly trying to find imports that can transition into the aesthetics of what we're selling. And it works. I do feel guilty, and I get into a lot of interesting conversations with customers who say things like, "You don't have as much pottery as you used to." This is not a museum, and we have to make a living. I think that although our hard-core old-time customers

People just don't want to pay $15 for a set of chopsticks.

are sad to see the direction of our shift, we have to change. You don't change, and you die. I mean that's really what it comes down to. You've got to keep reinventing yourself and trying to figure out what's going to work. I'm sure that's true with every successful store in America. You just have to keep figuring what new direction to take, and what people are looking for. Play to your strengths.

Do you suppose there is the bigger message in the public's reluctance to buy $15 chopsticks?

Tara: Well, I think that you have to look at it as the march forward. I think the crafts world will get divided up, and I think that the people who are producing at the high end are going to fare much better than the people making lower-end items. However, I think lower-end items have their place, but I think that as a retailer it's just become more and more challenging to sell it.

In the upper end, I've become savvy to the fact that if craftspeople want to get into my store badly enough, and that's now a factor, they're willing to work with me about giving us a big consignment package. I think that's going to be part of the wave of the future. People trying to break into that upper end need to be really aggressive about offering their work at consignment to get it in the door.

I think that what people really like about American craft is that interaction with the craftsperson. I think that's the key to the continued success of crafts sales. Retail shows with the craftspeople present where the customer can talk with the person who made the item will continue to be successful. That's what people really get off on, that whole idea that they're getting to talk to the person who's living this interesting life.

How do you decide what shows to attend, and how many do you attend each year, and how do you determine what to spend?

Tara: I think that realistically any jewelry buyer who's in her right mind would be attending the Rosen show in Philadelphia. In addition, I do search out small shows where I find people who are new, and I tend to shop the more interesting fashion shows. I do a bunch of shows in New York City where I don't see any craft buyers. A lot of people at these shows started out in the crafts world, or started out trying to do crafts jewelry through the crafts world and got completely disenfranchised. They've all abandoned it and gone into this other realm and are having tremendous success. I probably attend 20 to 25 shows a year. That's really how I shop. I don't have road reps come, and I don't really buy a lot of items through the mail. I like to go to shows. I think the interaction is interesting.

I try to show up with some idea of how much money I have that's open to buy new products for the seasons that are approaching. Generally, I go to shows with lists of things that I'm going to reorder, and ideas about new things to look for. Shows are a little bit more

stressful when I've got to find a jeweler that makes this kind of look at this price point. There are certain pressures you feel at certain times of the year that you don't feel at others. The winter shows definitely are the time when I tend to be a little looser with my discretionary budget. By the summer shows, money gets tight. I've got this much left, and I've got to make sure that I can fit all those old accounts back, and I've got to restock.

Does that mean you are a little more adventuresome in the first and second quarters?

Tara: A little bit more adventuresome, definitely. We'll often get things in the summer that are a little bit more interesting since it's a slower time for us, and so we bring in some wacky stock to try to liven things up, or use it as an experimental period just to see the buyer's reaction. Then I would reorder for the holiday if it did well.

As you walk around a show what attracts you, perhaps besides merchandise, what attracts you to a booth, or what makes you decide to stop?

Tara: Obviously, with bigger objects it's easier. People who sell pottery and glass have a much easier time presenting their work to somebody who's scooting down an aisle. It's big and you can see it, and it's colorful. The jewelers have a tougher time. When I buy into a line I like to have choices, and I like to be presented with a range of things that all make sense together, and relate on some level. Someone who attracts me is presenting something that really looks pretty cohesive. The booth display is certainly important; certainly the items and the booth are going to reflect the taste of the person whose work it is. The presentation is or is not going to attract me as the buyer.

We'll often get things in the summer that are a little bit more interesting since it's a slower time for us, and so we bring in some wacky stock to try to liven things up.

What makes your job as a buyer easier, and how is it different when you are working with other buyers?

Tara: Well, certainly putting the price tags on the pieces is incredibly important, so I can quickly tell if the price is right for my store. Making the work accessible so it's not too expensive is a great selling tool. Display items so people can pick them up, they can look at the craftsmanship. It's really smart to have extra clipboards and to put the code of the item on the piece along with the price, so if you are busy the buyer can write their own orders. I do it all the time. When you are really busy, offer to make an appointment. "Can you come back in 15 minutes? We're going to be done then, and I will hold this spot for you."

I'm pretty good at knowing what I think will work at The Clay Pot. I usually decide pretty quickly. If it doesn't immediately strike me, and I don't say yeah, I'm probably not going to write. I just kind of go with my gut, it's gonna work or it's not gonna.

It's completely different when we buy in teams. I find I'm less likely to buy risky things if I'm alone. If I'm by myself I tend to go really safe. I very rarely will buy a new line by myself. Occasionally I do, but I will often think, "Let's just wait and see how it goes, maybe I can see it again someplace else." My mom, Sally, and I have been buying together for so long we rarely disagree. However, I obviously bring a new eye to the table. I have been trying to work toward buying with a younger person on my staff to

bring another new eye to the process. It's such a smart thing to bring a new person onto your buying team since they will find things that you just don't see, and it's quite interesting.

I have found in the last year this whole explosion of people who have decided that they are only going to sell their work through credit cards. It's fine for an initial order; we're happy to do it. However, I have been getting calls from established accounts that we've had for years, asking if we want to switch to credit card terms. I'm like, "How am I going to maintain that many credit cards to be able to float a business of our size?" Do you think Fortunoff pays for their jewelry with credit cards? This whole thing is so crazy. It really is.

Do you need to look at something at more than one show before you're ready to buy it?

Tara: Well, often I'll see something at one show where it's impossible to buy it because of the booth chaos. And then I'll see it again and go, "Oh, yeah, that I really wanted." And then I'll stay and I'll write it there.

What advice would you give a craftsperson preparing to show his work?

Tara: I think that the best advice I could give anybody is: Present your work the way you would want to see it in the store, the way you would want it to be represented. Have it reflect your taste because it's obviously your taste that you are selling. Try to be as true to your own vision as you can, and put it out there and be as professional-looking as you can.

THRIVING ON
THE SHOW CIRCUIT

If the energy that goes into a vacation can leave us worn out after two weeks of fun, imagine how exhausting preparation for, travel to, and participation in a trade show can be. With this in mind, it's wise to plan very carefully to make the show experience as easy as possible on your body and brain.

ORGANIZE, ORGANIZE, ORGANIZE

Organization is the key to a smooth-running show experience. Whether you are a trade-show veteran or you are going to your first one, you'll want to make lists of the equipment and items you'll need to bring to the show. Your success and comfort level depend on having the right stuff.

*On with the show!
Ceramacist Steven
Forbes-deSoule knows
that good organization is
the key to success.*
PHOTO BY STEVE MANN

● Plan Ahead

Planning for the show begins the day you receive your acceptance letter. A good way to start would be to find another craftsperson who has done this show. Spend time finding out all you can about the physical aspects of the venue. Where are the doors, ramps, or loading docks for moving your booth and product in and out? Which one do they find is easier to use? Is food available at the show, or do you need to leave to go to a restaurant? Where are the restrooms? Are there lounges where you can get away from your booth for a few moments? This information will help you decide what to bring, and whether you can reasonably do this show alone. It's also smart to find out about the show's staff and how helpful they are.

Well in advance of the show, mentally organize your equipment by categories. For instance, think in terms of tools, paint and cleaning supplies, office supplies, shipping materials, drinks and snacks, and product. Then write a category heading at the top of a sheet of paper and put in everything you think you'll need and want in that category. As you spend time with these lists, think through the process of the show to understand what you'll need and when. Add or remove items until you have the final working list for each category. Use the same category headings to label your boxes as you pack them; knowing what's in each box is essential to a smooth setup. I've found heavy plastic storage boxes to be perfect for tools and supplies. They're reusable, and the things you use only at the shows can be stored in them between shows.

● Drive or Ship?

Once you have your equipment list, decide whether you're going to drive your own freight to the show or hire an art shipper to do this. If your pieces are very large, and you're not comfortable driving a big truck to haul them to the show, you'll want to ship. If you live within a day or day-and-a-half drive of the show site, it's probably cheaper to drive your own freight. If the drive exceeds this time, it may be cheaper to ship.

But when calculating the relative costs of each method, bear in mind that in addition to the gas, wear and tear on your vehicle, and any food and lodging costs associated with your travel, you also will lose this time in the studio. Lost studio time equals fewer goods produced and that equals fewer sales. With this in mind, it still may be more cost-effective to ship over a relatively short distance. Another positive aspect of shipping is that you do not have to handle your freight; it should be in your booth when you arrive.

The informational materials you receive when you're accepted into a show should provide the names of shippers

Heavy plastic storage boxes are the perfect tools for moving product in and out.

Heavy lifting is often necessary for set-up.
PHOTOS BY STEVE MANN

who will bring freight into the show. If the information is not there, call the show promoter to ask for it.

Contact the shippers early to find out if they are picking up freight in your area and the estimated cost for moving yours. You will need to give the shipper an estimate of how much space you will need, and since shippers charge by volume, you should plan to pack tight. Be sure to get an approximate date for pickup. Since most shippers consolidate freight they may want your boxes a week or more before the actual load-in day. If you need to purchase, order, find, or organize things, do this well in advance of your ship date.

● Counting the Days

Establish a timeline. Begin with your acceptance in a show, extend it through the show, and end it at least two or three days after your return. On this timeline, write down everything you'll need to do in sequence. Be realistic. Whatever you can take care of early, do. If you leave too much for the last few days, you will exhaust yourself before the show. The two or three days after the show are as important to plan for as the days before. You'll want to take time to store your booth and any unsold goods, and return tools and other equipment to their proper places. During the show, you will have

Getting the display you want is an intellectual challenge, much like that faced by a painter looking at a blank canvas.
PHOTO BY STEVE MANN

gathered information from a number of contacts. This is the time to deal with them. Don't put it off! Mail the requested brochures, call all the people you said you would, and enter the names of new customers, colleagues and suppliers into the appropriate database. Most importantly, you'll want to have time to relax and regroup before you begin the next production cycle.

● Almost There

In the days before, be sure to reread all the materials sent to you regarding the show. The load-in procedure will be spelled out; note if you have an assigned load-in time. Be sure you know the exact entrance you'll be using. Look at a map of the city and plan your route, or visit www.mapquest.com for door-to-door directions. If the materials don't mention a loading dock, ask the promoter. Even though loading docks are seldom the right height for vans and panel trucks, they usually provide the easiest access to the selling floors. If the show materials don't tell you whether there are handcarts or dollies available at the venue, ask. If they're not provided, you'll want to put them on your tool list or arrange to borrow one from another craftsperson who is going to the same show.

ORIENTATION AND SETUP

Once all your equipment is at your booth and your vehicle is safely parked, take a walk around the hall to get oriented. Find the show office and introduce yourself to the promoter. In particular, introduce yourself to the staff that will be providing direct services to the exhibitors and find out how to contact them during the show. Find the food areas and check out what they offer. You might want to find a deli outside the venue where you can buy lunch and bring it. Locate the bathroom nearest your booth. You also might take time to find friends and check in with them. After

taking your orientation walk, you'll find you are a bit more relaxed, and you'll be ready to begin setting up your booth.

● Setup

Even though you might have set up your booth many times before, it's never easy. Setting up a booth is hard physical work, and getting the display just the way you want it is an intellectual challenge. If you take the time to make a mock-up display of your product in the booth before you leave home, or at least plan your display on paper, your setup will go much easier.

It's a good idea to store your packing material in the booth as you unpack, so it's accessible when you are ready to pack up and leave. In fact, a good booth includes room for ample storage. You'll want to make sure you have the basic tools that you might need during the show and those you'll need for breakdown when the show is over. Once your booth is up and dressed with product, spend a few minutes taking photographs. Your booth won't look better than it does before the show opens—there's no dust, the flowers are fresh, and all the product line is there. Now, go back to your hotel, have a wonderful dinner, decide where you will have breakfast in the morning, and get a good night's sleep.

● The Show

The first day of a show is the hardest; the uncertainty about sales and the reception your product will receive is sure to create tension. Take care of yourself. Get up early enough to shower and dress and have a leisurely breakfast. Arrive at the show at least a half-hour before the doors open to give yourself time to settle in. You may want to dust, since other people have been moving in and stirring up dust over night. Freshen the flowers, check your office setup, and put on a smile for the first customer of the day. As the day goes on, be sure to drink plenty of liquids—the recycled air you're breathing is probably very dry. Make sure to change your shoes mid-day—sore feet can make you grumpy and though you might not notice it, your buyers will.

● Going Home

You've had a successful show with sales exceeding your wildest expectations. You're tired and exhilarated, and anxious to get on the road so you can get back and fill your orders or make new product for the next show. However, you're not alone. Breakdown is a mad dash executed by tired craftspeople who want to get packed and out the door. There are two ways to approach this unpleasant project. One is to slip into the bathroom and change into work clothes five minutes before the show closes, then jump into packing and accomplish this as fast as you can, no matter how tired you may be. The other approach is to go out for an efficient, but peaceful dinner and then return to the task at hand. I highly endorse this second approach. You've just worked long stressful days away from home; the hour you spend off your feet shifting gears might mean you get home an hour later, but you'll be in better shape once you arrive.

Take care of yourself.

87

As you pack, be sure to keep all orders and information about contacts for follow-up in your briefcase. This is especially true if you're shipping your freight. You'll want this information as soon as you get home, and your shipped freight will take a while to get back to you. You also don't want to risk losing this vital information. If you're using a shipper, find their representative before you leave the hall. Let them know your freight is ready and fill out any necessary forms documenting the number of pieces they're moving and get the approximate date they'll arrive at your studio.

Take some time for yourself away from the studio when you arrive home, but don't neglect the things that must be done right away. Communicate with the leads you picked up at the show; don't give them time to forget your products or buy from someone else. Make notes about things that went well and those that didn't, and note any changes you want to make next time, then file these notes with your other show information. After your intense week or two of preparing for and going to the show, take your rest time. Once you're refreshed, return to the studio and begin the next production cycle. As you settle back into your studio routine, know that you did your best at the show, and then promise yourself that you'll continue to grow and keep doing your best.

Jewelers need to provide mirrors and flattering light for the customer to try on wares.
PHOTO BY JOHN WIDMAN

YOUR BOOTH: THE CUSTOMER'S WINDOW INTO YOUR WORLD

Your booth is likely the first opportunity for your potential customers to see your product. Buyers walking a show aisle will look left and right and stop when either the product or the booth draws them in. However, it takes both great product and masterful display to keep them there long enough to do business with you. The design, color, and display arrangements you use provide a great deal of information about your aesthetic and your attention to detail. The customers will make instant decisions, sometimes unconsciously, about you and your product based on their perceptions of your booth.

Location, location, location is the answer. The question? What are the most important factors for a successful retail space? Your booth *is* your retail space. You want to locate your booth in the best show, locate your booth in the best place in the hall, and locate your product the best way you can in your booth.

DESIGNING YOUR BOOTH

To display your work to its best advantage, you need a booth that fits your product. For instance, booths where clothing is sold need a dressing-room space and a full-length mirror. Shoe designers need to have chairs for customers to try on their product. Jewelers need to provide mirrors and flattering light. Potters need sturdy and safe shelves and display pieces.

When designing your booth, remember that it's essential that the buyer can easily see into your booth and feel comfortable moving around without feeling trapped. Also, whether you attend one show or 20 each year, your booth design needs to be portable and easy to set up and break down. All these considerations for

booth design may seem like a tall order for a space that measures, on the average, 10 x 10 or 10 x 12 feet. However, a creative and clever craftsperson such as you can easily figure out how to design a booth that is both functional and beautiful.

Someone has to distill all the information and ideas you have about what you think your booth should look like. It could be you, or it could be you and an interior designer, or it could be you and the carpenter who will build it. If you're going to do it yourself, be sure you've visited craft shows and observed the booths of other craftspeople with similar display needs. If you're using a designer, it's essential for you to be clear about what you want and how the booth needs to function, both in place and in transit. Good carpenters often work with clients on the design elements of their projects. Once you understand you are essentially building a three-sided box, the rest of the work is about the way it's finished. If you're lucky enough to find a carpenter who has built booths before, you're ahead of the game.

The four major components of a booth are the walls, the floor, the display furniture, including shelves, and lighting. Your booth design must serve three major functions: displaying and selling your product, storing back stock and supplies, and providing space for carrying out office tasks. Keep in mind that you're paying a premium for each square foot you're renting and that you'll want to keep the storage and office areas to a minimum.

● Walls

Most producers divide the exhibition hall into booth space by marking the floor to designate the boundaries of each space. At some shows, this will be all you'll get for your booth fee. However, some producers contract with exhibition-service companies that will, for a fee, provide the other amenities to you. These can include anything from lighting, carpeting, furniture, display pedestals, and pipe-and-drape-walls. Assuming that you need to provide the walls for your booth, the first design decision will be the choice of the materials you will need for their construction.

The first consideration when deciding the type of walls you need is the product you make. The second is your budget. Craftspeople displaying soft goods such as clothing, wall hangings and quilts, or those with jewelry or small items displayed in cases don't necessarily need hard

Your booth must have space for carrying out office and retail tasks.
PHOTO BY JOHN WIDMAN

89

You will need to provide sturdy and attractive shelving for your product such as these built by Doug Dacey, ceramicist from Columbus, NC.
PHOTO BY JOHN WIDMAN

walls. On the other hand, craftspeople displaying hard goods, such as pottery, glass, wooden products, and baskets, will need hard walls to which they can attach shelving units. It's possible to display these items on shelving that's set up in front of curtains. However, because hard walls provide a feeling of permanence and substance—attributes that enhance your product in the minds of the prospective buyer—they'll create a more effective display.

● *Pipe-and-Drape Walls*

The pipe-and-drape system is the simplest way to enclose a booth. As the name implies, fabric panels are hung from a system of pipes to create walls. It's an economical way to create a booth for the beginner, or to use if your product doesn't benefit from hard walls. You can rent the pipes and drapes from the show's exhibition services, or you can easily purchase the components at a home-supply store and fabric shop to make your own.

The fabric of the drapes provided by rental companies is generic and often has been used so many times that it's no longer particularly attractive. To avoid wrinkles, the fabric is synthetic and usually quite shiny—not necessarily a look that works with handmade products. While the rental drapes are available in many colors, they're usually extremely dull, making them visually dead and unresponsive to even the best lighting.

Constructing your own fabric walls will take only a few hours and requires a sewing machine rather than a hammer or screwdriver. If the show you attend provides pipe-and-drape walls as part of the booth fee, you can easily customize the look of the booth by replacing the panels with your own fabric, or by hanging or pinning your own fabric over them. You want to choose a fabric that will enhance your product but not overwhelm it. You can use fabric as purchased, or you can dye it or paint it to complement your product.

Cut and hem the fabric to the correct length and finish the edges that will hang from the pipe with grommets or buttonholes. Then use clips or shower-curtain rings to hang the panel/panels from a horizontal pipe. You also can sew fabric loops at intervals to the top of the drape so you can thread the drape on the pipe—though with this design you'll see the pipe. You also can make a sleeve for the pipe at the top edge of each panel. The sleeve must be big enough so the drape can easily slip completely over the pipe to conceal it.

The width of each fabric panel will determine the look of the walls. If you make the panel the exact width of your horizontal pipe, you won't have any extra width for gathering the fabric. This creates flat walls that are perfect for a cleaner, modern look. On the other hand, panels made to be three or four times the width of the pipe will create generous gathers that allow the fabric to fall in soft drapes. This treatment creates a more soft and romantic look.

There are several clever ways that you can adapt a generic pipe-and-drape wall system to better set-off your work, from building your own hard walls to covering them with your own fabric.
PHOTOS BY STEVE MANN

It's also possible to use bamboo shades to define your booth walls. They're available in many widths, and can easily be hung from the pipe system to create a personalized look for your booth. The range of colors and textures in bamboo shades is very complementary to a variety of handmade items. You also can paint the bamboo to suit your color scheme.

Fabric or shade walls are obviously very easy to move to and from shows. You can fold and box the panels, or you can roll them around a hard core, then wrap them with paper to keep them clean during transport. The advantage of rolling the panels is that it minimizes wrinkling and makes setup easier—no steaming needed. Your booth will appear far more professional and attractive without wrinkles.

Whatever approaches you take with fabric walls, remember the fabric must be fireproofed before it can be used in large public buildings. The local Fire Marshal checks every show before it opens. You don't want to lose your booth because it's not deemed safe. Make sure that the fabric you use is already fireproofed when you buy it, or look for a fire protection company in your area that fireproofs fabric. Not all fabric can be fireproofed, so make sure you buy one that can be.

● Hard Walls

There are a number of practical matters to consider before deciding on a design for a booth with hard walls. Since you'll be moving your booth around and setting it up several times a year for a number of years, you want to construct it with light and durable materials. It can't be too heavy or cumbersome to carry in your vehicle, and you'll need to be able to maneuver it into place at shows with crowded aisles filled with other craftspeople, booths, and product. When you collapse the booth, you want it to take up the smallest possible amount of space.

A modular approach to hard-wall construction will serve you well since it allows you to change the size of your booth to fit various venues. Booth space typically comes in 10-to-12 foot lengths, and booth dimensions are always in multiples of even numbers. This means that you can get great flexibility by building a mix of wall units that measure 4 x 8 or 2 x 8 feet. By building nine 4-foot-wide and three 2-foot-wide wall units, you will be able to configure either a 10 x 10-, 10 x 12-, or 12 x 12-foot booth. If your product is hung on the wall, you may want to have a free-standing section of walls that will give you added hanging space. Zigzag walls are another interesting way to create a number of isolated display areas without losing too much floor space. You also can cut slots in zigzag walls for inserting glass shelves. This creates a very unified display system.

Creating storage areas that consume the smallest amount of your valuable booth space is a real challenge. You'll find that craftspeople are particularly savvy when it comes to saving space. Many of your

Russ and Nan Jacobsohn of Sparta, TN, designed these beautiful hollow wooden pedestals that also serve as storage and transport cases for her figurative ceramics and his wooden horses.
PHOTO BY
JOHN WIDMAN

These clever display racks for the fishing lures of Charles Morrison of West Virginia, fold up like a book to be packed flat for transport. PHOTO BY JOHN WIDMAN

ideas for storage will come from observing how others solve this problem. You may want to build two more wall units to define a storage area in a corner of the booth. You also can build your display units to have storage in them or underneath. Or, if you can give up floor space, you can decrease the depth of your booth by two feet and store items in the space between your back wall and the back wall of the booth behind. And, if you think you can't live without that extra bit

TOUCH
OF THE ARTIST

If you don't need to hang product from your walls, you can borrow a simple idea for making walls from fine-art painters. Construct a system of large wooden frames, much like the frames artists use for stretching canvas, to the size you need. Stretch the canvas on them and paint them to complement and highlight your product.

of storage that sacrifices selling area, just remember the hefty price you're paying for every square inch of booth space.

● *Materials for Constructing Hard Walls*

No doubt the simplest way to build a hard-wall booth is to use hollow-core doors. These are available in many widths and heights, are relatively lightweight, and durable. You want doors that are high enough to enclose your space. I think walls that are 6 feet high are too short, and I believe that walls that are 8 feet high create a more effective enclosure. To make the walls, you hinge the doors together. To transport them, you can take them apart by removing the hinge pins, or you can utilize the hinge to keep them together and fold them flat.

Plywood, fiberboard and pressed fiberboard are good materials for constructing your wall panels. Fiberboard and ¼-inch plywood behave in much the same way, so the finish treatment you have in mind may help you with this decision. Unless you purchase expensive interior-grade plywood with a super-smooth surface, it may take primer to seal the surface and several coats of paint to get the surface as smooth as you want. Plywood allows you the versatility to hang shelves or display pieces anywhere you want as long as your product is not overly heavy.

Fiberboard has a very smooth, hard surface and will provide a super-smooth finish when painted. You can find fiberboard pegboard that can be very useful if your product requires hanging to be sold effectively. The downside to fiberboard is that it may mar and scratch easily and is also difficult to nail or screw into.

Both plywood and fiberboard can be screwed and glued to a support system of 1 x 2 pine to create panels, and, as with hollow-core doors, you can use hinges to connect them. It would be good to add molding on the return edges of the panels that face the aisle to hide the raw edges.

You may want to add crown molding or some other architectural feature to the top of each panel, which will add interest and provide an illusion of solidity to your booth.

Pressed fiberboard is a thick board made out of paper. It's lightweight, but not as durable as plywood or fiberboard. While you can paint pressed fiberboard, it's a perfect material for covering with fabric. Because it's often used for bulletin boards in offices and schools, it works particularly well if your product is best displayed by being pinned to the walls. If you use pressed fiberboard, you want to be careful when moving it since the edges are extremely susceptible to damage. You can minimize this damage by using duct tape to reinforce the edges before covering it with fabric, or by using a paintable tape before you paint.

● *Wall Treatments*

When you think walls—whether at home, the studio, or in your booth—you inevitably think of color. You'll find there are a number of factors to consider when choosing the color for your booth. First, you need to think of color in terms of your product and what color or colors will best complement it. Brights? Neutrals? Rich, dark tones? This is a place where you can apply the principles of color theory.

The first thing to remember is that the warmer colors—

Darker background colors convey a feeling of elegance for higher end product.   PHOTO BY JOHN WIDMAN

PRE-FAB
BOOTH SYSTEMS

There are a number of pre-fabricated booth systems available today. Basically, you order them from the manufacturer and set them up. Most of them are known as systems because they offer modular pieces that allow you to customize the configuration of your booth. Some are hard-wall systems made from tubular stainless steel with solid panels covered in various fabrics. There are systems made of stainless steel with built-in grids that are perfect for clothing because they offer endless possibilities for hanging the product. Other manufacturers provide tents or canopies that you can pitch inside or outside. The best place to find the names of display companies and their contact information is in the advertising sections of national craft trade magazines.

UNION
CONSIDERATIONS

The larger exhibition centers are often staffed with members from various unions. These venues have strict rules about who can do what work. In some cases, exhibitors can't use any power tools or even plug in their own lights. There's an extra charge for the work the union members do in your booth. Your show producer should provide information on any restrictions in the materials you are sent before the show. If you have any doubts, contact the producer before the show.

Willola Tyson of Clinton, TN, uses traditional Shaker colors in her display, and even in her attire, to complement her classic wooden baskets.

PHOTO BY
JOHN WIDMAN

reds, oranges, yellows, and colors containing large amounts of them—tend to advance in our vision field. On the other hand, the cooler colors—blues, greens, and purples—tend to recede. You can use these principles to create the illusion that your walls are farther away from or closer to the viewer.

The neutral colors—beiges, grays, tans, and colors containing them—are calming. If your product is in any way meditative or visually complex, you can use these colors to your advantage to create an environment where the viewer is apt to stay longer to take in the details. Choose darker colors if you want to convey a feeling of elegance that is very complementary to high-end product or product that you wish to present as elegant. You also can manipulate the viewer's sense of scale with color: Dark colors make spaces look smaller; light colors give a more expansive feeling.

Greens, ochres, and blues are associated with the arts-and-crafts movement at the beginning of the 20th century.

Throughout history certain colors have been associated with particular moments. You will want to consider this aspect of color if your product is reminiscent of another time. For instance, particular greens, ochres, and blues are associated with the arts-and-crafts movement at the beginning of the 20th century.

You may want to consider wall-treatment options other than paint. Wallpaper can be used to create different moods, from romantic to jazzy, as well as to evoke the feeling of various historical moments. Fabric, aside from making pole-and-drape panels, can be applied to wood panels using staples or hot glue. Wallpaper and fabric on panels create perfect displays for flat art since the nail holes nearly disappear when the display is reconfigured. Linen and burlap are especially good for disguising nail holes.

● Floors

For every venue with carpeting, there are dozens without. Therefore, you need to make provisions for a floor covering—and you can't put too much thought into choosing the right one. Why? Because if you don't have something cushioned to stand on for the run of the show, your feet are really going to hurt. Furthermore, your buyers, who also may have sore feet, will be happy to spend more time on your cushioned floor, which gives you more time to sell them something. Aside from comfort, you also need floor covering for your booth because the floor, like the walls, is part of the total perception buyers will have of you and your work.

The color and design of the carpet are going to be determined by your product and the other design elements of your booth. You want the carpet to coordinate but never dominate the scheme. While you may be tempted to select that plush white shag, consider what the carpet will look like after hosting hundreds of buyers. Selecting a darker color or darker neutral will hide the dirt and cut your maintenance. Make sure the carpet you choose is manufactured for high-traffic areas and is stain resistant. Since the square footage of your booth floor is usually quite small, purchase the highest-quality pad available—the little extra money you spend will be more than offset by the added comfort.

Safety first should also come to mind when you think of flooring. Take extra precautions to tape down any edges that might trip your customers. If extension cords need to run over your carpeting, tape them down as well. The right flooring can also provide a measure of safety for your product, since a soft carpet may save the breakable piece that gets dropped. Outdoor booths present their own set of challenges when it comes to flooring. You'll find more information on this in "Taking It Outside" on page 101.

● Display Furniture and Shelving

Now that you have walls and flooring, you need to provide display pieces and shelving for your work. Your products, and the walls you've chosen based on your product, determine your choices for these. Pedestals or display furniture will help bring your product away from the walls so it can be seen from all sides, and can add extra interest to your booth. Shelves allow you to maximize the use of your walls as prime display area. And, because you want your booth to have a unified look, this is the time to consider what your office space and the chair you'll sit in when taking breaks will look like.

● *Display Furniture*

Furniture can personalize a booth, for example, a small bench or chair can be used to display draped items. If it's important for the buyer to see all sides of an item, placing it on a pedestal will allow them to do so. When deciding on pedestals—whether columns, cubes, triangles, or rectangles—consider how they'll travel. Spending time designing collapsible pedestals that travel flat, or ones that will nest, can save you space in your vehicle if you're transporting them yourself, or save you extra freight charges when shipping to a show.

There are many manufacturers specializing in display furniture for general retail. Going through their catalogs may be well worth your time. You'll be amazed at the hundreds of configurations available for a simple free-standing hanging rack. However, you may not want your booth looking like it's mass produced with chrome and brass fixtures. In that case, use the designs as a departure for making your own fixtures, using materials that are more complementary to handmade items. For example, consider drilling holes for inserting dowels into a wooden closet rod. This makes a great display for just about anything that hangs, such as purses, scarves, or hats, as shown here.

● *Shelves*

If you have hard walls you can attach shelves directly to them. The multiple shelves may be attached with brack-

Dowels inserted into a stairway newel post create a visually appealing and easily accessible display for scarves.

PHOTO BY
JOHN WIDMAN

95

ets or you can hang individual shelves using French cleats, which do not show and make for a much more professional-looking presentation. You also can have shelves that are used as freestanding units. They can be built in many ways, and you can do it yourself, have a carpenter build them for you, or purchase them. One interesting and easy-to-make approach to shelving is what I call the ladder shelf.

Ladder shelves are a series of ladders with removable and adjustable rungs that are used to hold shelves that can be either wood or glass. A little cleat added to the bottom of the shelf just on the outside of where it rests on the rung adds a bit of stability. Units can be built in varying heights for added interest. You can also place a shorter unit in front of a taller one to create a stepped-back look. The length of the shelves determines the length of the display unit. These units go together easily without the use of tools and come apart quickly and can be packed with little or no wasted space.

● *Office Space*

You'll need an area in your booth to keep office supplies and selling tools, such as cards, brochures, and price lists. You can make your office in your storage area, or you can place it on the selling floor, allowing you to get an order form or business card without leaving the customer and losing a potential sale. If you decide to place the office up-front, you need to think of it as an integral part of your booth design.

The office can be as simple as a shelf placed below an important selling area. It could be a series of clipboards hung on the wall: one for order forms, one for catalogs, another for business cards, etc. Or, you could use a small chest of drawers to hold everything you will need while providing an uncluttered surface for items being considered for purchase.

The ultimate luxury would be to have an actual desk where you could sit to write orders and perhaps a second chair where the buyer could also sit while writing

You need to think of your office space as an integral part of your booth design.

PHOTO BY
JOHN WIDMAN

a check or an order. Several years ago, we had a carpenter design a collapsible desk. The top, the single leg, and the storage piece were all independent, allowing the whole thing to fit in a reasonably sized box.

● *The Chair*

Effective salespeople go to the customer; they don't make the customer look for them. Therefore, you would be smart to put your chair in a very accessible and visible place near the front of the booth, just out of the aisle. If you choose this position, you'll want to sit in a relatively tall chair. Bar-height director chairs are comfortable, inexpensive, and fold up for ease of packing and travel. Of course it goes without saying—always stand when greeting or talking to customers.

● *Signage*

Clear and accurate signage is an important tool for turning lookers into buyers. You will want several types of

signs in your booth, including signs with your name or the name of the business, and signs that clearly show pricing and terms of purchase. As part of striving for high-quality booth design, you want every sign to look good and be easy to read. You may want to consider having your signs professionally made. Since you want them to hold up to years of use, have them made from durable materials.

The design for these signs should incorporate your logo, if you have one, and use the same typeface you use on your stationery and other printed materials. Keep in mind that you're making a name for yourself, and your customers will remember what your name looks like the more they see it. It's a good idea to have more than one sign with your business name on it.

Having one large sign and several small ones gives you the most versatility. Consider placing the largest one on the back wall and having a smaller one on each of the side walls where they will be visible to people approaching from either direction. It's a good idea to hang these signs high enough so that they can be seen over the heads of people in and around your booth.

If you're going to a wholesale market, you'll want some extra signage for your booth to help the buyers. In addition to displaying the price for an object, you'll want to indicate any multiple purchases that you require. For example, you want the buyer to know that the breakfast bowl must be purchased in multiples of four, or that the napkins always come in an assortment of six designs.

I suggest you also post your terms including where you will ship from, opening and reorder minimums, and the types of payment you accept. You could include the standard lead-time for an order, your packing fee, and any return or trade-back policies you may have. In addition, all buyers like to know about the process, and need information about the care of the products, so plan a way to include this in your display. This signage can be generated on a computer, just be sure to use a font size that's easy to read and make it all a bold typeface.

● *Price Tags*
There are many different theories about where to place the price tags on objects. Some people prefer not to price things so they can engage potential customers in conver-

sation. Others choose to place price stickers where they won't interfere with the design of the object, which often means they end up where they can't be seen.

My advice is to put the sticker front and center. Here's why: You don't want to upset or embarrass a potential retail customer who misjudges what an object may cost and then has to talk himself out of the situation when he realizes it is too expensive for him. Conversely, you don't want to lose a sale because the customer assumes an object is too expensive and walks away without knowing the real price.

Wholesale buyers are working and have to make many buying decisions in a short period of time. They must be able to quickly decide whether your product is priced correctly for them. You don't want to keep a buyer waiting while making other sales, only to have the buyer find out that the product is not suitably priced for their needs.

There are some shows that have wholesale and retail days. In this case, you must replace the stickers on your work for each segment of the event. It's too awkward and unprofessional to tell the wholesale buyer the price is half the marked price and then they have to do the math in their heads. Again, these are busy people who can buy product from many sources, and it's important to make shopping with you easier for them.

We are an aging population, and some of your customers may not see as well as they used to. Be sure to use stickers that allow the price to be large enough to be easily read. Price stickers can be made on the computer or written by hand. If you write by hand, please write clearly.

97

Clear signage can make it easier for the browser to become your customer.
PHOTO BY JOHN WIDMAN

South Carolina furniture maker Robert Garrett displays his work in the best light possible. PHOTO BY JOHN WIDMAN

● Lighting

You don't want to go to a show without your own lights. While you can always rely on a venue to light the hall, subjecting your product only to the harsh glare of impersonal fluorescents is not putting it in the best light, literally or figuratively. Lighting your product correctly and adequately is crucial to your success. Simply put, if people can't see it, they can't buy it. Just as with every other element of your booth, buyers will look at your lighting, or lack of it, as a measure of your aesthetic.

Washing your booth with the right light will bring in the customers and keep them interested in your work long enough to buy it. Even figuring out a simple, portable track system for your booth will be a vast improvement over the house lights. But don't get carried away. While lighting is one way you can create a dramatic mood or atmosphere for your booth, never sacrifice clear lighting for the sake of special effects.

With dozens of lighting systems and hundreds of different light bulbs available, how do you get the right one? It's important you do a lot of homework before you make a commitment. Go to the home stores in your area, get on-line to check out the offerings, and send for catalogs. Talk to other craftspeople about their experiences with lighting. If you see something you like in a booth, ask about it. How did they do it? Where did they get it? Find an electrician who can offer some design assistance, one who knows more than which wire goes where.

As with pre-fabricated booth systems, you can find complete lighting systems that are ready to go. There are many companies that are trade-show specialists that can put together a lighting package tailored to your needs. However, if you need to keep costs down, explore options from your home-supply stores. You may be surprised what you can do with clip-on photographer's lights or hanging lights used by car mechanics. Just be aware that a booth typically gets one outlet, and the number of plugs in your power strip will limit the number of lights you can use.

● Arranging Displays

With your booth up and the display furniture and lighting in place, it's time to dress the booth with your product. The principles you learned in basic design will apply to the way you arrange your product in your booth. Plan to make at least one fantastic vignette using your product so that it tells a story and captures the attention of the prospective customer. For instance, if you make clothing, plan to display your jacket with a scarf and hat, or if you make dinnerware, set up a place setting.

Feel free to include props, even if they're items you don't make—use jewelry with the jacket or a napkin and cutlery with the dinnerware. In addition to getting the prospective customer's attention, this approach makes it clear to wholesale buyers that there's enough depth to your line for them to tell a story with your product in a shop. It also can show the retail buyer ways to use your product. Your vignette should be in a prominent place in the booth and needs to be very well lit.

Remember, it's important to vary the sizes of items in a group. However, if your line includes many variations on one item, it can be fun to display them together. It's also important to display items within each grouping at different levels so the viewer's eyes will move through the display. It's usually true that we are more comfortable viewing a group of similarly colored items than many different colors in one group. In the same fashion, it's easier for us to understand an item when it's displayed in the context of similar or related items—all the coats together, all the rings together, or all the casseroles in the same general area.

Our eyes follow any strong lines, so make sure you use any directional clues your work may give. For instance, if you chose to extend the sleeve of a garment, make sure it's pointing into your booth or toward another important item. And always use the spout of a teapot or pitcher to point the way into your booth, and to another important product.

You'll want to plan for a dense display of product at a retail show. The shopper needs to know that you have the jacket in her size or that you have eight of the wine glasses she likes. At a wholesale show, the display can be less crowded; since you're taking orders, displaying multiples is typically not necessary. The wholesale buyer knows you can produce the quantity of product they

want. Exceptions to this would be to show all the colors available and any variations they might expect to see in individual pieces of the same item.

Only fill your booth with perfect examples of your product. I was once told by a jeweler at a show that the stone in the piece I was looking at wasn't as good as the stone in the pieces I would get, and by a potter that the plates I ordered wouldn't be warped. This is nonsense and a total turnoff for a buyer. How can the buyer have confidence in you and your product if you are showing

Only fill your booth with perfect examples of your product.

defective or inferior work? Excuses on your part are sure to motivate the buyer to walk away.

You might want to offer add-on products to your retail customers. Woodworkers can sell the furniture polish they recommend for use on their product; jewelers can offer good jewelry cleaner, etc. If you have such add-ons, plan to make a small display of these items.

● *A Floral Flourish*

A beautiful plant or floral arrangement can be the flash of color and touch of warmth that lures a buyer to your booth. It's impossible to over-emphasize the importance of placing flowers or plants in your booth, regardless of your product. Certainly, if you make vases or flower pots you'll want to display them in use. If you don't make those items, it's relatively easy to borrow containers from those who do in exchange for displaying their business card and booth number.

Most show producers will direct you to a good nearby florist; some even have florists at the venue during setup. Don't compromise your booth by using inferior plants and flowers. As with everything else in your booth, the plants and flowers you display should reflect your attention to detail. Decide at the end of each day whether

99

Include props, such as the faucet with this hand-crafted basin, to demonstrate how your product can be used.
PHOTO BY
JOHN WIDMAN

Robert Bondi inspires budding young craftsmen with his woodworking skills.
PHOTO BY
JOHN WIDMAN

you need to purchase fresh stock the next morning on your way to the show.

● *Watch Your Back!*

Keep in mind that the back wall of your booth is very important. Shoppers at craft shows walk an aisle until they see something that catches the eye, and then they stop in front of the booth and survey the contents. Perhaps they saw something on a side wall that interested them; now the back wall needs to draw them in. Typically, your sign will be there, and this will provide name recognition or introduce you to them.

● *Picture This*

Demonstrating your craft may be the best way to bring potential customers into your booth.
PHOTO BY
JOHN WIDMAN

One of the reasons people shop both at retail and wholesale crafts shows is that they get to meet the maker. A large color photograph of you working in your studio could be a part of the back wall display. This humanizes the product and gives the buyer instant visual information about the process.

Photographs give you another design element to work with. A photograph provides a lot of information quite quickly. You can use them effectively to add interest to your displays and, in turn, add to your sales. However, you want to be sure to use very simple frames that won't distract from the message of the image and any product displayed nearby.

● *Demonstrations*

Since we all enjoy the positive feedback we get from the captivated audiences that gather around demonstrations, you may be thinking of demonstrating your craft in your booth as part of your display. However, you need to consider the price you might pay for the praise and the feel-good moment. First, the space given over to demonstration is taken away from your selling space. Second, demonstrating takes you away from selling—the primary reason you came to the show. And third, a demonstration can distract the shopper from buying—the reason they came to the show.

On the other hand, at the right type of retail show, demonstrating your craft may be the best way to bring potential customers into your booth. Be aware of the show's demonstration policies before you apply. Some crafts shows encourage demonstrations as part of their mission.

If you're going to demonstrate your craft, make sure you have an extra large booth to accommodate tools, materials, and adequate selling space. You'll also need enough sales staff to handle the sales area while you're demonstrating. Don't hide yourself behind the demonstrations—remember that customers would rather interact directly with you, the artist-craftsperson.

● *Booth Maintenance*

During the show, you want to stay focused on selling and making contacts that will lead to future sales. However, you also will want to maintain your booth so that it is impeccably clean and orderly. In addition to keeping your product displayed perfectly, this may mean dusting more than once a day and tending to plants and flowers as needed. The appearance of your booth will enhance your ability to sell your product, and that is what you need most to do at the show.

TAKING IT OUTSIDE

If you're attending an outdoor show, there are specific factors you need to take into consideration when it comes to your booth. For example, how do I design an outdoor booth with the feel of indoor space? What flooring is best to use at an outdoor show? What if the terrain is uneven? What happens if it's windy, or it rains?

As you prepare for an outdoor show, be sure to have an equipment box that contains tools that will help you set up your booth outdoors. A good level will help you straighten your booth as you set up. Bring four-inch squares of wood for use under any poles. They'll prevent the poles from sinking into ground that's too wet, and can be used as shims when you're on sloping or uneven ground. A plumb bob will be helpful in getting the poles up straight. If your floor covering is plastic, carpet, straw mats, or fabric, consider making ground staples from metal coat hangers. The staples will sink into the ground and hold the flooring in place.

Choosing the right flooring for an outside booth is a real challenge. If you're sure it isn't going to rain, you could use carpet. Straw mats work well, as does indoor/outdoor carpeting, or you can have a wood floor. A wood floor should be close to the ground so you don't have customers falling in and out of your booth. You may want to create

a threshold using rubber mats that will ease the transition from soft or uneven ground to the harder floor.

Whatever flooring you choose, I suggest placing it over a rubber carpet saver, the kind that goes under a carpet to keep it from sliding. This will keep any residual moisture from soaking into your flooring. Once your floor is in place, check your shelving before dressing your booth to make sure it's totally stable. Use the level to ensure the shelves are as level as can be. You don't want your product crashing to the ground because the shelves are uneven or unsteady.

Prepare yourself for different weather scenarios. Bring a clean, fresh tarp to use just in case you need to quickly cover your product in case of rain. Prepare yourself for rainy days as well. Pack rain gear, including raincoats, umbrellas, and waterproof footwear. If you use cardboard boxes to transport your product, make sure they stay high and dry. On hot days, drink plenty of water and stay in the shade as much as possible. If there's an air-conditioned building nearby, take time to cool off every few hours.

Provide comfortable seating for yourself, including protection from too much sun, or shelter from rain, for a successful outdoor show.
PHOTO BY
JOHN WIDMAN

101

Perspective from a Life in Crafts
Stacey Jarit

Stacey Jarit is co-director of Artrider, a company producing several well-respected New York craft shows annually. A former enamelist, she has focused on refining the shows to make them work best for the craftspeople involved. She has also served on the board of the Craft Emergency Relief Fund (see page 45).

How long have you been producing shows, and how did you begin?

Stacey: Everything I ever did seemed to lead to this career. My very first jobs were working in my father's photography studio. Then I worked in a commercial arts studio; next I managed a gallery in Soho. I started making cloisonné enamels; which led to doing craft shows as an exhibitor. My husband Jeff, an urban planner, worked the shows with me. We had a lot of business experience. An opportunity came up when a show that I was going to do was suddenly canceled. It was a Tuesday in the summer of 1982. Jeff said, "You know, we can pick up the show." We had that combination of Jeff's business savvy, and my aesthetic sensibility, that allowed us to make good decisions. Jeff is still my partner, and we're co-directors of Artrider [our show production company].

How many shows do you have now?

Stacey: We have seven shows in four different venues. There are shows in March, April, May, and then September, October, and December. Our two biggest events, with 325 booths each, are in May and September at a 70-acre estate in Tarrytown, N.Y. It's called "Crafts at Lyndhurst." Although our show season ends in December, our applications are due the first week in January; therefore, we're busiest in January and February because of the paperwork.

When people apply to your show, do they apply per show, or do they apply to Artrider and then pick how many shows?

Stacey: They can apply to one show or they can apply for seven shows. It's one application, one set of slides, one due date, and one application fee. We ask people to prioritize how important each show is to them, and we try to accommodate people when we can. We get about a thousand applications, and I think the average show request is between two and three per application. We ask for five slides of the work, a slide of the booth, and we request a resume and any other promotional material that applicants want to send us. In 2005 we began accepting digital images. It was inevitable. I think it's happening much faster than any of us expected it to. I know there is some proprietary software on the market the very large craft shows are using now. But I don't think we're going to go in that direction. It's very costly. We think we can do this really well internally.

Can you talk a bit about the jury process you use at Artrider?

Stacey: We currently jury in-house. We had a jury of craftspeople for the first few years, but it became logistically very difficult for such a small staff. So now I approach it as a gallery owner might. However, I always had a group of advisors among the craftspeople. When I was really stumped I would call and ask them if they knew the work. As time went by I institutionalized that, and I created an advisory group I could ask when I was in the process of deciding who was in the shows. I score the applications numerically like a term paper with cutoff points for applicants who get in, get put on the waiting list, or are rejected. And, of course, within the media I have to balance the show, and this is always the biggest challenge. It's not necessarily everyone who has the best score. It's everybody in their media who has the best score. If I have 75 jewelers who have higher scores than everyone else, I can't put them all in.

What do you think are the hardest things for the new exhibitor to feel comfortable with?

Stacey: The application process and the display part are just technicalities. You can learn how to fill out applica-

tions and get good slides. You can go to a workshop; you can talk to other craftspeople. I always send new exhibitors to a craft show when they say, "I don't know what to do with the display." I say, "Walk up and down those aisles, and you'll see hundreds of different displays." The harder things are knowing how much inventory to make and having enough inventory. I will walk into a booth and realize that if the craftsperson sold everything in the booth, they still wouldn't make enough money to make a profit. Often they don't understand the subtleties of pricing, they tend to under-price, undervalue their own work.

What's the most rewarding part of your work?

Stacey: There are two very distinct areas. One is the creative piece. I get to select the artists; I get to design our ad campaigns. I actually design the way the show will appear to the public. Then there are the personal rewards I get because of the community of craftspeople I work with. I feel unbelievably blessed and privileged to have worked with thousands of artists over these 22 years. Yet, there are challenges working with artists on a business level.

American craftspeople are competing globally with often wonderful work that's being made abroad.

And what are those challenges?

Stacey: I think there seems to be a negative correlation between creativity and business savvy. So here I am working with all of these incredibly talented people who have a lot of trouble keeping their records straight. We have to be very flexible from our end. I was just talking with one of our exhibitors about how many hats a craftsperson needs to wear. We were looking at some of the top artists in the country and realized that

they need to be very savvy to get to that point. They need to be good businesspeople. They need to have a lot of self-discipline, and they need that on top of all their talent. They need to understand their own strengths and weaknesses. I'm amazed at how many people can't do the most basic things, like get work photographed, and get their applications in on time. If you don't do those basics, then you're not in the game. A lot of people have a business partner, often a spouse, who handles the non-creative part of running a business. Very often those are the most successful craftspeople. They're a team, but one of them is creating, and the other one is making the business happen.

If there are two artists who are equally skilled and whose work is equally well designed and executed, but one of them is a better public-relations person, will that one rise to the top?

Stacey: Absolutely. It's about marketing, and understanding the partnership involved in coming to a craft show specifically. To be successful at any show, craftspeople have to maintain and use their mailing lists to keep their customers informed. They need to announce in advance at shows where they're going to be next. They can use e-mail. They need to have a constant

flow of information going to the people who buy their work. They come to a show expecting that we will do our part in promoting them by advertising and doing public relations, and all the different things that we do to make the show successful. But they should realize it's a partnership, and it's a disadvantage for them to not do their part. We encourage people to cultivate mailing lists, and explain to them that their customer at this show needs to get a postcard about the next show. These are proven craft buyers. These are the people that you need to get to come back. We send them a list of zip codes so they know which of the people on their mailing list are in our area who would come to the shows.

So now, what about the future, the state of the crafts world?

Stacey: I think most of our parents never considered the career choices that we made. They just didn't have that luxury because of the economy. So we are products of the healthy economic conditions that existed in the United States when we were growing up. This was a phenomenon of the bourgeoisie really. We very rarely meet working-class people who become potters. Most of the potters that we know come from middle-class families. People who were struggling and needed to support their brothers and sisters became accountants. They didn't become potters. It was just too risky. I firmly believe that as the culture becomes more technological, and things become more and more mass-produced, the handmade object will continue to be valued. I don't think that it will ever lose its importance. I do think, though, that there is great design being done all over the place, and that American craftspeople are competing globally with work, often wonderful work, that's being made on the other side of the planet. I think in the end that the people who have exceptional work are the people who will really survive and thrive in this kind of a climate. In addition, having all the business skills we talked about is what's going to make a craftsperson successful.

The crafts phenomenon of the second half of the 20th century is really changing now. I think that the history books are going to look back on that period and say there was a flowering of American studio crafts. I don't think any of us know what's going to happen in the next few decades, but I don't think that we're going to see what we saw in the last 50 years. So craftspeople are going to have to be much more savvy and deal with a much more competitive climate. American crafts are not as popular as they were. I don't know if young people in their 20s and 30s find what we do as compelling and interesting as people in their 40s and 50s. Certainly one of the comments that I hear all the time from the craftspeople is that not only are the craftspeople graying, but also the buyers are graying. It does concern me that there are so few young people who seem to appreciate what we do. American handmade items have become pricier, and I wonder if that eliminates the population of young people because they can't really afford what we make.

Where do you think the next market is going to come from?

Stacey: Unfortunately, today our culture seems to be very superficial in regard to the importance of design and the integrity of handmade objects and the appreciation of the arts in general. I do think that the biggest burden for creating this appreciation really falls on the educational system. Art is barely taught in school anymore. I have a college student working for me who has never taken an art course in her life. She's a business major, but how you can get to college and never have taken an art class is incomprehensible to me. We need to educate a new generation of people about the arts, and that means we have to advocate for art in the schools.

Any last words?

Stacey: I started out as a craftsperson myself, and I was showing my work in a gallery in Soho where I was working. I just happened to go into a craft gallery and show the owner my pieces, and he loved them. He started selling them, and he said to me—it was the best advice I ever got—he said, "Just continue to make them as beautiful, as original, and as exciting as you can. That should be your only goal." It was great advice.

OPENING THE GALLERY DOOR

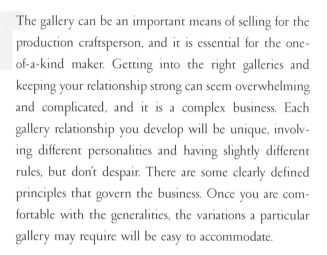

The gallery can be an important means of selling for the production craftsperson, and it is essential for the one-of-a-kind maker. Getting into the right galleries and keeping your relationship strong can seem overwhelming and complicated, and it is a complex business. Each gallery relationship you develop will be unique, involving different personalities and having slightly different rules, but don't despair. There are some clearly defined principles that govern the business. Once you are comfortable with the generalities, the variations a particular gallery may require will be easy to accommodate.

First and foremost: This is a system built on trust. Galleries do not buy art; they accept and show work from artists. When it is sold they pay the artist. The artist trusts the dealer, gallery owner, and personnel to handle her work with respect, to invest time in building her career, to actively seek to make sales, and to make payment for work sold in a timely manner. The gallery trusts the artist will deliver work at agreed upon times and will participate in the process of career-building and selling work. Without trust, this relationship cannot be successful.

Browsers and buyers alike flock to the American Folk Art Gallery in Asheville, NC.
PHOTO BY JOHN WIDMAN

TYPES OF GALLERIES

Galleries can take a number of forms; it's important to know what the differences mean to you.

● The Value of Nonprofits

Not-for-profit galleries account for a large percentage of the galleries operating today. They are typically a component of a larger nonprofit organization. For example, art and crafts schools often have galleries that provide faculty and students with a place to show their work as well as to see the exemplary work of professionals working in their field. Since the primary function of these facilities is to enrich the educational programs of the school, selling and career building are not a primary concern. Therefore, there may not be a paid staff; volunteers often handle gallery functions including sales.

Similarly, many colleges and universities have a gallery. Larger schools, and those with strong art departments, may have more than one. As with arts and crafts schools, these galleries primarily function as educational tools. They may specialize in showing faculty and student work, or shows exploring media that are important components of the curriculum. While the staffing and sales arrangements here are similar to the art and crafts schools, the big difference may be that budgets exist for printing catalogs and promotional materials.

There are also galleries in arts centers that are similar to museums. The art center might provide the community with a number of activities including theatre and the lively arts, and educational opportunities as well as a schedule of gallery shows. Notable in this respect is the John Michael Kohler Art Center in Sheboygan, Wisconsin. This center presents an ambitious schedule of one-person and group theme shows each year. Although the point of these shows is not to sell art, artists actively seek to have their work shown in centers like Kohler because of the prestige and future career benefits.

The nonprofit status of these facilities allows them to seek grant monies to enrich their budgets. This money makes it possible for these venues to take risks and to show work that is more controversial, too innovative, too large or otherwise not particularly salable and therefore not viable to the for-profit galleries. In this way these centers provide a great service to our field by allowing us to see work we would otherwise not be able to experience.

Participation in shows at non-profit galleries is important to every craftsperson's development. Often your first opportunity to show work is in a group show in one of these facilities. As your career grows you might be asked to have a one-person show in conjunction with a teaching engagement or because the faculty or exhibition committee recognizes and wants to honor your excellent work. Although these shows may not return much to the craftsperson in financial terms or career development, they are a way for emerging artists to show their work and for master craftspeople to have retrospectives and to give something back to the community.

● Questions for Cooperatives

There are thousands of gallery cooperatives of all kinds in the United States. These venues only show the work of their owner/members, and their members pay dues and provide volunteer time to support the business. Individuals may be invited to become members or may ask to be considered for membership. In either case there are important issues to consider and questions to ask.

You want to know how long the co-op has been operating. Obviously, longevity is a plus since it indicates that the cooperative has built a client base and served its members well enough to last. The size of the membership and the range of media included are also key questions. If the membership is large, you will want to know how often individual members get a one-person show in addition to regular representation. You also will want to know how decisions are made. Is there an elected board whose responsibilities include streamlining the decision-making process? If there is a board, do they keep minutes? They should, and you should ask to read a year's worth.

In addition, a co-op could be operating as a partnership with many partners, or it could be incorporated. You will be wise to give careful consideration to the legal structure of the co-op and any financial obligations you may be taking on with your membership. If the co-op is incorporated, your personal assets will be protected from any legal problems the co-op may have. You will be asked to complete an application that becomes your contract with the co-op and spells out your responsibilities. Read it carefully, and perhaps have your lawyer read it if you have any questions.

Each gallery relationship you develop will be unique and have slightly different rules.
PHOTO BY
JOHN WIDMAN

Ask to be given information that will help you determine the financial health of the co-op. Ask for accurate information about your financial commitments. Will you be assessed for costs other than your dues? It might be policy for individual members to pay the printing and mailing costs of a postcard for their solo shows, and this is understandable. But, will you need to kick in money in addition to your dues if the roof leaks or the furnace dies?

Most co-ops do not have paid employees; the members share the workload. Find out how the work is distributed. Are there clear, written job descriptions that allow members to understand the expectations for the various jobs? What arrangements are in place for situations when members can't, or simply don't, do their share?

Selling the work of the members is the primary function of the organization and the reason you are interested in joining; examine this area very carefully. Are shows installed professionally in a well-maintained and lighted gallery? Is the signage and labeling well done and in a manner conducive to sales? Are the exhibiting members encouraged to provide written statements about the work they are showing? Is there a budget for paid advertising? Does the co-op print high-quality artist cards for each show, and is there a mailing list and is it maintained? Does someone produce press releases and aggressively mail them to the media in the region, especially to free listings on the radio and television as well as to print media? Are the galleries open any evenings and on the weekend? It's important to be open when customers can visit and shop.

Has the co-op prepared a sales manual to help artists who are minding the store tackle the task of selling artwork? There is more to making a sale than opening the door and smiling. There are proven techniques for beginning a selling conversation and also for closing the sale. Some artists are not instinctively good at this, so a good co-op will provide tools to help.

Get your intuition involved in making this decision. Look for indications the membership is open-minded and welcomes new ideas and energy. Then, realizing this is an important ongoing relationship that should get better over time, decide whether you like what this organization has to offer. The co-op you are considering may not offer everything outlined here, but you might still feel like it's the place for you. If so, you could volunteer to write the needed sales manual or to keep the galleries open on Friday nights or Sunday afternoons, if necessary.

● The Private Sector

The privately owned gallery often bears the name of the owners or founders of the gallery and totally reflects their tastes and interests. Very often they specialize in just one or two media. Most of their shows are one-person presentations, and although selling is just one of the services they provide their artists, they can seldom afford to show work that does not sell. There are a limited number of these galleries and therefore they can be quite selective when choosing artists.

It is possible that a gallery may find you in a first-rate juried or nonprofit gallery show. But for most craftspeople, gaining representation by a private gallery requires a great deal of persistence and stamina, not to mention having great work. The competition for the few spots in the really good galleries is intense; however, having your career in the hands of the right gallery can change your life. But it's key that the gallery be the right one for you and your work. As you begin this process, remember that your expectations and those of the gallery need to be aligned. This will be a personal, as well as professional, relationship. The essential attributes of a good gallery/client relationship include trust and a mutual commitment to building your career.

● *Looking for the Right Place*

The best way to get information about a gallery is from someone who is, or was, represented by that gallery. Trade publications are also a source of information in their editorial content, reviews of shows and display ads. Advertising rates are very high in these four-color glossies. Only galleries that have achieved some level of success can advertise there.

When you have a short list of possible appropriate galleries, or maybe a gallery has approached you, it's time to begin getting specific information. You will want to consider the location of the space. Is it on street level? This is very important except in large cities. It should be in a commercial district with other galleries within walking distance. It is absolutely true that foot traffic drives sales, and that other businesses in general, and similar businesses in particular, generate foot traffic. The space needs to be able to accommodate your work, whether that means large ample wall spaces, or small intimate showcases, or pedestals with vitrines. You are looking for a well-maintained space with freshly painted walls and good gallery furniture. Look for indications that someone thinks the details are important. The labels, or price lists, need to be well done; the graphics should be clean, neat, and, along with signage, written in a typeface that complements the overall image of the gallery.

A look at past and future show schedules is a great source of information. You will learn who has, and will, show there, and you should be able to discern a point of view, a focus. Does the gallery specialize in narrative work, minimalist objects, sculptural forms, vessels, or perhaps just one media? If the gallery's offerings are too broad, you may want to keep looking since it won't be a likely source for collectors because it isn't clear what they will find there.

It's always good to find a gallery that presents events related to their shows. Artist talks, panels, films, and slide shows are all sure signs of a vital and lively business. Find out if the gallery does temporary shows such as SOFA, the

International Exhibition of Sculptural Objects and Functional Art in Chicago and New York. These shows draw international audiences of collectors who are predisposed and prepared to purchase the things you make. They provide priceless opportunities to get your work before this audience and to enrich your bank account and career.

One of the most important assets to any retail business is its staff. The most important staff member is the gallery director or dealer. Dealers are creative adventurers seeking talented young new artists to represent. When they find one they often provide encouragement in the form of moral and financial support. They work to generate interest in the new talent by bringing the work to the attention of the three Big Cs: collectors, curators, and critics. Collectors are generally quite knowledgeable about what they collect; you want your gallery staff to know more about your work than they do. This means there has to be adequate staff so they can spend time learning about you and your work. The gallery staff must understand your work and be able to convey that information to current and prospective collectors. Knowledge lets the gallery staff interact easily and confidently with your collectors, and this is really important for your career and sales.

The best work in the world isn't going anywhere without an audience. Without adequate public relations the audience won't know to come. I consider every printed piece produced by a gallery to be part of, but not all of, a publicity plan. The most essential component of the public-relations package is the mailing list. Find out how many names are on the gallery's list, how names get added, and how they get removed. You'll want to know how the list is used and maintained. For instance, do they do a mailing every couple of years with a mail-back card so people can identify specific interests? Are those who are no longer interested removed? A large list that is badly maintained is not as useful as a small, carefully maintained and targeted list.

Take the time to review the gallery's recent print ads. You are looking for consistent graphics and a layout that clearly presents the craftsperson's work. A strong gallery will have ads in national magazines dealing with specific media, such as *Ceramics Monthly*, and also in broadly based national magazines such as *American Style* and *American Craft*. This is the paid side of the public relations picture; anyone can pay and have an ad published. Much more difficult to get, and of equal if not more importance, is the free press a gallery receives.

The ability to produce well-written press releases and informative and complete press kits are the keys that open this door. Ask to review some. Then look at the gallery's press clippings. At the very least, every show should be listed in every free calendar, both local and national. Ideally you will find the majority of the gallery shows have been reviewed in the local press, and some have gotten national attention. You might ask questions to learn how comfortable the gallery director is about communicating with the press.

The gallery's relationship with collectors is of the utmost importance. Collectors are the engines that drive the gallery train. People become collectors for various reasons: the love of the work, social connections, investment, or simple desire. Whatever the motivations, collector dollars and moral support are essential to the craftsperson. They are the repeat customers, the ones who commission objects for their homes, or jewels for their bodies. Collectors are the informed individuals who join and participate in the numerous collector organizations that spread the knowledge about our field. The intrigue of the hunt and the thrill of discovery energize collectors and, of great importance to you, they can't resist sharing the news about their newest find. You don't want to work with a gallery director who does not have ready access to the potential collectors of the objects you make.

In addition, the purchase of your work by a museum, or its being chosen for a museum show, will provide a major boost for your career. An effective gallery director will be comfortable approaching institutions and making presentations of the work of the craftspeople the gallery represents. Find out if the gallery contacts museums about their artists' work and if the director has any relationships with curators. Further, find out if the gallery has placed any work with museums, either in the permanent collection or in an exhibition.

● *Approaching the Gallery*

After you have done your research, what is the best way to approach your chosen galleries? Your initial contact with the gallery is crucial. I don't know any gallery director who wants to deal with unexpected visitors who are not there as customers, so simply showing up to chat about representation is out. If you have a friend, or even an acquaintance, who is known to the gallery director and who feels good about your work, see if he will make an introductory call for you. Nothing opens the door faster than an introduction.

With or without an introduction, you will want to call the gallery to make an appointment to discuss your work. Make your initial telephone call brief and efficient. Introduce yourself, state the purpose of your call, and ask for information about the gallery review procedure. Galleries are beginning to post this information on their websites, so check there before you call. Traditionally, galleries reviewed work from hard copies, i.e., slides and paper. Increasingly, galleries are able to receive this information via the Internet, and so you should find out the preference of each gallery you approach. Follow the phone call by sending a well-prepared presentation that introduces you and your work, clearly and in depth. Be aware that gallery directors are busy people, and therefore it is important that the cover letter be well-organized and to the point. Refer to your phone conversation;

restate your interest in their gallery and why you think your work is appropriate for the gallery. End with your action plan: for instance, "I trust it will be appropriate for me to phone in two weeks; I will be able to provide any additional information that may be helpful at that time."

Your packet also must include visual images (see page 149). Slides are the traditional form and may be the preferred way for a gallery to view your work. However, more and more galleries are reviewing artist's work on CDs or via e-mail. Send slides if there is no stated preference. The gallery director will want to know the title, size, materials, and price of each piece presented. If you are not confident about pricing your work, say so and perhaps set forth a range for each piece.

The color accuracy is far superior in professional quality slides than it is on a computer screen where the color may be incorrectly balanced. If the color is very important in your work you might want to send slides in addition to other presentations. Deciding what images and how many to send takes some serious thought. You might want to prepare several presentations and show them to another artist for feedback before making the final decision.

The best work in the world isn't going anywhere without an audience. Blue Spiral I in Asheville, NC.
PHOTO BY JOHN WIDMAN

You do not want to send images of unrelated work. Galleries are looking for artists with mature concepts, which means they need to see related pieces that demonstrate you are working through an idea, exploring all its possibilities. You might consider sending a group of images representing each body of work that you have completed in the past five years, but not more than 20 images. Include an up-to-date resume, any reviews of your work, and any essays or articles written about you and your work. If you are sending hard-copy materials you will want to provide a stamped envelope for the return of your materials. You might have to wait up to a year for their return.

After your stated waiting time, phone the director to ask if the materials have arrived and been reviewed. Offer to provide any additional images or information that might be helpful. If the gallery is nearby, offer to drop off an actual sample of the work. There's nothing like the real thing. Try to set up an appointment for an interview and plan to bring several examples of your work at that time. If the gallery is a great distance away, offer to ship work and arrange for a longer phone call to discuss it.

As with any interview situation where rejection is a possibility, this process can be very stressful. Go into the process mindful that dealers need to find new people to represent and fresh work to present to the clients of their galleries. Therefore, getting to know you and your work is as important to them as getting to know them is to you. You may think I've suggested you ask too many questions. Let me assure you, smart dealers are seeking and impressed by business-savvy artists eager to promote their work and career. Ask away!

● *Working for Your Art*

Once you and your work have been accepted by a gallery, be prepared to go to work for your gallery. It is essential that you communicate clearly and regular-

ly regarding your work plans and the nature of your new work. Provide the gallery with a status report regarding the availability of all work, both old and new, and provide images of this work. It is essential to photograph each one-of-a-kind piece as it is finished. This could be a digital image you make yourself for pieces of lesser value, but it should be a professional image for the more important and pricier pieces. This lets you maintain a record of your work and provides the gallery with an essential selling tool. Many collectors today purchase work from photos mailed to them by the gallery, or that are posted on a gallery website or attached to an e-mail.

Let the gallery know immediately when any problems occur with your work schedule. They must know if the piece the collector from out of town wanted to see won't be there on the day he will be. Provide the gallery with a list of any collector contacts you may already have, and if possible, images of the pieces they own, where and when they bought the pieces, and what they paid for them. With this information, the gallery can present your new work to collectors with knowledge and confidence. Now that you have a gallery, you won't be contacting these collectors except to send out personal e-mail invitations to your gallery shows, or holiday greetings and family announcements. A good gallery invests considerable amounts of time and money selling an artist's work and building her career. Nothing will destroy a gallery's trust in an artist faster and more completely than to learn that the artist has been selling work directly to collectors.

From time to time you will be asked to provide other information. Your gallery may need a new, or more in-depth, artist's statement, or a statement about the new body of work you have just given them. Provide these tools as quickly as possible.

To the collector, the artist is the most important person.
PHOTO BY JOHN WIDMAN

And last, show up when it counts! To the collector, the artist is the most important person. They almost always want to establish a relationship with the artist, to ask questions and know more about why you do what you do. Always attend your show openings. It's also smart to attend other openings at your gallery. Seldom do collectors look only at the current show; they almost always want to see the back-stock. You never know when someone will find your work, and your presence can help make the sale. Make yourself available for visits with collectors, and consider letting your more important collectors visit your studio. They will love it and share what they learned and saw with their friends and colleagues, who also may decide to collect your work.

It is important that you understand that you are there to help promote your work, while the gallery is there to relieve you from conversations about money, selling, and the payment arrangements for your work. Often the dealer will talk to you privately about possible financial arrangements of a sale, but you should refer any collector questions, particularly those about money, to the gallery staff.

● *Your Gallery Working for You*

Just as you are working for your gallery, you can expect the gallery to provide you with many services. If you are granting a gallery the exclusive right to show your work, they should provide you with a written contract setting forth the responsibilities and expectations of both parties in this relationship. The contract will vary depending on whether it covers a specific show and period of time, an ongoing relationship, or an exclusive relationship. In addition, the gallery should maintain an accurate inventory of work that is in their possession, and a really effective gallery will maintain a database of information about all your work including that which has sold as well as the pieces that are still available.

The gallery director, your dealer, should stay in touch with you regarding any activity or lack of activity with your work. He should communicate the reactions from the public viewing your work. The other personnel of the gallery should know as much as possible about you and your work. Many galleries maintain a binder of materials about each of their artists. If your gallery does not provide this service, consider putting a booklet together for them and be prepared to update the contents in a timely manner. In addition, take every opportunity to talk to the staff about yourself, your work, and why you make it.

Every gallery artist should have her work considered for the photograph on a group show card and in print ads. Since you have regularly been providing high-quality images, you should be in the running here. The materials prepared need to be well-conceived and printed in a quality consistent with the gallery's standards of excellence. Well-written and informative press releases must be mailed for each show. An e-mail release also could go out to collectors and the press announcing the arrival of a new body of your work at the gallery. Early in your career you may be asked to contribute to the costs of producing

113

An effective dealer will use all the avenues available for selling your work.

PHOTO BY JOHN WIDMAN

some promotional materials, but be sure your career will benefit from the materials you are paying for. Often these payments will be deducted from future sales; this should be spelled out in your contract. Don't be shy about offering to contribute or match gallery spending to increase the size of ads or the number of cards printed to promote your show. Remember, your contribution will help build your career and sales, and that's what it's all about.

An effective dealer will use all the avenues available for selling your work. They will show it respectfully in the gallery and temporary art shows. They also will be in touch with your collectors in an ongoing way, not just when you have a solo show or are in a group show. Good dealers travel. They show up at collector events at art centers, museums, and other art-related venues. Sometimes they sit on panels at these events and take this opportunity to show slides of their artists' work. Good dealers make presentations of their artist's work to museum curators for consideration for group or solo shows, as well as for purchase.

Finally, your gallery should pay you in a timely manner following the terms spelled out in the contract. Typically, payment is made in the month after the sale was made. If the buyer is making payments over time, and this is quite common on high-priced items, the gallery may not pay you until they have been fully paid for the work.

You should not enter into any financial arrangement that pays you less than 50 percent of the selling price. The one exception to this relates to the universally given "collector's discount." Collectors are most commonly given a 10 percent discount on work costing more than a certain amount. The discount is split equally between the gallery and the artist. Sometimes the gallery may give a bigger discount to their really good customers to ensure customer loyalty. This benefits the gallery, but may or may not benefit you specifically. Be smart: make it clear to the gallery that if they choose to offer a larger discount, the difference must come from their share.

● *A Good Choice*

The last gallery decision is one that every craftsperson should be lucky enough to encounter: How many galleries should you allow to represent your work? The answer is not simple, but it is discernible if you consider certain factors.

An exclusive contract with one gallery provides focused career development.

The number of galleries you can have will first depend on the amount of work you can and want to make, and how well it sells. For instance, if you produce 20 objects a year and you have a gallery that can sell most of them, then you should choose to be in that one gallery. Craftspeople who make many more objects in a year than a single gallery can sell might want to have more than one gallery and more than one show in a year.

If you decide you need to have more than one gallery, geography must be a consideration. You neither want, nor will galleries agree, to multiple representation in one city or area. You will want to spread your work around the country. A plan could be to seek representation in a major city on each coast, Boston or New York, with San Francisco or Seattle, for example. If you are prolific, you can add cities in other regions. Be mindful of where your client base is the densest, and be sure to secure representation there.

But more is not necessarily better. An exclusive contract with one gallery will provide you with the most focused career development, and will make numerous services available to you. In this relationship the gallery expects to receive all the work you produce, and expects your total cooperation in selling it. In trade for this exclusive access to your work, you can expect special treatment. In an exclusive relationship, your gallery will take on the task of managing your career, as well as selling our work. You would ask your dealer to help make decisions about the requests you might get for teaching workshops or speaking engagements—are they advantageous to your career, or is this time better spent producing more work?

An exclusive relationship will mean that the gallery will keep a definitive inventory of current work, and records of work that has been sold, including who bought it, when, and for how much. Your dealer will also be instrumental in establishing the prices for your work based on your sales record, the prices being paid for the work of other craftspeople of similar caliber, the demand for your work, and the quality of the current body of work. Although it's smart for you to leave these decisions to the professionals, you certainly can make your wishes known.

The number of galleries you have will depend on the amount of work you can and want to make.
PHOTO COURTESY OREGON COLLEGE OF ART AND CRAFT

115

In addition, your gallery will respond to requests for loans of your work from other galleries, typically choosing only those that can enhance your career or sell your work for a premium price. This latter benefits the gallery directly since normally galleries split the commission on a loaned work 50/50.

Any gallery relationship—nonprofit, cooperative, or private—is a give-and-take proposition. You will be expected to do your part to make the relationship work, and that will mean work above and beyond simply crafting your products. The return is having someone else committed to seeing you succeed and doing all he or she can to make that happen.

Perspective from a Life in Crafts
Leslie Ferrin

Leslie Ferrin is the director of the Ferrin Gallery in Lenox, Massachusetts. She gave us an inside, in-depth look at the world of the gallery professional.

What in your background led to a life in craft?

Leslie: My mother is a painter. I was raised in a household that had artists and musicians coming in and out of it. At one point, when I was four or five years old, we rented our house to a potter and folksinger. My mother's artist friends would stay with us when they had shows in New York. I always had the example of a professional artist as a career model.

My mother encouraged me with regular art classes. Like many young girls, I read the *Little House* series of

books, obsessively rereading them four or five times. It was the 1960s, and the back-to-the-land movement was a strong influence. I enjoyed making things by hand and wanted to be self-supporting, even live off the land, as did the pioneer families. When I was a teenager, I started to attend the American Crafts Council shows in Rhinebeck, New York. It was at that time that I focused clearly on my idea to become a potter and a self-supporting crafts artist. The many successful artists exhibiting there each year provided me with a clear career model to focus on.

And then did you study pottery in a structured way?

Leslie: I went to Hampshire College whose motto is "to know is not enough," and the philosophy was to teach lifelong learning, how to ask and answer questions. By the time I finished I had it in my mind that not only was I going to be a potter, but I would balance that with the idea of being an "entrepreneur." Northampton, Massachusetts was in the midst of a downtown renaissance, and many of the players were my age. I came up with the idea for a place called the Crafts Market where there would be studios and showrooms in the same spaces

So let's go from the Crafts Market to being the director of Ferrin Gallery. Why would you want to do that?

Leslie: I started Pinch Pottery in the Crafts Market in 1979 with the vision of myself as a self-supporting artist. The Crafts Market was a floor in a renovated department store that housed various stores and restaurants. In addition to ceramics, we had woodworking, weaving, and stained glass studios on our floor, which was independent of the rest of the building. My dream was that you would put your artwork in the kiln, and as you opened it there would be people waiting to buy what was in it. I was always tied to the idea of making a living and keeping it as simple and direct as possible. However, it quickly became obvious that to support myself, I was supposed to efficiently reproduce objects again and again. That was not my forte.

On the creative side, I had come to the end of a set of ideas. On the professional side, it turned out that I enjoyed selling art made by other people, and Ferrin Gallery began. I look at that whole period of time in which I produced artwork as a training period for what I do now.

So it was your entrepreneurial spirit and your interest in providing good representation to young artists that motivated you to become a gallery director?

Leslie: Right, my father is a businessman; my mother is an artist. I got the best of both worlds. I want to represent artists in the way I never was. I want to provide opportunities for artists to grow creatively through exhibitions and experiences where, at times, the product or its sale is not necessarily the only end result. I use my experience as an artist to guide me in terms of what we do for artists: prompt payments, proper promotion, advocacy to the collector, press and museum communities.

What do you find most rewarding about the experience of working with artists?

Leslie: We recently promoted a group of artists in a show and called it "The Next Generation." The exciting thing about putting this group together was watching these artists from afar, one by one, get to the point where they had a body of work they could show. It is very different from when we started out and were building careers the first time around. This next generation of 20 to 30-year-old artists is able to

follow in the footsteps of the now 40 to 50-year-old artists we represent, specifically, in terms of introductions to collectors, curators, and residency programs.

Another area that has developed over time is the cross-fertilization between artist careers, such as when one of the gallery artists gets invited to an exhibition, and I can provide a group of images of work by other gallery artists who might fit into that show. Another is when one artist gets invited to a residency situation; then a year later I can suggest the name of another artist. With the emerging artists that I present, it is more a process of watching their work over time, their dedication to their work, and seeing that work grow and emerge. When it starts to work, when the fit is right, it is very exciting to see those artists take advantage of the opportunities offered and move forward due to the financial stability offered through sales.

What is the process for choosing an artist for representation?

Leslie: The artist's role is to create the artwork and to provide the necessary support information, slides or digital images, statements, and resumes. When initially reviewing work, I can look at those three parts and make a judgment about how to proceed from there. I look for a related body of work up to 10 pieces. Along with this I need an artist's statement, a resume, and a price list with materials and sizes. You can't imagine how rare it is for the combination of those four things to arrive on my desk at the same time. If they don't, it tends to reflect poorly upon the work, and it goes in the pile of "Do Later" instead of "Do Now."

I have to analyze how the new work will fit with the rest of the stable, the group of artists that one gallery represents. I ask if it fits into the interests of our collectors, is it a good partnership for us and our existing community of artists, is the work the right scale, and other practical questions such as how fragile is it, and what will it cost to ship back if we are not able to sell it?

Is it important for an artist to be present when their work is in a show?

Leslie: It's so much easier for me to work with the artist who immediately falls into a pattern of being able to show up at an exhibition, either at art fairs or at the gallery. It's not to say that the work doesn't speak for itself, and if an artist never shows up that I wouldn't show their work. But there is an excitement to the community aspect of artists working with one another, sharing ideas, sharing technique. And it is important when we start the introductions that the artists are there for the public openings whenever possible.

How do you see your role in the marketing of artists' work?

JASON WALKER
Nest of Conduit
7" x 14"
Porcelain
PHOTO BY
MICAHEL MCCARTHY

When you look at our relationship as a partnership, my role is promotion, and the artist's is to produce. One of the things I try to do is take care of setting up the extracurricular activities so the artist can spend her time in the studio, not on the phone. I do

this by planning and arranging lectures, panels, visiting artist activities, and either solo or group exhibitions. The artists and I work together to decide which offers are accepted, how they are balanced out year to year. In making these decisions, we discuss what they are getting out of it that is additional to what they can do in the studio or that our gallery can pro-

vide in terms of publications, professional affiliations, and travel experiences.

The other part of marketing is more direct. It is our job to promote the artist's work in magazines, through ads and articles, and to produce mailing cards. To do this, I work with the artist to create imagery and information that is used in these materials and becomes the press release about their work and exhibition. I communicate with a large number of press contacts and maintain an active relationship with institutions and independent curators. It is our job to get the work into the public eye and to place artwork in public and private collections that will provide the longest possible public life.

What's "the longest public life"?

Leslie: This starts at the time when I first receive an image of an artist's work prior to the show, ideally, four to five months prior to the opening date, so I can create the ads and marketing campaign, the press releases, get the images duplicated and out to the various appropriate publications. The earlier I have that image, the more that piece will be published, and the piece gets the longest public life. The next step is the "adoption." We are all temporary custodians for the artwork we own. It is my job to work with my list of collectors who are waiting to buy a piece by that artist and make the placement. In a case where an artist has a waiting list, I think about who has supported the artist's career, who's supported the gallery, who's going to share the work with others in their home, or lend it for exhibitions. Most collectors understand this part of the hierarchy of buying things. They might not like it, but if they are experienced buyers, they understand and are usually willing to wait. It is in the artist's best interest for me to consider these factors.

But the exhibition is five months down the road, and we need an advance image of a completed piece that would be available for sale and on view during the show. It almost requires someone—and the gallery does this from time to time—to prepay the artist for a piece that will sell during the exhibition so that they can continue to create the body of work for the exhibition, hold onto that piece, and eventually make that available. Fortunately, the gallery is mature enough at this point that I can send a check out prior to a completed sale. But not every gallery can, nor is every artist in the position to hold work. But it's very important to hold that piece and have a good image available so that the piece has the longest public life possible before it's sold.

What do you think about artists selling their own work?

Leslie: There are artists who are very good at selling their own work. It makes no sense for us to represent such artists as it is a duplication of effort and can create conflicts when the sales are to an overlapping clientele. The time an artist spends selling is time taken away from the studio, which can add up to more than the commission taken by the gallery. The question is: When is it more important to let the gallery sell so that the artist can focus on producing? When is the time, money, and energy spent on marketing less important than using those resources to focus on the creative process?

Do you give your artists feedback from clients that might influence their work?

Leslie: Absolutely. And in some cases I feel guilty about it because I don't want to tell an artist what to make or that they should create based on the demands of the market. On the other hand, as long as the request has integrity and it's not compromising the artist's point of view, what is the harm in understanding that the commission process and patronage are important, and that

RED WELDON
SANDLIN
Miss Ettaquette
10' x 18½' x 7"
Porcelain
PHOTO BY
MICAHEL MCCARTHY

there are times when you respond to that? There are all sorts of requests that are presented to an artist. An artist could be asked to make something on a miniature scale for a benefit, or they could be asked to make an installation for a museum. These are no less invasive than being told, "We have a client who wants one in blue." The final decision is up to the artist, and it's up to me as a gallery director to steer things in a way that's appropriate for the artist's career. In most cases I advise, "Don't make anything you wouldn't make otherwise."

I think if artists put themselves into the marketplace, then they need to pay attention to the marketplace. The feedback from their dealer is a direct connection to the marketplace. I would like to think that the feedback I give them is: 1) not offensive; 2) constructive; and 3) an opportunity to move in a direction that they might not have thought of on their own. It's something that is beneficial to them in terms of the longer view of their career.

Perspective from a Life in Crafts

Kari Lonning

Kari Lonning has been a full-time contemporary basket maker since 1975, and is the author of The Art of Basketry, *a comprehensive resource on the design and construction of contemporary fiber vessels and sculpture. She lives and works in Connecticut. She spoke with us about working with galleries.*

PHOTO BY BETSY HOLLOWAY

At what point in your career did you decide you were ready for a gallery?

Kari: I didn't make the decision: A gallery found me. After I had been exhibiting at the Rhinebeck craft fair for a few years, a gallery I had been selling work to asked me to do a one-person show. That was 30 years ago, and I am still friends with the owner, although she no longer has the gallery.

How do you find a gallery, and what factors do you consider when choosing one?

Kari: Usually they find me through juried craft fairs and exhibitions, or as a result of publicity or other media coverage. Often a friend's recommendation or introduction to a gallery owner works well for both the gallery and me.

The first thing I consider is if I have seen or heard about them in print, or through other artists. I try to find out what other work they show, and the price ranges of that work. Then I try to talk to other artists who have shown with the gallery. Word-of-mouth is important. If possible, I try to visit the gallery myself.

How many galleries do you work with at one time, and how do you balance them?

Kari: I only work with two or three galleries at a time, unless I am participating in an invitational show. I try to reach a wider audience by not working with galleries in the same geographic areas. Galleries appreciate this, as well.

How do you help your gallery sell your work?

Kari: When I give work to a gallery, I give them photography to use in publicizing these pieces. I also give them as much technical information as they are willing to take in, understand, and talk to their collectors about, especially in the case of an invitational exhibition, or one-person shows. I give the gallery names of collectors who may be interested in buying my new work.

Under what conditions would you want an exclusive relationship with one gallery?

Kari: If one gallery alone could sell enough work to support me, that would be great, but it would put a lot of pressure and expectations on the gallery. Since I don't produce a lot of work, and no single gallery gets more than a few pieces at any one time anyhow, if I made a commitment to show and be shown by two galleries, each would be able to show a representative body of work. These galleries would have a vested interest in knowing what I do and would be able to talk knowledgeably to their collectors about it. Finding the gallery who would be willing to develop a long-term relationship with me would indeed be a joy.

I have started working with a small gallery. When the public looks to that gallery for my newest work, then everyone—the gallery, the public, and I—all benefit. If they sell well, I will be able to focus on the creative aspect of making a living, of weaving new work.

Do you see any conflict between selling your own work and having gallery representation?

Kari: If I were working with one gallery and they were doing all of the publicity, they would deserve to reap all the benefits. Unfortunately, I don't have that luxury, so I do a lot of advertising and publicity myself. Some galleries feel awkward about their artists selling through juried fairs. I see this as an opportunity for me to meet the public and introduce them to my work. The larger the ticket, the less likely people are to buy on the spot, anyhow. Since I don't encourage visitors to my studio, I direct people to the gallery I am working with. This works well for everyone. Handled carefully, the potential conflict becomes a respectful balancing act between artists and their galleries.

KARI LONNING
She Met a Wall and Other Stories
he: 18½" x 9" x 10";
she: 14½" x 9½" 10"

121

KARI LONNING
Holding Thoughts of HM
18" x 15"
PHOTOS COURTESY
OF ARTIST

SPINNING THE WEB

Shopping on the Internet can save time, is extremely convenient, and is changing the way Americans buy. It is also changing the way crafts are marketed. The web has the potential to serve as a virtual press agent and shop for the Internet-savvy craftsperson. You need to learn everything you can about how to use it.

THE VIRTUAL PICTURE

A survey by the Pew Research Center found that two-thirds of adult Americans use the Internet to buy consumer items. Although there is no hard data on craft sales specifically, it's reasonable to assume that e-shoppers are spending money on handmade items. Internet shopping will surely have an impact on the already changing craft market. A study completed by Jupiter Media Metrix predicts that the online shopping population will grow to 132 million by 2006. According to Forrester Research, online spending will reach $172.4 billion in 2005, up 22 percent over 2004. This same research predicts the purchase of jewelry and gifts to grow 33 percent. Now, wouldn't you like to have your share of this marketplace?

Wouldn't you like to have your share of the growing online marketplace?

The millennials—children of the baby boomers who sparked a dramatic growth in handmade buying at the end of the last century—number 71 million. They rely on the Internet for communication, as a source of information and for dealing with their shopping needs. They are very image-savvy and can make decisions about objects they view on the screen. Consequently, careful photography and multiple images of an object, including close-ups, are essential to selling to this Internet market. And the millennials are not the only age group shopping online. In 2006, customers over age 50 are expected to account for 30 percent of online shopping, according to the Jupiter research. Jupiter also predicts that by 2008 each e-shopper will spend $780 annually.

Thomas Mann, a New Orleans-based jeweler whose work is sold in shops and shown in galleries all over the country, describes the role of the Internet in the craft business this way: "The nature of craft marketing is changing, and we must do everything we can to retain the interest of a declining customer base. The Internet is an important way to do this. I have in-house staff whose responsibility it is to manage my site on a daily basis. I am very clear that to be a successful tool, it must be managed like the best brick-and-mortar stores. I also believe we have to find a way to make the Internet a win-win situation with our wholesale accounts and galleries. They feel threatened by our online presence, yet they are not using the Internet to sell our products. Retailers have to understand that people who buy online have seen the work and likely own a piece they bought in a shop or gallery." You might want to visit www.thomasmann.com for a look at a site that is well-done and easy to use.

WHAT FORMAT?

There are several general website formats that can work for craftspeople; you'll have to choose the one that best suits your business. Artists are beginning to create websites and are posting images of their one-of-a-kind work, creating a virtual portfolio. Proper marketing and promotion of these sites will ensure that a surfer will find them and make a purchase or go to a gallery link to purchase an item. Savvy craftspeople are also sending out e-mails inviting galleries to review their work online rather than mailing a portfolio. This approach is very efficient, uses

no paper or stamps, and allows the gallery owner to review the work and respond in a timely manner.

Production craftspeople may want to design a site to be used by wholesale buyers, just as they would use a printed catalog. Typically, the buyer registers to use the wholesale section of the site, and the registration restricts the use of the site to qualified buyers. Buyers choose a user name and are given a password that is used to gain access. They can then place orders for product online, something that is happening with increased frequency. Or the site might be set up so the buyer has to call in an order. This will allow you to interact with your customers, and add a personal touch to doing business online. You could also use this time to talk about new product not yet posted on your website.

A well-designed website is like a beautiful store.

You might choose to add another section to the same site and offer products at retail. This means anyone can use this area of the site to place an order. To do this, the site must be set up with a shopping cart system that can take orders and securely handle credit card information.

IT'S ALL IN THE PRESENTATION

Just as with booth and shop displays, you must present your online product correctly if you want to attract and sell to buyers. The first step is to find an experienced web designer/web manager to prepare your site and maintain it. Just as with anyone you're considering working with, it is important to check his or her references. Marjorie Clark of Little Fish Studios, a web designer/manager, suggests you search the web for sites you like, and find the designer's name at the bottom of the home page. Then contact their clients and ask about their experience working with the designer. When you have narrowed the search, it's time to contact the designer and interview them. All of this can, of course, happen via e-mail.

● The Domain Name

One of the first things the web designer will do is help you develop your domain name and get it registered. These are the words people will type in to reach your site, or a page within your site. It is called a Uniform Resource Locator (URL); simply, it's your address online.

Think carefully about the name you are choosing. Luann Udell, a New Hampshire artist, shares this advice about domain names: "I recently went back to using just my name for my business and my website. I am much happier for it. I think artists can get carried away coming up with a cute business name, and trying to revert to your own name later can be problematic. Stick with simple."

Simple, yes, and descriptive, surely. If your name gives a clue to the nature of the contents, it will pop up when people are searching for your product. Glassblower Josh Simpson is well-known for his planets, his site is www.megaplanet.com. Perfect. Even more perfect; he has another site, www.joshsimpson.com that is linked to the Megaplanet site for people who don't know the planet connection but know his name.

● A Host of Information

The information on your site has to be stored somewhere and made available when requested; this is called hosting. (In this case, the host is not in a dinner jacket, but rather is a computer in a plastic jacket.) The annual fee for hosting a site is typically $15.

You have to decide the services you want your site to provide your business and your e-shoppers. A good web designer will help you understand the ways your site can function to deliver those services. He will know how to build sites that are not only beautiful but that also move quickly. The latter is essential. How many times have you clicked off a site because it was moving too slowly? Having a website that pokes along is like having a retail store with a clerk who is too busy reading a novel to wait on your customers.

Your web designer will be most effective when you are clear about the business you are trying to build. This means you need to think through the marketing strategies for your business. Your web designer should be able to help you craft a strategy that will attract the web surfer and turn them into your e-shopper.

● Home Run!

A sample home page is the first thing the designer will do. This will take into account your aesthetic considerations, marketing strategy, and product information. You will then discuss the design, and changes will be made until it has the look and information you want. This page will act as a template for the rest of the site. The most important part of the site will be the product pages that may show one-of-a-kind pieces or production items. At this point you will have to provide the images you want included. These could be digital or slides; however, there may be an extra charge for scanning slides. In either case, you must provide complete descriptive information about each image, including: size, materials, date created, title, weight, price, and units that must be purchased, as well as any special features and benefits the item may offer. If you are building an online portfolio site, or one you will maintain in-house, be sure it is set up so images can be changed easily. Remember, a website is an active form of communication, unlike printed materials that are finished when they return from the printer. A great website is always a work-in-progress.

Your designer should suggest you include links on your site. For example, you might link your site to that of a show where you plan to sell your product or a gallery that shows your work. Many websites have an "about" section. Yours could include an artist's resume and statement, or a business history and philosophy. You may want to have a page of new items or best sellers, allowing the speed shopper to see what's new and hot very quickly. Another section of your site will allow visitors to leave messages and feedback. You will want to decide what kind of information you want from this section of the site.

● A-La-Cart

Sites that actually sell online do this using the shopping cart system. It's important that the appearance of your cart match that of the rest of your site. Your web designer should help you find the fastest and most user-friendly cart system. E-shoppers want the check out process to be easy, and countless online sales have been lost by a shopper frustrated with a complicated, slow or annoying check out system.

Here's what happens when an e-shopper clicks on an item, puts it in her cart and completes a sale. Briefly, the shopping cart sends a message to your payment gateway which then sends a message to the cardholder's bank asking if the credit card is valid, etc. The bank then sends the appropriate message back to the payment gateway, which in turn sends a confirmation message to the customer. The payment gateway also sends a message to you telling you what was purchased, how it is to be shipped, any special requests, and how much will be deposited in your bank.

Some shoppers may leave a site because of the cost of shipping. Be fair with shipping costs, both to the customer and to yourself. Shipping is expensive and seasoned e-shoppers know this. They are willing to pay for the convenience of shopping from home, but they won't respond well to being overcharged.

● Start Your Engine

Getting your site into search engines so it will be seen by the most e-shoppers is the work of your web designer. You want maximum search engine optimization, i.e., you want your site to appear in the top ten responses to a search request for your type of work. In an effort to make this happen, you will be asked to provide a list of words and phrases

A great website is always a work-in-progress.

es that you believe will help lead visitors to your site. Surfers initiate a search of the Internet by entering words related to what they are trying to find. These are called keywords. For instance, a potter's site might include the keywords "mugs," "dinnerware," "porcelain," or "majolica." Keep in mind that a study by Vividence, a market research firm, found that 52 percent of search requests leading to a visit to a shopping site used only one or two words. You have to get yours right.

THE PRICE OF GLORY

You will need to have a budget for all this. As with everything else, you get what you pay for. In this case, you can choose a simple site or a complex one, managed in-house or by a web manager, professional photos, or high-quality in-house photos. At the most basic level it should cost about $1,500 to get the site designed. Basic hosting may cost as little as $10 a month, increasing to as much as $25 with a shopping cart. In addition, there may be a one-time set-up charge of $30 to $50. Your domain name registration could cost around $25 a year.

You will also need a budget for promotion. Initially your best e-shoppers will be people who know your work. Therefore it is essential they receive mailings inviting them to visit your site. Since you will continually change your website to keep it interesting and profitable, you will want to send mailings several times a year. Further, any printed materials you create, including brochures, business cards, show cards and print ads, should include your web address. You will want to begin collecting e-mail information from anyone who expresses interest in or purchases your product. When you have enough of these addresses, you will want to send e-mails with news about your product and a reminder to visit your website.

Your web store is a separate business and must be treated as one. It will need to be given ongoing attention if it is to grow and be profitable. Just as with a physical store, profitable websites are the ones that change frequently, letting the e-shopper find new things to purchase. This can be done in-house or by your web manager, but either way, you will need to budget for this maintenance.

It is also going to require staff time to download, process, and ship orders.

You must be prepared to monitor the site each day, to collect any orders that have been placed, and to respond to any e-mail inquiries promptly. People are shopping on the Internet because it is easy and quick. The credibility of your business depends on your ability to ship purchases so they arrive in a timely manner. You will want to have in stock the items you show on-line so you can ship in a timely manner. You need to be prepared to handle increased shipping. These shipments will be smaller than your typical whole-sale shipment, which means you will need to order a supply of boxes suitable for shipping one or two items at a time.

ETHICAL COMPETITION

The pricing of your work online will require some serious thought. It needs to be priced at a level similar to the prices charged when your work is sold in a retail store or gallery. Today most retail stores mark the retail price at two-and-a-half times the wholesale cost. It is tempting to offer your work for less than it sells for in a retail store. After all, you'll still be making more than if you sold it wholesale. But this is unfair competition to the retailer who is carrying your work, and may make them decide to drop your line. It is reasonable, however, to factor in the cost of shipping to the overall price when you compare it to that of your retail outlets.

You may have given exclusives to some shops; now your website is going to be available to customers from those areas also. This can create problems with some of your shops. You will have to be clear with them that your site is designed to send business to them. One way to do this is to list the shops that carry your work and where they can be found. This way shoppers who find you online may chose to visit the store to see your work in person. E-shoppers living in out of the way places without access to a gallery will still be able to buy your work as well, and these are the people who will buy from your site most often.

It is best to discuss your plans for an online presence with the major accounts that carry your work and to consider ways to make this work for both of you. Many retailers understand the necessity of having a venue for shoppers online. Many galleries will encourage you to have your own website. Nevertheless, you may lose some accounts, and you should know this up front when deciding if a web store is the way to go. Another option is to have a website that displays your work and talks about you, the artist, but instead of selling the work directly, has links to the shops where your work is sold and that have e-stores of their own.

You can also offer your work online without incurring the added expenses and doing all the site work. There are two sites that might work for you. To arrange for retail sales consider www.Guild.com. This is a large site presenting the work of hundreds of crafts people and artists, something of a virtual craft fair. Or to find wholesale buyers there is www.wholesalecrafts.com. This site presents the work of crafts people for purchase by buyers who register to use the site.

Perspective from a Life in Crafts
Toni Sikes

Identifying a need for artists to reach new audiences, Toni Sikes founded THE GUILD publishing company in 1985 as a way to connect artists with architects and interior designers. In 1998, she launched www.Guild.com, an e-commerce and catalog company. Today, THE GUILD presents the work of more than 1,000 artists.

What is your opinion of the Internet as a selling tool for craftspeople?

Toni: I think the Internet is the most important new channel for sales and distribution to come along in our lifetime. Note that I use the word "channel." The Internet is not a market unto itself, but rather another way to communicate with potential customers, and a new way to conduct transactions.

And I believe that we are just beginning to understand its real potential. Retail sales at THE GUILD are growing 35 percent a year, and we expect that to continue. But there are other, more powerful possibilities. The Internet has become our greatest source of information. So, when I want to find out about an artist, the first thing I do is go to Google to search for artist links. I often will find the website of that artist (which gives me an e-mail address to contact the artist), as well as links to exhibitions of the artist's work, or articles about the artist.

One of the results of this information is a new kind of consumer. She's powerful, demanding, and has access to nearly everything she needs to make a buying decision. And she insists on being satisfied with that decision once it's made. As a result, there has to be a strong commitment to customer service. And I think this new, more sophisticated consumer has a genuine appreciation for the work being done by artists and craftspeople. She knows quality, and she understands that there's value in a piece that's been produced with care and creativity. She's a perfect fit for artists!

Any words of advice?

Toni: The same rules apply when marketing artwork on the Internet as with other channels, even more so! Quality of photography is incredibly important. A simple and clean image shows up much better on a screen.

An artist should edit his website in the same way that he would edit a brochure. Don't put everything you've ever made up for the world to see. Just feature your very best pieces that you will be proud of 10 years from now.

The Internet provides a way for people to find artists, but it also allows artists to easily and inexpensively stay in touch with customers and potential customers. A regular e-mail sent to customers is a wonderful way to keep them apprised of new work, awards, and other news.

At the end of the day, the real power of the Internet lies not in the technology behind it, but in the profound changes it brings to the way people interact with one another.

127

Perspective from a Life in Crafts
Jean McLaughlin

PHOTO BY ROBIN DREYER

KJean McLaughlin is the director of Penland School of Crafts, which has thrived in western North Carolina for more than 75 years. She spoke with us about the evolution of the crafts school.

How do you see the role of a crafts center in the life of the professional craftsperson?

Jean: Mentor, friend, and family are the words that first come to mind. Perhaps our most important roles are providing historical and contemporary contexts for object making, and being nurturing and supportive of creative explorations. Penland School of Crafts serves artists at every stage of their professional careers. Our programs, like those of other educational centers, are designed to guide and assist artists who are starting out and asking those early questions about materials, tech-

niques, and processes. We know that artists want to learn about lifestyles, making a living in this field, and other practical aspects of being a professional craftsperson. Most important to us is helping artists as they grapple with questions about meaning—what do they want to be saying through their work. "Who am I, and what do I have to contribute through my work?" are underlying questions on the minds of most students. We also serve professional craftspeople throughout their careers. Many intermediate and advanced artists take classes to be in a community and out of the isolation of their studios, to learn new skills, and to experiment in a new medium. We have an artist-in-residence program that provides time and space for artists in some stage of transition into full-time studio practice. We provide professional craftspeople with opportunities to teach, exhibit, and sell their work. We function as a social center and gathering place where artists, collectors, and curious, interesting people from all walks of life can come together. We hear from our instructors how they value the quality, enthusiasm, and energy of out students—it is important in this field to be able to give back. Penland and other crafts centers enable relationships to develop among artists who then become ongoing resources for information, encouragement, and connections to professional networks.

What is the place of a formal education for people planning a career in crafts?

Jean: I am a firm believer that we must never stop learning, and that, in order to be successful, we must continually grow. I also believe that a career in crafts will only come through practice and application. The learning sets the stage for the practice, and that learning can come in many ways. Certainly there are excellent, successful craftspeople who have learned their craft primarily through apprenticeship and independent exploration. However, formal education, both through the university model and the workshop model, can be very helpful. Classes such as ours offer information, a chance to practice skills, and the inspiration and excitement of being around other people interested in the same materials and forms. A more formal education will give an artist important feedback on their work and provide models of successful practitioners. MFA programs are known for helping artists achieve the kind of focus and discipline needed to create distinctive work. All opportunities to learn can be invaluable for someone attempting a career in crafts.

Does your center offer classes to help a craftsperson market work?

Jean: Yes, to some degree. Our classes are small, so the instructor-to-student ratio enables much one-on-one learning to take place. We find that our instructors are generous with their time and experience, so when a question arises about marketing, instructors (and other students) freely share what they know. At other times instructors include marketing as a formal discussion topic. Periodically we offer a summer workshop that focuses on professional practice. Twice each year we offer an evening or weekend workshop on the business aspects of being a studio craftsperson, and often this workshop includes information on marketing. The Penland Gallery is also available to students and instructors as a place, not only to market their work, but to seek advice on marketing.

How would you describe the nature of the Penland student, and are there differences in the motivation of the short- and long-term student?

Jean: Students attending summer sessions and concentrations are highly diverse in their backgrounds and skill levels, and they represent every age group, from 18 to 90. What serves as the common denominator is the seriousness of their intent to learn. Many of our students make some, or all, of their livings as craftspeople, while others are attending Penland to find new ways of self-expression. All walks of life are represented

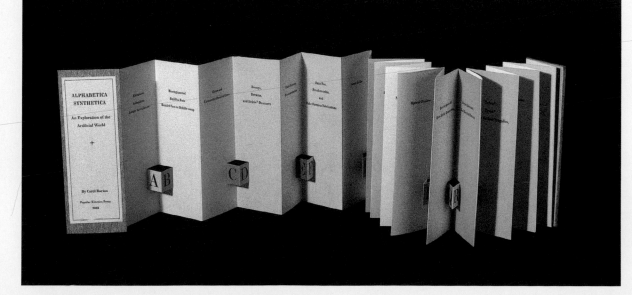

CAROL BARTON
Alphabetica Synthetica
7½" x 2½" x 70"
Paper
FROM THE
PENLAND BOOK OF HANDMADE BOOKS
PHOTO BY THE ARTIST

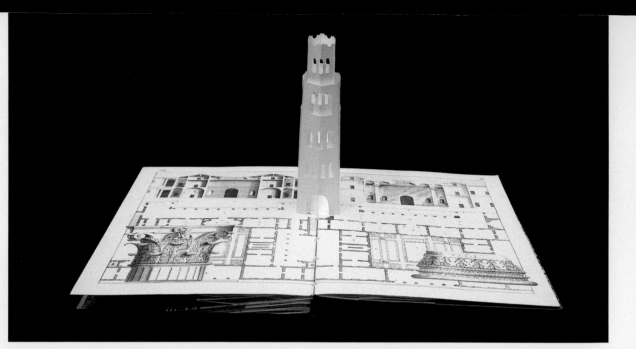

CAROL BARTON
Five Luminous Towers
11½" x 7½" x 3"
Superfine paper, light
bulbs, batteries, fiber
optic filament
(FROM THE
*PENLAND BOOK OF
HANDMADE BOOKS*)
PHOTO BY THE ARTIST

among Penland's student body. In addition to professional artists, our classes have attracted engineers and architects, lawyers and surgeons, and principals and teachers in all disciplines. Each year we have about 1,200 students from almost every state and numerous foreign countries. Most of our students would be considered short term since our classes last between one and eight weeks. However, we do have one two-year program for nine students, and each year about half of our students return. Some students will take several consecutive sessions.

What activities does Penland undertake to educate the public about crafts?

Jean: As an educational institution, Penland sees learning opportunities in all its activities. Through exhibitions, sales spaces, and a reading room, Penland Gallery provides the general public, school groups, and our own students with information about artists and the objects they make. We discuss the concepts behind the work and the technical processes involved in all the work we exhibit. Students use the gallery as a resource, for example, to study how a pitcher pours or a pin clasp works. People are able to touch the objects to understand the importance of texture or weight.

The Penland Gallery also provides tours of the campus and reference information on the artists affiliated with the school. Artists participating in Penland's Resident Artist program open their studios to the public and explain their processes and knowledge of crafts.

Penland also produces publications and implements other activities to provide lifelong learning opportunities. In collaboration with Lark Books, we have recently published *The Nature of Craft and The Penland Experience* and a series of media-specific books of master classes. Each of these books was conceived as a way to share information about the contemporary studio craft movement and to bring the voices of artists forward. In *The Nature of Craft* we wanted to share the breadth and depth of the crafts field with the public and particularly to look at craft with a fresh critical and interdisciplinary eye. We also produce a newsletter, *The Penland Line*, which reaches more than 5,000 former students, instructors, collectors, and friends.

Our staff plans and participates in educational panels at conferences, give talks to various groups, and curates exhibitions that travel or occur off-site. We provide general information on our website and links to Penland instructor sites and other craft-related sites.

We work with various media contacts that often lead to newspaper, magazine, radio and television stories on craft. Each year we host a community open house that provides hands-on activities in our studios for the general public. Our Hands-on-Learning program reaches local schoolchildren with skills and information that will enhance their lives and enable them to see the value of craft and creativity as they become adults.

Each fall and spring, Penland hosts various groups at the school to widen the reach and impact of our programs. Our facilities provide a unique opportunity to gather, explore craft, and have dialogues in a retreat environment. Hosting special groups deepens participants' connection with and understanding of craft processes.

What are the educational considerations that influence the decisions about class offerings at Penland?

Jean: Penland classes represent multiple points of view and a broad spectrum of making. This variety demonstrates that craft, at its best, embraces a deep history and a wide range of responses to materials and ideas. The Penland experience includes classes rooted in tradition and classes that break new ground. We invite instructors who will help students carefully hone techniques and who will engage with us in pure exploration. We welcome the co-existence and intersection of functional work and sculptural work. We tailor some classes for beginners and some for artists with more experience. With all our classes we think about where craft has been over the centuries and where it is going. We pay attention to what crafts artists are making, listen to them, and give them a place to experiment and push their processes and ideas forward. We want to respond to new directions in the field. We think it is important not to define "craft" but to allow it to evolve.

What do you see as the role of the crafts center as we begin the 21st Century?

Jean: I have always regarded craft history and craft activity as a great connector. Craft connects us as people across time and across continents. As our culture becomes ever more mechanized and our economy more service- and information-oriented, it becomes even more important to develop hand skills, tool skills, communication and problem-solving skills which engage our physical and intellectual spheres. These things remain integral to a broad education and to the development of knowledge, patterns of thinking, and a sense of basic competence—which is, in turn, a key component of self-esteem.

In a mobile and often socially fractured society, crafts centers offer a real sense of community—an anchor. The physical community experienced during a class may be temporary, but the greater community of craftspeople to which one remains connected through the craft workshop experience is vital to one's well-being. We know that lifelong friendships begin in our classes, and we know that many of our students and instructors value the opportunity to meet people who are different from them, while still sharing common values and interests.

Craft connects us as people across time and across continents.

Despite the general availability of just about every commodity in manufactured form, handmade objects of all sorts still function as a humanizing force, as carriers of individual expression, and cultural information. Crafts centers encourage, through all their activities, both the creation and the appreciation of the handmade object.

DEVELOPING POSITIVE CUSTOMER RELATIONSHIPS

In whatever venue you choose to sell your work, your ability to develop positive working relationships with your customers will be the cornerstone of your successful business. It is important to see the consumer as a business partner, an ally, and the final part of the process for getting your product out to the world. When this relationship is built on positive experiences, everyone involved is happy.

There are two basic categories of consumers: wholesale and retail. Although the end result is the same for you, there are major differences between wholesale and retail selling.

Your consumer is an ally, the final part of the process of getting your product out into the world.
PHOTO BY
JOHN WIDMAN

THE WHOLESALE BUYER

The primary mission of the wholesale buyer is to select items that will sell in his or her shop. One deciding factor in taking on a new product line is that it's complete so the buyer can use it to "tell a story" in the shop. You can't predict how a buyer will use your work, but it is important to provide the correct components. For instance, if you make dinnerware, you must offer multiple patterns, and you need to make all the pieces that make up a place setting. If you make scarves, they need to be available in a range of fashion colors, and they will be more marketable if they come with gloves and hats. Get the picture? The wholesale buyer wants to select from enough product so your objects will make a statement on his or her store shelves. Shoppers in stores buy from rich displays that offer product depth and diversity; consequently, wholesale buyers buy from craftspeople whose product line provides these attributes.

Unique work also can convince a buyer to take on a new product line. There are thousands of people making mugs, so a wholesale buyer is likely to choose the ones that are in some way special: unusual color combinations; a quirky, but functional shape, or a special size.

● Exclusive or Not?

To be successful, a store, or a department in an upscale department store has to have a point of view, and suc-

The wholesale buyer wants your work to make a statement in his store.
CONTEMPORARY QUILTS AND FURNITURE BY NIKI BONNETT AND ROBERT GARRETT

only certain kinds of stores. You sell to only one shop per zip code, or sell a soap line only in bed and bath stores, but not souvenir shops, for instance. Dealing with exclusives ethically and legally can be very tricky. For instance, it is illegal to refuse to sell to a buyer. Most buyers know this, but it is unlikely that anyone would try to force you to sell product to them. (Although I did once hear a buyer who was told he could not purchase a line say to the craftsperson, "I need your business card so my lawyer can contact you.")

It's more likely that the buyer will ask you what shops in their area are selling your work. It is your job to know the answer to this. If your business is small, you are likely to know your accounts and where they are. If it is larger, your records should be computerized, and you can pull a list of accounts to take to the show. If for some reason you can't confirm this information at the show site,

A positive working relationship with your customers is the cornerstone of your successful business.

cessful buyers seek out items to support it. They want to find product that is new and is not going to be everywhere else. One way to appeal to these buyers is to offer exclusives. An *exclusive* means you make an item or a line available only to one certain store in an area, or to

you can take the buyer's order with a note to check when you return to the studio. If you discover that a previous commitment prevents you from filling the new buyer's order, you must contact the buyer. It is essential that you follow through on this. First, it's fundamental good business practice to do what you said you would do. Second, the buyer needs to know if he or she can expect product from you in order to plan for his season. And third, while you may choose not to sell to this account at this time, you don't want to cloud the future.

Offering exclusives is most common when you are selling to a store in a small town (who would sell to only one account in New York, Chicago, or San Francisco?), but there are times when you might sell to multiple shops in an area. For instance, your purse line might be in a shopping district store, but also in the shop of the art museum of the college up the road. This works since the museum is a destination and that visitor is unlikely to also go to the shop on Main Street.

Some craftspeople have developed elaborate systems to determine what accounts may be given an exclusive. Often these are based on sales that favor the largest accounts. Unfortunately, this makes them of little use when dealing with smaller shops. I find it is more helpful to determine if an exclusive is warranted by the commitment the shop has made or is willing to make to your work, both financially and personally.

● What the Wholesale Buyer Wants

The wholesale buyer's job is complex. Good buyers must be aware of selling patterns in their stores and their geographic areas. In addition, they have to be aware and track the development of trends in the industry. This includes staying on top of news about the consumer's spending patterns as well as tracking new developments in styles. Buyers also are responsible for communicating information about product they have purchased to sales staff and the marketing and display departments. A catalog with clear images and descriptions of your product, explaining any special features, will help your buyers with this task. If you've recently seen an article in a magazine that features an item like yours, you might want to display it in your booth so the buyer gets the message that the quality and design of your work has been recognized by the media. It also may help sell your work to a buyer if you provide printed information that fully explains how it's made, what makes it special, and how best to display it. This will make it easier for the wholesale buyer to do the job of communicating with the sales staff back at the store.

● *Price Point*

Every buyer has set price points that dictate wholesale costs, and they will only be interested in buying items in that price range. You should ask for this information upfront. Neither of you should waste time if your items are too expensive or, as is sometimes the case, too inexpensive. Second, every buyer wants to be "sold." This means you need to be prepared to talk about your items, including the price points, the processes used to produce them, and the customers who buy them. It is essential that prospective wholesale buyers understand the quality you have built into your product and any advantages or limitations related to its use. It is important for them to know the success other shops have experienced selling your line and how those shops and customers compare to theirs. Buyers will want to be shown your best-selling items and to talk about why you think they sell well. You need to let them know why they should buy your salad bowls and not the ones in the next booth.

● Utilizing the Order Form

The wholesale order form should contain key information about the transaction that is taking place. It also should help you continue selling your product to your buyer after this purchase. The name of your business, address, phone and fax numbers, websites and e-mail address, and any terms you have can all be preprinted on the form. If your product line is really large, the items,

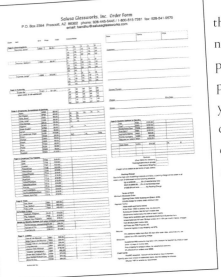

their item numbers, and prices can be printed so all you have to do is write in quantities. In addition to items ordered and quantities, you will have a place to record the name, address and phone numbers of the business ordering, their purchase order number, if they are using one, and the name of the buyer and any other contact person they indicate. It is helpful to get the name of the person in accounts payable should you need to make a collection call later.

The order form needs a place to indicate shipping information, as well, since many businesses have different mailing and shipping addresses. Remember that you cannot ship to a post office box unless you are shipping with the U.S. Postal Service.

The order form should have a place to record the details of when they want you to ship their order. This can be confusing: Be sure they are being clear about the difference between "in-store" and "ship" dates. The former is the date that the wholesale buyer expects to see the product in their store, ready to go on the shelf. The latter is the day that you will actually ship the product, and there can be a great difference between the two. If goods are coming across the country, that can take eight working days. If your buyer needs product for graduation weekend, it must be shipped early enough to arrive on time. The shipping information also should indicate if they want

you to hold the order until you have all the items, in other words, to "ship complete."

In the course of selling the items you should discuss your payment terms and then the arrangement you make needs to be noted on the order form. For a description of the terms you may wish to use, see sidebar on page 137.

● *Communication is Key*

Clear communication between you and your wholesale accounts is a key element in building long-lasting positive relationships. There is an ongoing flow of information each of you can and should expect to get and give to one another. A good buyer will communicate any changes needed in the order or ship date well in advance of the date you are to ship the order. You should also expect an account to inform you in advance of any delay in payment. Established accounts should be able to provide you with a tentative annual order schedule including dates and amounts. It is not typical, but is the sign of a good account, for a buyer to call you after your order is displayed in the shop to forward comments from their customers, especially about design and pricing. They also might share information about sales. Conversely, it would be appropriate for you to phone them a month or so after they receive the goods. They may be surprised to hear from you, but just let them know you typically check in with your accounts after you have shipped an order.

● *Good Housekeeping*

Remember that it is five times more expensive to replace an account than to keep an existing one in good order. There are things you need to do to assist the wholesale buyer, and shipping their order on time is the first essential. If an account places an order for June 1, that means their records indicate they need products in your category

It is five times more expensive to replace an account than to keep an existing one in good order.

to sell during the month of June. If they are not going to get your product in June, they need to replace it with like product to make the income they have projected for that month. Therefore, it is crucial that you deliver the goods at the agreed-upon date or notify the customer at least a month ahead of time that their order will be late. They can then decide whether they still want the items. It is possible that they will have to cancel an order so they can replace your item with other product and meet their customers' expectations and their projected revenues for the month. But if you have given them fair warning, they may be willing to reschedule delivery of your product at an appropriate later date, or purchase from you again. If you

simply ship the product late with no warning, they may well be reluctant to ever do business with you again. Additionally, the buyer expects the product you deliver to be the same design and quality they saw when they placed their order. If for any reason this is not going to be the case, they need to be notified and given the opportunity to keep or cancel their order.

It is always a good idea to keep your wholesale customers informed about any new products you have put into production since they last saw your line. This can be done with a color sheet that can now be produced using a digital camera and computer. Some really smart crafts makers send their accounts a survey within a month of a shipment. It asks for feedback about the quality of the packing and shipping and for any feedback from customers about the product. To increase responses, they include a coupon good for a discount on a subsequent order, not only collecting important marketing information but also encouraging re-orders.

Providing full information about you, your work, how it's made and can be used is smart marketing.
PHOTO BY
JOHN WIDMAN

TERMS
OF PAYMENT

Typically you will ask new wholesale accounts to pay for the order when it is delivered. This is called C.O.D., and in this process, the shipping company collects a check on delivery that is then forwarded to you. Another option growing in popularity is credit card payment. This can save you paperwork. Many sellers write the credit card number on the order form, but I think it is preferable to phone for the number just before shipping. Credit card fraud is on the rise, and this assures you will not be a part of any misuse of the account number. This also gives you the opportunity to confirm that the customer still wants the goods. The use of credit cards has made *pro forma* payment, requiring the buyer to send a check before the work is shipped, nearly obsolete.

The most complicated, scary and trusting of the payment terms is *Net 30*. Net 30 means that the account will pay you for the goods within 30 days of the invoice date. Unfortunately, most accounts consider Net 30 to mean payment is due 30 days from the receipt of the goods. This can add as much as a week to the payment time on goods shipped a long way. If this were your only problem with Net 30 accounts you'd want to thank your wholesale stars.

Allowing a customer to have 30 days to pay for merchandise is, in effect, giving them a no-interest loan that is contracted when you ask the buyer to sign the order form. The craft economy has been built on the Net 30 payment plan. It would be difficult to run your business without offering this payment option, but you need to do so with extreme care. There are a number of factors to consider before establishing credit. Ask for a credit sheet from new accounts. Make sure it includes the shop's bank name, the bank account number, and contact person's name. In addition, check the credit sheet for the names of businesses similar to yours and ideally ones you know.

You will want to call all the references given. Do be aware this is a list chosen by the buyer; any shop can come up with four or five accounts with which they have a positive payment record.

There are a number of additional things you will want to consider as you do a credit check. The first is the amount of cash a business has at a given time. You will get this information from the bank when you talk to them. The age of the business will be an indicator of how much collateral they may have and a long history suggests they must regularly pay their bills. Your feeling about the character of the buyer is also important. Although subjective, I think it is important to listen to any "gut" feelings you may have as a result of your interaction with a new buyer. The size of an order and the amount of credit granted should determine the time and energy you put into a credit check.

The order is a contract between two parties. You attest that you will make and deliver the listed items at the listed prices and at the agreed-upon time. The buyer agrees to pay you in the agreed-upon way and at the stated time. Always have the buyer sign the contract just before you hand her a copy.

There is no foolproof way to guarantee you will always be paid on time or will not encounter slow or non-paying accounts. Some of our major department stores are famous for late payment. A well-established shop may pay late, but they always pay or they would not be in business. Events out of the control of a shop owner, such as a natural disaster or a family tragedy, could prevent them from paying you, or delay payment considerably. This is a system built on trust. You need to do the best credit check you can and then proceed with caution. It is smart to build a cushion in your business plan for uncollectable debts, because at some point you will have them no matter how careful you are. The object is to keep them to minimum.

THE RETAIL SHOPPER

The retail shopper has very different motivations than the wholesale buyer. Most shop because they enjoy the activity. They are seeking the perfect item for themselves or to be given as gifts. The retail shopper also needs to be "sold," just like the wholesale shopper. In both cases, knowledge about your product and related merchandise is key. Retail shoppers will want to know about any special features of an item and the benefit they will derive from these features. For example, if your clay pot is made using flameware clay that can be used directly on top of the stove as well as in the oven, you need to inform the buyer; or if the silk was pre-washed and the blouse does not need to be dry cleaned, that information should be conveyed. Printed materials—hangtags or brochures—that your retail customer can take with the product are good ways of communicating, but you should also talk about your work to establish a rapport.

In addition, the retail customer may expect and request services not required by the wholesale customer, such as a gift box or even gift-wrapping. They may be shopping for a gift for an out-of-town friend and want you to ship it for them. They may want an item, but need it in a different color or size. The successful retailer is the one who says, "of course!" and then makes these things happen.

WHEN GOOD SALES GO BAD

Even with the most careful attention to details, things do go wrong from time to time. The attention you give to your customer's complaints will pay off in the future support you get from that customer.

There are some interesting statistics about the way we respond to bad news. One is that we are four times more likely to share bad news than good news, so word of a bad experience with your business will

It's never to early to learn that taking good care of your customer is the best selling technique of all.
PHOTO BY
DANA IRWIN

spread more rapidly than news of a good experience. The White House Office of Consumer Affairs also reports that 91 percent of those customers who have a bad experience will never work with the offending business again. According to the American Management Association for a healthy business, 65 percent of sales are to existing customers, so it is in your best interest to build repeat business by keeping your customers satisfied.

Resolving complaints from both wholesale and retail customers requires the same skills. The first, and most important, is prompt attention. Carol Sapin Gold, a customer service consultant in Del Rey, California, describes three stages the complaining customer passes through: First, disappointment that something has gone wrong; second, frustration and questions about whether the problem will be resolved; and, finally, there is loss of control and anger. You have a chance to build a great relationship with your customer, despite a problem, if you can address the issue in the first stage.

● Whatever It Takes

It is really important to let the customer tell their story. As you listen, be understanding and try to put yourself in the customer's position. Then, without making excuses, move as quickly as possible to do whatever is necessary to correct the problem.

It is possible there is a defect in your product that you didn't catch before you displayed it. This is easy: Replace it or refund the customer's money, whichever they want.

Sometimes people purchase things they realize are not right for them or that they shouldn't have purchased This creates a difficult situation for them. It's hard to say, "I've made a mistake in judgment," and therefore they may try to create a problem with your product. This won't happen very often, and the smartest way to deal with this is by quickly doing what the customer wants. This will avoid a confrontation in your booth that would create a negative situation that could be observed

Move as quickly as possible to correct the problem.

by other potential customers whose feelings about you—and your product—will be colored by the way you handle the difficult situation. If that potential customer observes you dealing quickly and cheerfully with a problem—even one that only exists in the disgruntled customer's imagination—it will reflect well on you and the idea of doing business with you.

139

Perspective from a Life in Crafts
Elizabeth Stahl

Elizabeth Stahl has been a crafts buyer and collector of fine crafts for many years. She has a large collection of artist books with an emphasis on Western Massachusetts bookbinders. She spoke with us about buying crafts from the customer's perspective.

How did you begin to collect fine crafts?

Elizabeth: I actually got started when I was growing up making things for myself. I always made my own clothing, and I think that I initially went to crafts shows for inspiration. But at the crafts shows, I realized that although I liked to make things, these people were artists. So at some point my motive crossed over from inspiration to wanting to appreciate, and eventually acquire, the things these artists were making. It was an appealing new area of artwork that was very enjoyable to me.

What attracts you to an item?

Elizabeth: If I am approaching a booth at a crafts fair, certain materials attract me first. Then it's the presentation. There's a way to present more or less similar items that attracts you, and there are ways that will turn you away. If everything looks the same and not handmade, that's not good. If you can show similar items in the different ways your mind worked on them, that's good. I think it's always nice to see the thought process that artists use. You don't want to sees lots of any particular item. If you are a crafts customer, you are looking for things that distinguish themselves from everything else that is out there.

What attracts you to a shop, and how do you like to be treated in a shop?

Elizabeth: A certain level of quality attracts me to a shop. It is important that something resonates there. For me that would mean something that crosses over to fine art work. I want to be treated as a person who would appreciate it and enjoy it. Sometimes you need to be educated about the work, and the person helping you needs to be knowledgeable. I always like to have information about the artist, for instance, how long they have been working, their educational background, and where they are from.

How important are the displays in the shops you visit?

Elizabeth: Displays are somewhat important, but when I'm shopping, I'm like a missile. I have an idea about what I want, and I will either see it, or I won't. It's always good to have a lovely presentation that is interesting. I like to see things put together that work well with respect to color and that show how the object might be in a home setting.

How important is the staff's knowledge of the items you are considering?

Elizabeth: Many of the things I purchase are utilitarian, and I want to know how I can use them; for instance, can they go in the dishwasher or the oven?

When do you typically decide to make a purchase?

Elizabeth: I might go looking for a present, and I want to give something beautiful and handmade. How do I decide if something is beautiful? I'm attracted to color and classic forms with some whimsical attributes. I'm attracted to fine crafts because I am not going to give something that my friends could see everywhere; I want something that's one of a kind. If I am shopping for a holiday I like to go into a shop that has items in a wide variety of media.

You are a docent at an area museum. Do you have any thoughts about the role of museums in crafts education?

Elizabeth: I am noticing that museums are beginning to reinstall galleries and include not just the so-called fine arts of painting and sculpture, but also the decorative art of the same period. I also think that museums are beginning to show more of what was called crafts as art.

Would you like to say anything about the separation of crafts and art?

Elizabeth: Well, I'd say there is a continuum. Certainly there's a level where people are making utilitarian objects, and they sell them at crafts fairs; then you get to the point where people are doing utilitarian objects that are extremely beautiful and precious, and you begin to think of them as art objects. And then there are people who are artists with a capital "A" who could have chosen any media to work in and what they do would be art. It is hard to draw the line, but I definitely believe there is a continuum.

LASTING IMPRESSIONS

Selling your work at a store, in a show, and from a gallery affords your potential customer the opportunity to see and hold the piece and to discuss it, either with you or your representative in the gallery. But to be successful in the contemporary crafts market, you must be able to "sell" your work from a distance, as well. This is when good printed materials and excellent photography are essential.

PRINTED MATTERS

The printed materials you create for your business are powerful memory tools for your current or prospective customers. Each piece of paper a customer carries away or each print ad they read contributes to a memorable identity for your business and your products. This is not just about content, or what the materials say; the quality of the design and its execution sends a clear message about your professionalism. Great design generates positive associations with your work, and good execution contributes to a feeling of confidence about your products and your skill as a craftsperson. This results in stronger sales.

To get these essential materials right, you will want to work with a great graphic designer. Your colleagues can steer you in the direction of professionals they've worked with before, and in a moment we'll discuss what you need to do to assure a good working relationship with them. But first, what do you need them to design?

The Sybaris Gallery
202 East Third Street, Royal Oak, Michigan 48067
Telephone 248-544-3388 Fax 248-544-8101
sybarisgallery@msn.com

Garden of Dreams
May 24 - June 30, 2001

Diane Echnoz Almeya
Heinz Brummel
Sarah Hood
Micki Lippe
ROY
Kiff Slemmons
Christina Smith
Roberta & Dave Williamson

Opening Reception
Thursday, May 24
5:30 - 7:30 p.m.

● The Catalog or Line Sheet

Ads, business cards, and show announcements are all significant components of your print arsenal, but the most important tool is your catalog or line sheet. All of the printed materials remind your buyers of your work and give them access to information, but the catalog or line sheet does it most directly and is the tool that is most often used for reorders. Reorders are essential to any healthy business.

● *Line Sheets*

A line sheet is what it's name implies, a sheet or several sheets that describe your line of products for the purpose of selling and ordering. These are not bound, but typically stapled together. The line sheet is perfect when your line does not contain enough items to fill a catalog, or if you are working with a limited budget. In its simplest form, it can be printed in black and 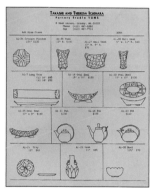 white using line drawings to show your products. A color photograph or a sheet of color samples will give your buyer a more realistic sense of your work and also show the options available.

A line sheet also can feature a composite photograph or a collection of photographs arranged on a page. There are photographic houses that specialize in composite photos 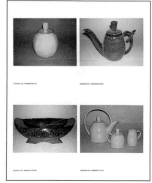 that can contain a dozen or more items, depending on their sizes. Unfortunately, these photos can "feel" generic, not the image you want to project for your handmade items. However, if your line is large and your budget limited, this is a way to show lots of product for a reasonable cost. Typically, the photo house will take the pictures and provide a number of printed sheets for a fixed price. They can provide all this at a reasonable cost because they use a standard setup for the photo. In addition, there is only one color separation, and you will not get a proof to check color before the job is printed. If at all possible, it's better to work with your own photographer and do your own composites. This will reflect your aesthetic and present your product in a manner that says it's special.

A line sheet with a series of photographs that group related products is a more upscale approach. In this case you will want all the backgrounds to be the same, and the items to be shown at the same scale; otherwise, you will have a page that is visually very jumpy, and you may confuse the customer about the sizes of the items. Because you need to pay for each picture, and also for a color separation for each of the pictures, the cost of the printing will increase. You can justify the added expense if the items on the sheets will remain in your line for more than one show cycle, or if you believe you are likely to sell large quantities of the items.

● *Catalogs*

A catalog shows your line in the most professional way. A catalog conveys more than its content, the images of the product. A catalog speaks of stability and success, attributes you want your buyers to associate with your business. A catalog can be as simple as a few sheets of paper folded and stapled, or it can be bound with many pages. It can be printed with one or two colors, with full four-color pictures, or with a full-  color cover and one-color contents. The size and type of printing used for your catalog will depend on the size of your line and your printing/promotion budget.

LUANN UDELL
polymer and fiber

You will need to determine how long the catalog will be used. The number of catalogs you plan to print in a year influences the way the content is presented. For example, if you are going to print one catalog a year, you will want to avoid any references to seasonal imagery in your photos. The summer photo doesn't sell in December and vice versa.

You don't need to know how to build a catalog; your graphic designer will. However, there are some important decisions only you will make. You will choose the items to be included. Since inclusion of each item adds to the cost, you will not want to put an item in your catalog that you have not test-marketed somewhere, either at a craft show or according to sales from your own studio. Work with your graphic designer to determine the number of pages your budget will allow, and determine how many items you can include overall. List the items you make, then look at their sales history and rank them in order of sales. Obviously, the best sellers all get in. Then choose other items that sell well and complement the best sellers, or that display something unusual or specific about your work.

You have two choices about where to print the prices in a catalog: next to the pictures of the items or on a separate page with references back to the photo and description. As a buyer, I like the prices on the page with the items. It's distracting to have to go back and forth from the price sheet to the catalog, and I resolve this for myself by penciling in the prices of the items I might buy next to their pictures; and every buyer must have some such plan. Since your job as the seller is to make the shopping process easier for the buyer, you might wonder why all catalogs aren't set up with the prices right there with the item. Cost is the obvious reason for keeping prices separate in an expensive four-color piece, and many sellers have an inexpensive black-and-white sheet with prices that can be replaced whenever they need to change their prices. Catalogs without prices are also useful if you sell to both wholesale and retail customers. You can print a price sheet for each and distribute with the same catalog accordingly.

If you are going to print separate price sheets, be really smart about the way you organize them. The best way to organize a price sheet is to list items by ascending item numbers. Another acceptable approach is to organize item numbers and prices by page number. Although the price list seems pedestrian, it is important to have your graphic designer put this together for you so it is clear and easy to use, and it enhances your image as a professional.

● *Don't Forget*

There are a number of other pieces of information that you must include in the catalog or on your line sheet. If certain items are only available in multiples (soup bowls by fours, earrings by four pairs per style, or lamps in pairs), you must include this information with the price per unit. In addition, you will want to state your terms of sale, including when and if you will offer Net 30 terms, in the catalog. Clearly state your packing charges and where you are shipping from. Your price sheet is also where you will state your minimum opening order amount and reorder minimums. A clear return policy also belongs with pricing information. Also explain your procedures for dealing with defective, broken, or damaged merchandise. You also will want to include any disclaimers you need to make about your products. For instance, you may want to say that each piece is made by hand and will vary slightly, each dye lot may produce a slightly different color, or the shape of the freshwater pearls may not be exactly the same.

Hangtags and Care Cards

The hangtag doesn't need to literally hang, but accompanies your work to identify who made it and perhaps give information about the process, the product, or the craftperson. The care card, as its name implies, gives any information that might be necessary for taking care of the object. They are important selling tools, particularly for your retailers. The typical buyer of handmade items is making a conscious choice to buy and perhaps pay more for your item than for a comparable mass-produced one. Part of the rationale to buy includes feeling that the item has a "story" attached to it, and the hangtag is a way to enhance that, even when you're not around to tell the story personally. Often a buyer's purchases are gifts, and they want the recipient to know they made a handmade choice and to convey information about the maker. An attractive, thoughtful hangtag gives you the opportunity to influence the buyer and enhance your work. The care card reassures your buyer that he will be able to keep your work in good condition, and it also implies that the work is special. It is essential if your work can in any way be damaged by what the uninformed buyer might consider a normal process of care; in other words, if fabrics must be hand-washed and dried flat instead of thrown in the washer and dryer.

Brochures

You will want to consider adding a brochure to your package of printed materials. There is a reason why most brochures are the size and shape of a roadmap. Brochures are often distributed at tourist facilities that rack them in displays with slots to accommodate this size. If your studio is in an area with major tourist activity, you will want to consider having a studio shop that will be open during the heaviest tourist time, and distributing your brochures to the visitors' bureau, highway welcome centers, lodging facilities, and places where tourists naturally seek such information. Having an open studio won't generate any sales unless the people know they can come by and buy.

You will want your brochure to "pop out" and catch the eye of the viewer when it is placed among a collection of brochures, each vying for attention. Color and photos will do this. The brochure should include at least one photo of you at work in the studio, since a major part of what you are selling is your personal touch. Other photos should show your shop and specific items from your line. To make it easy for people to find you, include a simple, but accurate, line map to your studio keyed from a major local tourist attraction or the nearest well-traveled highway. Include a thoughtful statement about what

Stuart Nye
SINCE 1933
Originator of the Dogwood Jewelry

In the depths of the depression, Stuart Nye bought some second hand tools and a little silver. Without any experience in jewelry or metal work, but with good taste, an eye for beauty and faith in himself, he began to make a few simple bangle bracelets. Through trial and error he learned the nature of his materials and began to fashion silver into the leaves and flowers so characteristic of our jewelry today.

From that day in 1933 when Mr. Nye began, our shop has changed in many ways. It has moved from an attic room, you do, why it is special, and the rewards of a visit. Clearly state the hours you are open and if there are special times when the visitor can watch you working. If you include your show schedule for the year, perhaps your tourist customers will be able to shop again at a show near their homes.

● Newsletters

Keeping in touch with your existing customers will result in increased sales. Use a newsletter to stay in touch and to encourage your customers to buy more items. A newsletter is useful with both wholesale and retail customers; however, the same piece can't go to both.

● *Retail News*

The newsletter for the retail customer can be chatty and more personal. It can contain news about you and your family; it should include information on any recent honors you have received or special projects you've been involved in. Use the newsletter to highlight items that are selling well or new to the line. Include a calendar of shows you will be doing. It is wise to offer a discount on something in your line to newsletter recipients. This not only encourages them to buy, but it says they are valued customers and a part of your community. But be sure the discounted price and the total price, including packing and shipping, are clearly stated. A spring newsletter can feature items that make perfect wedding gifts, and the fall issue can highlight items for holiday

giving. Be sure to list the last possible order date before the holiday to guarantee timely delivery.

● *Wholesale News*

Wholesale buyers are looking for product information and tools to make their work easier. You can use a newsletter to provide this information. Feature new items and include information on delivery availability. Use the newsletter to make a solid pitch about why these items will be great sellers in the buyer's store. Share information on successful selling tactics you have used to sell particular items. You can include reprints or quotes from articles about you or your product. You also can include quotes or stories from retail sources that support the sell-through strength of your product category. You could feature one of your retailers talking about your product in each issue. This would give your buyers the opportunity to read great things about your product without your explicitly saying them.

Include contact information and an order form. If you have established order dates to guarantee specific delivery dates, list these. The more information you can provide the wholesale buyer to make ordering easy, the better your newsletter is working for you.

● *Mail and E-mail*

In addition to the costs of printing a newsletter, mailing can be expensive. If you are going to do several large mailings each year, get information about bulk-mail rates. Preparing a bulk mailing takes a bit more time since the pieces must be sorted by zip codes, but it can be worth it. Mailing first-class bulk does not require sorting, and the cost is still less than mailing straight first class.

Savvy craftspeople are sending e-newsletters to the growing audience of web users. E-mailed newsletters need to be formatted to download quickly. (In the past we were most impatient in restaurants; now it's when we are waiting for e-mail to open!) Your e-mailed

MARSHA ELLIOTT DESIGNS

MAKING
A STATEMENT

The artist's statement is a valuable promotional piece that supports your ability to sell your work. An artist's statement is not a resume or list of accomplishments or an evaluation of the artist's life and work; rather, it is a reflection on what you do, how you do it, and why you do it. Remember that consumers of handcrafts are buying more than an object; they also want to connect with and support the philosophy behind the work. The more they know about you and your work the more likely they will be to support your career. In addition, you will be asked for an artist's statement by galleries, educational institutions, and the press. And you will have to include one with any applications you make for grant money and applications to show at major exhibitions.

Craftspeople accustomed to being creative with tangible materials are often reluctant to take on the intangible word; however, no one knows your motivations, the production processes you use, and your products as well as you do.

To begin, use a writing process that is much like sketching. At the top of the page, write the beginning of a statement: "I make these things because..."; or "There is something in me that causes me to..." Then for the next 20 minutes, just jot down all the things that come to your mind to complete this thought. Don't censor. Don't worry if it makes sense. Don't be surprised if it takes you someplace unexpected. And don't stop writing until the time is done, even if for a moment all you write is "yadda, yadda, yadda." Often the most startling ideas come after just such a riff.

When you finish, you will have several usable ideas from which to build your official statement. This is an excellent exercise for any artist. The product (your statement) of this soul searching will be an important tool for you, your galleries, and wholesale accounts, but far more important is the process of thinking through your work and putting what you do into words. In this process, you may very well discover some surprising things about yourself and your relationship to your work.

Draft a statement from the notes you have made. Keep it simple and direct. Use words that you would use in conversation. Try to write it as if you are writing a letter to a friend who has asked you about your work. When you have drafted the statement, ask a friend who writes or a fellow artist who has a statement you admire, to look it over and give you feedback. Don't be dismayed if they don't understand something or if what you have said is not exactly clear. Writing about what we know instinctively and feel deeply is often the most difficult. A question from your reader is simply a signal that you need to clarify something a bit more.

Before you commit your statement to print, have it proofread for grammar and spelling by someone who works with words. Don't rely on your computer's automatic spell-check program, which sometimes allows incorrect words to pass as long as there spelled correctly. See what I mean in that last sentence?

newsletter should be mostly text and should be short and to the point. This is where you announce upcoming shows, new product, or a significant award. Then provide a link directly to your website, or ask for a reply requesting follow-up information to be sent in hard copy. Other than your time to prepare it, the e-newsletter is free, and an indication to the recipient that you are

Choosing the right designer is a bit like choosing a therapist.

up-to-the-minute in your marketing approach. As an extra bonus you might want to consider including a special offer only available to this audience, providing a code number to be referenced so you know the order came as a result of the e-newsletter, even if it's placed by phone or regular mail.

● Miscellaneous Materials

In addition to the printed pieces that will be used directly to sell your work, you will want a number of other printed materials to back up your selling activities. Office or business items include stationery, business cards, order forms, and invoices. Each of these should be professionally done. If you haven't developed a logo for your business, your designer can work on this with you, and can recommend the typefaces and colors that best convey what your business is about. Many craftspeople recognize the importance of having a well-done business card, but consider that your invoice may spend more time in front of your wholesale buyer. All of your printed material deserves serious attention.

● Getting Good Help

Since creative design is a large part of what you do, you will very likely have good creative ideas about printed materials, but a talented professional graphic designer will be able to augment and implement them for you. Choosing the right designer is a bit like choosing a therapist; when you get it right the results are very satisfying, when it's wrong you feel you have wasted your money. To find the right designer, talk to colleagues in your area whose printed materials you like. Do you see anything you like in the mailings from local galleries? Call and ask who does their work. If you have no other leads, turn to the business listings in the telephone book. If you are cold calling, ask if the company has done work in the past akin to what you are looking for and request that they send examples to you. Even if you are going on the recommendation of a colleague, ask for other examples of the designer's work relative to your needs. After looking over the samples, choose at least two designers to interview so you can compare what each has to offer you.

● *A Productive Interview*

You will need to bring materials to the interview to demonstrate what you want. You can take materials you have used in the past, noting what seemed to work well, and what didn't. Take examples of brochures, catalogs, and cards that you like, and be prepared to say why. The designer will want to know something about the look you have in mind, the message you want to convey, your budget, timeline, and, most importantly, your projected audience. Make time in your schedule to prepare this information so you can present it in an orderly manner. Arrange for the interview to take place in the designer's office. This will allow you to look around and get an idea of the scope of their operation and probably to see their work displayed.

Bring a list of questions to the interview. You will want to determine that they have worked with clients with similar needs, and that they can produce the range of product you need. Be sure to look through their portfolio carefully with a particular focus on these pieces. You want a designer who can take a project from conception to delivery, so be sure to ask about their relationships with printers. The material being designed may need copy; do they have a copywriter available? If so, be sure to read some of the pieces they have written. If not, think how you will handle this situation.

Lead-time can vary, so find out how much time is required for various projects. Discuss the fee structure. Some designers work on a quote-for-the-job basis while others charge on an hourly basis. If it is an hourly rate, you will want an estimate of how much time the job will take, and you will want a clear understanding that the designer will contact you should something unexpected arise that would make the job take considerably longer to complete. Most designers charge different rates for conference time, design and production time, and may charge an extra fee for rush jobs.

● *A Productive Relationship*

After you have chosen a designer, have your first work meeting in your studio, so she can see the full range of what you do and the processes you use. The agenda for this meeting should be to work out a long-range plan for the printed materials you will need, and to establish a timetable for when you will need them. These could include postcards announcing shows, or new product, line and price sheets. Be sure to have your show calendar handy. Be very clear when you will need each item. It's a good idea to ask to have it at least a week before it is actually needed. Your long-range design plan will allow you to work backwards and establish your personal lead times for providing the designer with the necessary materials so you can meet your deadlines.

Establish an agenda for the next meeting before the end of each meeting to maximize the use of both your designer's time and yours. This will save you time and money, but also allow you to think in advance about what you will be doing. Working with another creative person developing an image for your business can be an important creative process, providing you with a richer understanding of what your business and craft are all about.

PICTURES WORTH $1,000

It's true that a great image can convey as much or more than a thousand words. It's also true that great photography can open the door for you to thousands of dollars in sales. Your photographs can go where you can't and can get you where you want to go. You will want to begin developing a library of images as soon as you begin completing product. The planned use for the images will determine if you or a professional photographer should take them. In the course of your career, you will need images ranging from simple shots you take in your studio to carefully lit and composed shots taken at the photographer's.

149

STEPHEN MICKEY
Squared T-Pot
9" x 7" x 4½"
Stoneware
PHOTO BY
RHUE BRUGGEMAN

JOHN POLLOCK
Untitled
5" x 14" x 7"
Claro walnut burl,
black walnut
PHOTO BY ARTIST

● You as Photographer

Although you are most likely not a photographer, and you don't have the necessary equipment to take the sorts of serious shots I'll discuss in a moment, you certainly can take your own photos of your work for some purposes. You should photograph every new item (or item representing a line) you produce using a simple 35mm camera or, better yet, a digital camera. I can't say enough about the quality of the pictures you get with the new, simple-to-use digitals. Nor can I speak enough about the money they will save you. Free of film and processing costs, a digital will pay for itself in a brief period of time. Within seconds of placing your camera on the port, the photos are stored in your computer. You can then access them on your computer screen, or you can print them. You can also e-mail them to fellow craftspeople and ask for their response to the new product. These photos will be your documentation of what you have done. They are an invaluable reference when you are designing new product. It's always good to be able to look back at your old designs and to borrow an element here and there. They also are useful for insurance purposes, or simply to archive your body of work. But these photos would never be used for jury submissions or be used for publication. For that you will need professionally produced photographs.

● Photos by a Pro

All the images used to present your work to the public—including jury submissions, printed materials you produce, and any requests for images for publication—must be taken by a professional. Yes, it can be expensive, but it is money spent to generate money, and it is worth it.

These images can be slides or digital, but you should note that Kodak no longer manufactures slide projectors. I think there's a message for us in that news. It's time to start thinking digital. While juries and shows still request slides for review, it is very possible that they will begin requesting digital images in the near future. Many publications prefer them now. The wise craftsperson will get both slide and digital images of work.

Most publications have specific guidelines regarding digital images for their publication. In general, they require very high-resolution shots. A professional photographer can provide you with these.

Finding the right photographer is no different from getting the right employee, graphic designer, or doctor. You need to begin by asking people you trust for recommendations. You can inquire about the photographer of images you see and like. Remember that you produce objects, and you will want a photographer who does excellent work photographing objects. A great wedding photographer or terrific photojournalist won't necessarily be able to give you the shots you need. If you can, work with a photographer with lots of experience creating images to be submitted to craft show juries.

Review several portfolios and interview the photographers whose work you like. Be sure you clearly convey what you want the images for, and in what form(s) you need them. Know what you can spend, and determine whether each photographer can provide what you need and want at a fee you can afford. It is possible that you will find a photographer who is willing to forego some portion of their fee in exchange for your work. Ask.

Typically, photographer's fees are determined in two parts: a day rate for the part of the day your job requires, and a fee for all the materials used to produce your images. Materials may include Polaroids needed to check the composition, any 35mm film and film processing, and CDs, since you will want to get the images that way also.

When you have chosen a photographer, bear in mind that the best photographer will only be best for you if you communicate exactly what you need and want from them. The photographer will need to know what the image will be used for, when you need it, and in what formats. He also should have an understanding of your work and the mood that you want to convey with the image.

● *Trial by Jury*

The most important images you will need are those you will submit for jury selection into select craft fairs and shows. These images will be your pass into the show circuit. You will want to put as much thought into them as you put into creating the items being photographed.

You should think of this set of images as a suite. Begin by choosing a related group of items to be photographed. If your line is large and includes a number of different looks or styles, don't try to show them all. A jury wants to see a cohesive body of work that represents a mature understanding of the media you are working in. Concentrate on the items that will make the strongest group impact. Choose a range of items that tell your story and represent your point of view. Be absolutely certain each item is perfect. Remember, there can only be one item in each shot, no groups here. Remember also, that it's your product that you want the jury to focus on; therefore, any props you use must be secondary in visual impact, and should only be there if they enhance the presentation of your product.

Work with your photographer to be sure the background color sets off your work and is not distracting. You will want to photograph all your items with the same background. Different background colors are very distracting when simultaneously viewing multiple images. Relative scale is also important. The jury will react most favorably if the mug isn't larger than the bowl, or the placemat is seen in correct size relationship to the tablecloth.

Lighting needs to be set so that the items pop out and radiate life. No flat or dull images will do. If your items are three-dimensional, they need to be lit so they come

151

DANA ROTH
Beer Can Rings
$^2/_3$" wide
Sterling silver,
aluminum
PHOTO BY ARTIST

away from the background, and so the viewer will sense their volume. The viewer must know in an instant what they are viewing. Any confusion in the jurors' minds, and you're out.

Talk to your photographer about the negative space in each picture. You want some "air" around each item, but you also want the item to fill the frame. Let the photographer know that the quality of the images she produces will determine your future, since a jury unconsciously responds favorably to good photographic art. And if your work is selected, be sure to let your photographer know with thanks.

Although you only need five images for jury consideration, have more items photographed. This will allow you to select the five that make the best composition and work best as a group. In addition, while you are having this work done, you might want to have your photographer take a group of shots of you with your work. These may be enlarged and displayed in your booth, or be useful in any printed materials you may produce. It's also good to have images on hand that can be sent to magazines or newspapers.

Preview the images before you accept them from the photographer. Be sure they are what you asked for and expected. If not, discuss the procedure for retaking any images that are not acceptable. If you were totally clear

Always be sure you are getting the originals and not duplicates of slides.

about what you wanted, you should not have to pay for the photographer's additional work. Always be sure you are getting the originals and not duplicates of slides.

● *Sliding by*

As soon as you receive the slides, label them. If you put this off, you may sell the objects and not have the information for labeling later. You also run the risk of accumulating so many slides that the task of labeling them all at once may overwhelm you. It's important to have all of the information clearly on the slide and ready to go if you need to produce it quickly for, say, a magazine story. (See "Ownership Issues," next page, for the protocol on reproduction.)

Each original slide should be labeled "master" in addition to the other pertinent information. That info includes your name and the completion date, title of the work, size, materials, and construction techniques. You will want to indicate the correct viewing direction by placing a mark, preferably a red dot, in the bottom left-hand corner of the slide when viewed with the image right-side up. Once labeled, these slides go off to be duplicated. As soon as they return, use them to label the duplicates, then put the master slides in a safe place. Never send the masters out; they will become the photographic documentation of your career.

Gold Is in the Details

Call the promoter's office before you make the final decision about the images to be included with a specific show application. Ask about the order in which your images will be viewed: It could be five across, or two stacked rows. You will want to play with different arrangements until you get the one that works the best. This is somewhat like analyzing the composition of a picture in art history class. You want the juror's eyes to travel around the images and be brought right back in for further study. Be sure there are no strong directionals that will lead the viewer's eyes and mind out of your presentation. Typically, the description of one image is read to the jury. Find out the placement of this image and be sure the description you provide for it will enlighten the jury about the rest of your items being viewed.

The same guidelines apply for digital images on disc, except these are labeled in the computer, and you can make your own copies since each will actually be of master quality. Promoters are not asking for discs yet, but it's likely that they will soon. When they do, you will want to know how they will be viewed. Just remember that the images must be of the same high quality as slides.

Ownership Issues

The photographer retains ownership of the reproduction rights to the images he has made of your work just as you retain ownership of reproduction rights of your items even when someone buys the original. Some photographers will convey ownership of the images to the craftsperson, so it pays to ask. If the photographer chooses to retain these rights, you will have to ask permission before allowing the images to be reproduced in any form or used in any way other than the one stated at the time they were made. Most photographers working with craftspeople will readily grant this permission without cost. Some may have an additional fee when their images are used in print or on the Internet. In any case, never use—or allow a publication to use—an image without crediting the photographer.

MARCIA LAGING CUMMINGS
Follow the Yellow Brick Road
9" x 8"
Seed beads, bugles, assorted beads
PHOTO BY ROGER BRUHN

Perspective from a Life in Crafts

Tim Barnwell

Tim Barnwell is a commercial and art photographer working in North Carolina. In addition to 25 years' experience photographing craft and art items he is the author of The Face of Appalachia: Portraits from the Mountain Farm. *His photos have appeared in dozens of national magazines and are in the collections of major museums around the country.*

Are there things a craftsperson can do to help ensure they get the right photographer?

Tim: The key thing when trying to select a photographer is finding someone who has experience photographing the kind of work you do. Generally that is going to be a commercial product photographer, not one who takes wedding or portrait pictures. The studio must be set up to do what you need done. At Barnwell

Photography we have table setups and wall setups ready to go when people walk in, so there is no set-up time that they have to pay for. Most photographers don't want you there during the shoot, so it's important to get this information before you make a decision.

What role do you think digital imaging will play in product photography?

Tim: There is a problem as far as film vs. digital because we are stuck between two worlds. Most shows are still requiring slides but some of the bigger shows are asking for digital and will charge you to convert your slides to a CD. Using CDs saves them money because they can send them out to jurors to review from home. The problem for the artist and photographer right now is that you almost need to have both. You cannot generate good slides from digital files, although you can work the other way, but it is almost as cheap to shoot both ways at the same time.

The real question about using digital is: How much knowledge and capability do you have on the computer? Can you resize a file? Can you put images on the web page? Do you have the software, or do you need the photographer to do these things for you? Can you size a file for an application? Just now there is very little standardization of digital requirements on applications. I see a lot of confusing things about digital applications just now. A serious issue with digital images is how much retouching is being done. It's nice to be able to remove reflections or dust spots, but where do you stop? This was not an issue with slide film because it was nearly impossible.

Are you doing a lot of digital work?

Tim: Currently 75 percent of my work has a digital component as compared to two years ago when it was 10 percent and that was mostly scanning. I'm in a dilemma when people say to me, "What should I shoot?" The answer is, "What is your ultimate goal?" For most applications you need to have slides, but I think in the next few years that will be the exception rather than the rule. If you just want to put images on a web page or use them for jury applications, then digital may be fine. If you want your work published, or if you want to create a portfolio that you can use to have 8x10 prints made from, then you are going to need high-end corrected digital files or more traditional slides and negatives.

The artist has to know what the end uses are, whether it is only web and e-mail or electronic applications, or if the images have to be on a CD and slides or everything on a CD. The artist also should be prepared to listen to the photographer's advice about this since the artist may not be technically savvy enough to make decisions without the photographer's input. It's bewildering to me, and I deal with it every day. There are so many variables to consider. The best scenario is to ask for the highest file size and then scale it down later, but you have to have the computer skills to do this. If you can't do that, ask the photographer to provide you with a high-resolution, print-quality file and a low-resolution, web-quality file.

Do you have any tips that will help a craftsperson get the best images?

First, it's a mistake to assume you can do digital yourself just because you own a digital camera. It's not about having the camera; it's about composition and lighting and all the things that photography is all about. There's also the post-production processing of the images that typically have to be sharpened, color corrected, and resized to make them right. Most artists don't have the computer skills to do this.

Second, hire a photographer. Perhaps five or ten years ago you could have gotten away with shooting your own work, but the jury process has gotten so competitive now that they'll use any excuse to narrow the field, and poor photography is one of them. If you are

applying to a show that could result in 50 to 75 percent of your wholesale work for a year and you try to save $100 on photography, and you don't get in; that's false economy. It's okay to do the day-to-day cataloging, but the important stuff should go to a professional photographer.

Third, prepare for the shoot by grouping your work into similar sizes to save time. If you won't be at the shoot, be sure to mark the side of the work that you want shown; leave a note about angles you want and if there are blemishes you want to avoid showing. Cut photo samples out of magazines that show the approach you like, the way it's lit or the background used. It's also good to provide photographs of your work that you like that you would like to match.

Ask to see samples of a photographer's work, either on their website or in their portfolio in the studio. It gives an idea of backgrounds and the lighting approaches that can be used.

Fourth, be aware that magazines can print from digital files but what looks good on the computer screen will not necessarily print well. The image on a computer screen has the resolution of newsprint, 72 dots per inch, but print quality for magazine reproduction would be at least 300 dots per inch, and that's going to be a high-end digital image.

Fifth, you cannot e-mail top-quality, printable images; they have to be on a CD.

Top to bottom images by Tim Barnwell: Ceramic vessels by Michael Sherrill; woven scarf by Vickie Vipperman; woven scarves by Kathryn Scott.

NOTHING BREAKS

Think of packing as part of the creative process. You have put your heart into producing your work, and now its time to put the same energy into getting it safely to its destination. I'm always saddened when we get a box that rattles at the store. It is painful to open a box from a craftsperson and find the pieces of what must have once

been a beautiful object. You must be as skilled at packing your work as you are at making it, and obviously, the more fragile the work, the more skilled you need to be.

The objectives of safe packing are the same, whether the piece is breakable or not. It must be safely enclosed, protected from other objects in the box; it should not move in the box, and it must be protected from liquids or odors that can permeate from outside.

Smart, attractive packaging and packing can be another opportunity to use your creativity
PHOTO BY JOHN WIDMAN

AN INSIDE JOB

The actual wrapping of the object will vary depending on the media and the value of the piece. We'll start from the inside and work out. What follows are some inner packing suggestions that I have arranged by media.

● Jewelry

● Earrings: each one in a small zip bag, then the pair placed in a larger bag zip bag, or mounted on cardboard, then placed in a zip bag.

● Necklaces without delicate surfaces: rolled in tissue, then coiled in a zip bag.

● Necklaces with delicate surfaces: arranged in a zip bag large enough for them to lie flat and be pinned in place.

● Bracelets with strung elements: rolled in tissue, then coiled in a zip bag.

● Bracelets from solid metals: in a zip bag.

● Extremely fragile jewelry: placed between layers of foam with tissue for extra padding as needed, then placed in its own box.

● Fine jewelry with precious metals and stones: always in a presentation box with cotton or fabric, or attached to a card to prevent movement.

● Fiber

● Small wearables such as scarves, hats, gloves: neatly folded and in a plastic bag.

● Large wearables such as jackets, skirts, blouses and shirts: neatly folded with tissue, then placed in individual bags.

● Decorative textiles, pieced or woven: rolled, and in a plastic bag. If it is necessary to fold, it's best to fold with the right side out because this reduces wrinkles on the viewable side.

● Ceramics, Glass, Fragile Wood, and Baskets

● Each piece must be individually wrapped using newsprint, foam, bubble wrap, or a combination of the three. When combining, put the softest material closest to the piece.

● Very fragile pieces, or parts of pieces (for instance, handles on a ceramic piece, or delicate fiber extending from a basket) can be easily protected using toilet tissue as a cushion.

● *Metal and Sturdy Wood*

Each piece wrapped in newsprint, foam, or bubble wrap to protect the surfaces from scratching.

MERYL WAITZ
Mini Geo Earwires
3/8" x 3/8"
Sterling silver,
gold vermeil

Wrap in many layers when packing fragile objects such as glass.
PHOTO BY TOM STEVENS

EXTRA! EXTRA!
READ ALL ABOUT IT!

The daily newspaper is a handy wrapping item that most of us have lying around the house. It can provide a good cushion around an object, or can be used as stuffing inside a box. But the ink on newsprint easily rubs off, so never, ever use it as the first wrapping around the item you are shipping. If you do, the object will arrive with black smudges and streaks. And if you are using newspapers for the outer layer, be sure to wash your hands between items, since they will be stained and can transfer that ink onto the next item that you touch.

THE INNER SANCTUM

Once you have each object individually wrapped, it's time to put them into inner containers. Again, this process differs relative to the fragility of the work.

● Jewelry

Individual jewelry bags go into a larger bag that holds several of the smaller bags. This goes into an appropriately sized box. There should be a bit of room in the box for packing peanuts to cushion the work.

In the case of boxed jewelry, assemble the boxes and choose an appropriate outer box that can accommodate them with room for a layer of packing peanuts on the bottom and another at the top. The object is to guarantee that nothing inside moves while shipping.

● Fiber

Individually bagged fiber items should always go in groups into larger plastic bags. The purpose of two bags is to protect the work from outside invasion from liquids or odors, which may be released if something in another package breaks during shipping. The bags also may be useful for protecting your work in the store, since most store owners do not keep bags on hand for this purpose and will appreciate having them with the piece. The double-bagged items now can go into an appropriately sized outer box; no other packing materials are necessary.

● The Rest of the Story

The next categories need particular care. Items must be packed into an inner box that is, in turn, packed into a larger box to ensure their safety. Most shippers will no longer consider a breakage claim unless items are shipped in an inner box.

Think of the outer and inner boxes as sets, with the outer box six inches larger all around than the inner one, i.e., a 12-inch square inner box with an 18-inch square outer box. Pack the wrapped item in the inner box with several layers of bubble wrap or at least two inches of packing peanuts. Larger, or more valuable items should be packed one to an inner box, while other items can be nested together. All items should fit snugly in the inner box with packing materials. You can use more packing peanuts, crumpled paper, pieces of cardboard, or even egg cartons to stabilize the items and keep them from banging into one another. Remember: Nothing moves. End with another layer of packing peanuts or bubble wrap.

Begin filling the outer box with a layer of packing peanuts three inches deep. Place the inner box on top of this layer and fill the area around its sides with crumpled paper to the top of the inner box. This is to keep the inner box from moving and to add additional protection from outside invasion. Then fill the remaining top area with packing peanuts, shaking it all down and adding more peanuts, if necessary. When it is filled so that nothing moves, you are ready to seal and address.

● Enclosures

Before you seal any inner box, include: hangtags, care cards, artist statements, and a stamped post card for return comments about the quality of the work or the packing. Since it is the shipper's responsibility to contact the freight carrier about any breakage claims, you will want to include information about how you want the recipient to notify you should any damage occur in transit.

It's savvy marketing to also add a "what's new" sheet and an order form to this collection of enclosures. It may be months since your buyer saw your line. Take this opportunity to introduce them to new work. This is a simple way to keep your buyers informed and motivated to buy. It is true that the buyer may not be the one to open this box, but the paperwork it contains will find its way to her desk.

It is important to include an invoice, or a copy of the invoice, even if you intend to mail the original invoice for later billing. The store will use this information as a reference to price items for the floor. Mail doesn't necessarily travel at the same speed as the box, either outside of the business or within. I can tell you from experience how frustrating it is to have an eagerly awaited shipment arrive only to find the items can't go immediately to the selling floor because there is no pricing information in the box. Be thoughtful of your accounts, and quickly get your work on the market by putting the invoice in the box with the goods.

KEEP IT CLEAN

Using clean, fresh packing materials will endear you to your wholesale accounts and further emphasize your professionalism. It's really unpleasant to unpack boxes packed with what appear to be scraps swept off the floor, including the occasional cigarette butt, candy wrapper, or empty envelope. If you want to be treated like a pro you need to behave like one, so no trash in your packing materials.

THE SHIPPING NEWS

You can ship using the United States Postal Service, but unlike many private shipping companies, the USPS will not come to your place of business to pick up packages. A private shipper is not able to deliver to a post office box address, however. Most shipping rates are comparable, and checking the websites of various shippers can be a good way to determine costs in advance. As a rule of thumb, the faster you send something, the more it will cost you. The choice of shipper is most likely to depend on what is available in your area and whose pick-up schedule is most convenient for you.

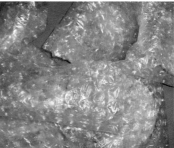

Individual items that are encased thoroughly in bubble wrap can be nestled together in the inner box.

A layer of packing peanuts in the bottom of the outer box will provide an extra cushion for unexpected rough travel.

Crumpled newsprint or more peanuts around the sides of the inner box will assure that nothing moves!

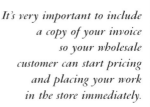

It's very important to include a copy of your invoice so your wholesale customer can start pricing and placing your work in the store immediately.

Perspective from a Life in Crafts
Carol Sedestrom Ross

Carol Sedestrom Ross is currently Director of Crafts Marketing for George Little Management GLM, where she oversees the handmade sections of the gift shows produced by GLM. Prior to joining GLM in 1992, Ross was the President of American Craft Enterprises and the senior vice president for the American Crafts Council.

You have been in this business for more than 30 years; how did you start?

Carol: In the late '60s, my partner, JoAnn Brown, and I created a line of women's clothing made from handmade fabrics. A friend suggested we exhibit in a craft fair in Bennington, Vt., which is where the ACC

Northeast Craft Fair was being held in 1969. Shortly after our huge success at that fair, we approached B. Altman's in New York City and had a very successful three years with them. I became aware that if we hadn't had such success at the craft fair, we would never have had the nerve to approach a major NYC department store. I knew there were hundreds of other creative people in the same situation—working away in their basements or garages, afraid to approach the mainstream—and based on my own experience I wanted to help them find their market.

So when the ACC Fair outgrew the town of Bennington in 1972, I suggested the Dutchess County Fairgrounds in Rhinebeck, N. Y. Within the year, I became the on-site management volunteer because I lived in the area. I discovered I was good at running craft fairs, probably because I had been an exhibitor and knew what exhibitors wanted and needed.

You seem to have always understood the importance of marketing as a part of the creative process. How did this affect your decision-making as related to the fairs?

Carol: I always thought (and still do) that if you make things, you should sell them. Craftspeople did want to sell their work; many of them had to sell their work, as it was their only means of support. I was very aware that not many people really knew about, or understood, handmade objects. Moving the fair from Vermont to Rhinebeck, only 90 miles north of New York City, had a huge impact on the attendance. In 1972, 17,000 people visited the fair in Bennington. The first year in Rhinebeck, the attendance was over 30,000, and during the next 10 years it grew to over

70,000. Craftspeople became a kind of '70s phenomenon, and everyone wanted to see, and buy from, people who could actually make things.

As soon as the Rhinebeck fair was running smoothly, I decided to start a winter event so that buyers and collectors could have access to crafts twice a year. I chose Baltimore, a city that was easy to get to that had an indoor facility, because that lent credibility to what I saw as an emerging profession. The first show in 1977 was a huge success, and from there I developed shows in San Francisco, Dallas, St. Paul, Atlanta, etc, etc. Crafts have become part of the fabric of our society.

The Internet is becoming a powerful marketplace: What are your thoughts on this?

Carol: People always ask me if the Internet is going to replace trade shows, and my answer continues to be "No!" The Internet is perfect for communication and makes life very easy for buyers who want to reorder. But I think people need to initially see and hold and touch a craft. And many people who buy crafts enjoy the relationship that develops between the maker and the buyer or collector. Because of the relationship aspect of buying crafts, I think trade fairs will be with us forever.

Our field has undergone vast changes since you began. What do you think is going on now?

Carol: There are two things taking place right now in the craft field. Because the market changed so dramatically after 9/11, buying habits also changed radically. Buyers don't want to hold on to inventory anymore. They want what we call "just in time" inventory: "Let me call you next week if the dozen I ordered sell." This is tough for American craftspeople. They can't afford to produce and hold unsold inventory, and they can't produce things in a week. This new way of buying has put quite a squeeze on craftspeople.

We are also facing a generational change. A lot of people who have been making and/or selling crafts for 25 or 30 years are ready to retire. With more difficult economic conditions, they are not making as much money as they used to make, and they feel like they are working twice as hard. As a result, I hear both buyers and craftspeople talking about selling their business or just going out of business.

Does it seem to you that there are very few 'pure' American craft stores left, that buyers are putting a mix of American crafts and imported handmade items in their stores?

Carol: It seems to me that this is the direction retailing is taking, and the future of the crafts movement will depend on selling to a broader market. We have become a global marketplace. Not everyone can afford to buy everything handmade—handmade things are more expensive. People buy their imported dinnerware from Crate and Barrel or Pottery Barn, and then buy beautiful American-made candlesticks or a fabulous centerpiece for their table. One of the things that will ensure the longevity of American makers is their flexibility, their ability to turn on a dime and change their work to fit current buying patterns. If they stay in touch with the market, read the trend magazines, shop their neighborhood stores, they can quickly change their direction. And also, many American craftspeople are producing offshore now so their prices can compete with lower priced imports. They take their designs and their creativity and go where they can find skilled, but less expensive, labor to do their production. Instead of complaining about the competition, they are becoming the competition. Rather than being knocked off, they are knocking themselves off. It is not necessarily the fingerprints on the object that are important to people; it's the design value, the look.

TRADE AND TECHNOLOGY

As the 21st century unfolds, you need to be aware of the impact on our field of the technical, social, political, and economic changes around the world. The way you make your living as an artist/craftsperson has already been affected by these changes and will continue to be. To be successful in this rapidly changing marketplace, you will need to remain focused on why you do what you do, at the same time that you learn how to adapt to the changes around you. Perhaps the most pressing issue for the contemporary craftsperson is to educate a large and loyal enough customer base about the value of handmade products. A clear understanding of the new worldwide marketplace, and what you can bring to it, will be essential if you are going to be financially rewarded.

THE GOOD, THE BAD, AND THE UGLY TRUTH

In the 1940s the marketing of handmade objects began in earnest in the United States. Their increased availability was the result of thousands of men returning from World

Ever newer technology is redefining the concept of "handmade" work.
PHOTO COURTESY
BROOKFIELD CRAFT CENTER

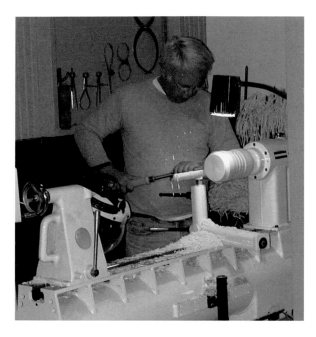

War II and studying art and handcrafts with benefits granted by the GI Bill. This peaceful army produced handmade objects that they introduced into the marketplace where they were a refreshing change from the mass-produced items so prevalent at the time. An appreciation of, and preference for, the handmade began to compete successfully with the previous interest in machine-made products.

At this time, the interest was focused on American handmade work. Many of the handmade items being imported from around the world strongly reflected the ethnicity of their source, and did not appeal in the same way that American handmade items did. This also was a time when huge numbers of factory-made items were imported into the United States, many of them plastic. American handmade items therefore had an automatic connotation of quality in comparison to many imported goods.

The handmade items found their ways into the lives of discerning buyers who insisted on them for their homes and wardrobes. The handmade trend has persisted for at least six decades, continually changing and evolving to meet the needs of three generations of consumers in the United States.

Major retailers are always watching trends as they move toward the mainstream and pick up mass. In this case, the interest in handmade goods for home and personal adornment grew in dollars spent as the baby boomers came of age. In the early 1980s, mass retailers began to realize there was a place for them at the lucrative handcrafts table. Spearheaded by the demand generated by hip home furnishing and clothing retailers who sold by catalog as well as at storefronts, factories on several continents began making goods that mimicked the American handmade look. Initially only small numbers of these goods were brought in, and the prices remained fairly high. This allowed items made by the studio craftsperson working in this country to compete quite well.

However, strengthened by technology and falling trade barriers, imports from around the world are creating a major challenge for the studio craftsperson. Asian countries, large and small, many of them fueled by very healthy economies, and a workforce that can be hired for very little, present a serious problem for the American craftsperson. Manufacturers operating factories there are able to access whatever technology and labor is needed to produce the items sought after by the rest of the

It's up to each individual craftsperson to decide how new machines and materials can, or can't, be accessed for his work.
PHOTO COURTESY BROOKFIELD CRAFT CENTER

163

Leicester, NC potter Matthew S. Jones utilizes video technology to tell the story of his handcrafted wares to visitors in his booth.
PHOTO BY JOHN WIDMAN

world. The workers in these countries come from regions that have a handmade specialty: pottery here, weaving there, metalwork over there. These traditions provide a springboard for training workers, and these workers can produce handmade versions of your product at prices far below anything you could match.

Inexpensive goods are flowing into this country at an unprecedented rate, and there is no reasonable way you can compete with these goods in price. The imported items are, in fact, handmade, although that often means handmade in a factory, not in the personal studio we have come to associate with that term. They are often well-designed and -executed, and can be strikingly similar to studio pieces produced here. (See Wendy Rosen's essay on page 47 for one explanation of how your artisan design can end up being mass-produced overseas.)

In the early years of the handmade movement, the way an object was made was the most important factor. As the handmade trend evolved, the method of manufacture became less important to consumers, and the look became the significant component. "Look" is the key word here. The products don't need to be made by hand, they simply have to *look* as if they were made by hand.

So, what's going on here? The future of the crafts movement in the United States is challenged as a result of our doing

Creative employment opportunities here at home are one result of educating the general public to the value of handmade American crafts.
PHOTO COURTESY BROOKFIELD CRAFT CENTER

both a really good and a really bad job of promoting our products to the buying public. On one hand, we have successfully convinced large numbers of consumers that handmade is a good and desirable attribute in consumer goods. On the other, we have not adequately educated the buying public to the value of goods produced by individual artisans working in the United States. Nor have we sufficiently emphasized the many negative effects that buying mass-produced handmade items from offshore manufacturers can have on the local craft economy and the larger economy that surrounds it. We also need to emphasize the importance of a healthy economy for the tradition of artistic innovation that is an integral part of our cultural history.

MAKING IT WORK FOR YOU

The future of our field depends on our ability as educators as well as makers.

We must undertake a grassroots public-relations campaign designed to educate the buying public about the way our products are made and about the difference between objects that are mass-produced and those that are made by hand in limited numbers. We also must create a connection with the buyer through our work. Because people like talking to the maker, you have a ready made audience. Be sure to engage your customers and share information about the handmade process and the nature of the items produced by craftspeople in the United States.

Think about your product and capitalize on the things that distinguish it from imported craft items produced in mass quantities. Do you use indigenous materials or a method that is distinct to a region? Tell the buyer with printed materials or a display. Create a story for your product. Don't just make lovely wooden boxes, but make lovely wooden boxes for specific purposes—to keep your wishes in until they come true, for instance. Create a feel good pay-off for buying your work—a percentage of all sales goes to a specific organization or group doing positive work in the community. Create a value-added service for your product that can't be replicated by a huge company whose workers live far away. One custom shoe designer in North Carolina will resole the shoes you buy from him for free throughout your lifetime, for instance.

Telling your story with printed materials that a customer or browser (think future customer) can take away with them is a really essential component of your PR campaign. Snappy images end up on the refrigerator to be seen again and again. Well-designed informative hangtags can be used to talk about the materials you use and why your processes make your product more desirable than an imported knock-off.

Other ways to spread the word could include a brochure to pass out that describes, not only your items but talks about the field, and the impact of the money spent on work that is made in the region where you are located, or in the U.S.

It is also to your advantage to become an integral part of your community. Sending out press releases anytime you receive an award or participate in a prestigious show is one aspect of this. But consider also going into the schools to demonstrate your craft. Do local businesses exhibit local art? Make sure that crafts are seen in these venues also. And, don't overlook the library! If they are not showing art, ask if you can begin to schedule shows that will include handmade items from the region. Offer to do demonstrations at town events and celebrations, particularly if your craft has some sort of historical link to the region. These may actually turn out to be venues for direct sales, but even if this is not the case, the object is to make a specific emotional connection linking you, your work, and your community in the minds of your potential consumer.

It's also important that we get involved with regional hand-

made organizations. Don't just pay your dues, but establish and work on committees whose purpose is to educate the public at large about the positive values of buying regionally made crafts, and the negatives of buying imports from stores, particularly if they are local and have a history or connection that makes the work more appealing.

And, finally, become a member of national crafts organizations. There are general ones and then media-specific ones. These organizations are able to call attention to what we do in the national press. Again, it's important to support them with more than membership money. Keep

165

Valuable time-tested tools and techniques do not need to be abandoned, even if we are open to new ideas and change.
PHOTO COURTESY
BROOKFIELD
CRAFT CENTER

The future of our field depends on our ability as educators as well as makers.

in touch. Write or call and make your ideas and views known. These organizations need input from members, or they can't serve the members' needs. If you have the time, get on a committee. Your efforts will help the crafts industry on a national level, but they also can be used to call attention to what you do in your own community.

● Continuing Education

In addition to educating the public, we need to continue educating ourselves about new and better ways to produce our work. Smart craftspeople will find ways to design, produce, and market their products using techniques that are not viable for the big retailers with factories here or offshore.

The successful crafts person will also make use of 21st century technology and materials in combination with

I wonder if the 17th century dyer would have rejected the washing machine?

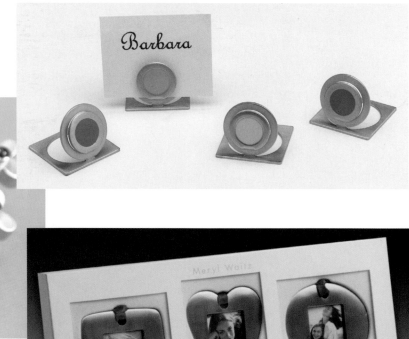

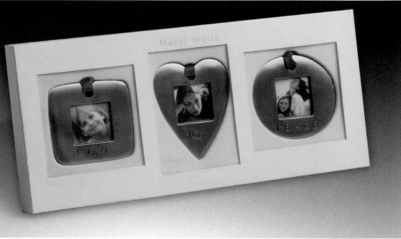

New York City jeweler and designer, Meryl Waitz (page 168) is hands-on in the design stage, but accesses new technology and the global work force to produce her work. Here is a mixture of both hand-crafted and mass-produced items from Waitz.

PHOTO COURTESY MERYL WAITZ

centuries-old techniques. Deciding the place for modern technology in our field presents major philosophical issues that each craftsperson must confront. Traditionally, the hand was the most important tool in the production process. Technology is now providing us with the methods to produce the handmade with less hand and more machine. How will you fit the new technologies into your work? Some of the new techniques produce items that reflect the 21st century; others allow the maker to make traditional-looking items more easily. I wonder if the 17th century dyer would have rejected the washing machine, or if the 19th century potter would have chosen not to use a pug mill? You must decide what and how much technology you are comfortable using. It is important, however, to be mindful that embracing new technology can increase your viability in the marketplace.

The old mill at Brookfield Craft Center, Brookfield, CT, where both old and new technologies are respected.

PHOTO COURTESY BROOKFIELD CRAFT CENTER

AID
TO ARTISANS

Founded in 1976, Aid to Artisans (ATA) changes the lives of thousands of artisans in developing countries each year through its empowering programs of product design, business skills training, and marketing. Historically, handmade crafts are legacies of cultural traditions. In developing countries, handcrafts continue to provide an important source of income, especially for women who have limited options and resources for productive employment. Working one-on-one with artisans, ATA acts as a catalyst to encourage artisan commerce in local, regional, and export markets.

ATA is best known for its commitment to making connections between craftspeople in developing countries and consumers in the United States. But ATA can also be very helpful to the American craftsperson interested in mass-producing products economically. Craftspeople interested in working with ATA should first telephone and discuss their plans with a staff member to determine whether ATA could make a connection. ATA will then ask for a more detailed proposal describing the products and outlining the work to be done. If ATA makes a match, the craftsperson travels to the artisans' country and works in their workshop with them until they can produce products to the American craftsperson's specifications. If ATA has an ongoing project in the country, they can oversee the work being done. Potter Jonathan Adler's line of pottery and textiles is produced in Peru as a result of a connection made through ATA. You can learn more about Aid to Artisans at www.aidtoartisans.org.

Perspective from a Life in Crafts
Meryl Waitz

Meryl Waitz is a designer-craftsperson working in New York City. Her designs include jewelry and decorative home accessories.

Were there early influences that led you to work in the crafts field?

Meryl: The household I grew up in had a "do it yourself" atmosphere. In my family, deciding you wanted to create something and just going ahead and making it were totally acceptable and encouraged. The concept was "nothing is impossible." When it came to creating things, there were no obstacles, you just figured it out, and you made it. There was no real focus on design, just on the joy of making things. My dad built the furniture, all the food was homemade by my mom, and we sewed our own clothes. We were a total craft house.

I often think I was attracted to jewelry-making and silversmithing because it was one medium that no one worked in at home and therefore was more exotic and attractive. I learned the technical skills in high school and was fascinated with soldering, polishing, and being able to make objects out of metal. I also loved wearing the jewelry I fabricated.

Can you discuss your education and if you would do it this way again.

Meryl: When I was getting ready to go to college, I was encouraged to pursue something academic. I discovered architecture as a field of study that incorporated both academics and creativity. An architectural education teaches you how to think, to problem solve, and to design anything, from a teaspoon to a building. It turned out I wasn't interested in anything as large in scale as a building. When I had an assignment to design a house, I was always thinking about the doorknobs and light switches. My craftsmanship in silversmithing provided me the immediate gratification of seeing my designs realized, something architecture does not do. In retrospect my education at Parsons was an excellent education, and I feel lucky that I stumbled upon architecture.

And what led you to designing household accessories like picture frames and canisters?

Meryl: My strong background in design allowed me to expand beyond jewelry into designing other objects for the home. I have no loyalty to a narrow set of techniques. I will use any skills and processes available to achieve the desired look of an object. A piece could be fabricated directly in metal or carved out of wax and cast.

Can you discuss the move from making your own work to having it produced by others?

Meryl: A few years into selling my handmade pieces, there was a shift in the consumer market that changed my approach to the work. The quality of overseas manufacturing was improving. The costs for these products were much lower than handmade items, and expensive handmade craft started selling less and less. Many imported products knocked off designs from craftspeople like myself and the look of the pieces was good enough for the customer. In addition, this type of manufacturing process could take the cost of a handmade item from $50 to $12 retail. This had an effect on the perceived value of my work; it watered it down. I had to make a choice as a businessperson, rather than as a craftsperson: Do I keep producing my work the same way, or do I join in this manufacturing craze? After much consideration, I made a conscious decision to change the way I was making my work. The design is the same. I never compromise on that. I did begin to manufacture the work differently. Keeping the craft as the inspiration, I moved away from making the products myself. For me, letting go of the techniques wasn't painful; therefore, letting go of making it myself was possible. I did miss the hands-on aspect, though. Ultimately the fact that I can design objects, have the prototypes made by another person, and then manufacture it in another country, is quite satisfying because in the end all I really wanted was for the piece to be the piece I designed. More people can enjoy my work because we can mass-produce it.

I know you design on the computer; can you talk about that process?

What I find I can create on my computer screen is amazing. For me it is the same thought process as sitting with a piece of metal and sawing out a shape. Now I am sitting at my computer and bending and manipulating shapes digitally. I can create presentations in a professional way for meetings. My clients can actually see the items they are interested in buying rendered in 3-D.

You have become a very good businesswoman as well as a highly respected designer-craftsperson. What advice would you give to someone starting out in this field?

Meryl: I think the best advice I could give is to encourage young craftspeople not to shy away from the business aspects of this field if the goal is to support themselves through their craft; to pay attention to shifts and changes in the marketplace, and to develop a way to respond to those shifts accordingly. It's not always easy to do this, but I believe if you understand that making big changes along the way might have to occur, it will make it easier when it does. And of course always approach your designs with integrity.

169

Perspective from a Life in Crafts
John Russell

John I. Russell is the executive director of Brookfield Craft Center in Brookfield, Connecticut, a nationally recognized non-profit school and gallery for fine craftsmanship. I asked John to comment on the role of crafts in the 21st Century and what he wrote follows:

Man is essentially a toolmaker, and a woman or man's ability to create life's necessities with his or her own hands has been critical in creating our civilization. Until the Industrial Revolution, everyone had some training in craftsmanship because most everything had to be made by hand. In today's world, I believe people have a spiritual need to reconnect with what is essentially one of the most human of experiences: to work with one's hands, mind, and eyes to create beauty and utility. People also need to maintain a reverence for materials and a respect for the skills and values of fine craftsmanship, as well as the highest consideration for those who will eventually use the object created.

The modern American craft movement has undergone a number of cycles. During the second half of the 20th century there was a tremendous resurgence in the interest in fine crafts. As we move into the early 21st century, we are seeing the digital information age move quickly into a digital-entertainment age. Today, students in high schools communicate on their cell phones or hand-held computers. They sit in front of screens to play games and search for information. Most decisions they make are digital: yes or no, go there or don't go there. Some people question whether making things by hand has any value, role, or place in post-modern life.

One of our missions is to reach younger generations with the message that the handmade creative process still exists and still has relevance; that it's something they should try, and that they may discover it offers another path they can take. One of the things we find at Brookfield is that when young people discover our "analog" world by making something using the hand-eye-mind linkage, they embrace it, and it enables them in powerful ways. They learn to "communicate" with the materials they use, and they find that these materials "talk back"—as they make adjustments; the materials make adjustments. The process of making an object with their own hands becomes a different process and a refreshing change from the yes-or-no, on-or-off digital world that is increasingly consuming their attention.

As an educational organization we have a heightened responsibility to augment the work of the public schools. Recently we received foundation support to provide tuition-free scholarships for area high school students to take classes at the Center. The creative processes they discover here are applicable in many other "real world" situations, not just in the artistic world. The high-tech industry wants creative, hard-working, skillful people committed to problem solving, people who can meet deadlines, and who can work in ensemble situations, and can innovate. These are the skills we provide to high-school students.

We believe a generational change is leading our industry away from that place in which it prospered during the 1950s through the end of the last century. In order to be relevant and viable in the future, we must make the essence of the handcraft ethic relate to the realities of our global popular culture without sacrificing the core values that have lasted so long.

Our organization focuses on what the fine crafts community has to offer that other "world views" can't provide. For us building community means educating and enfranchising people into our heritage and value system. While it's essential to teach the basic skills needed to make fine craftwork, we also need to focus on teaching values, particularly the intrinsic human values embodied by creating something with your own hands. After all, it's the rich human connection we derive from handmade work that separates the fine crafts world from the commercial world.

We don't feel that our mission of "preserving the skills and values of fine craftsmanship and creative design" is endangered in any way. In fact, it is perhaps more important in our post-modern, post-industrial world than ever before. As robotic assembly and computer-aided design create more and more of the products we use, the role of the handmade object becomes more and more essential to our quality of life.

America's fine-crafts community may, however, be endangered in the commercial business sense because it is becoming increasingly difficult for the creators of fine craftwork to make a living in their field, given the overwhelming pressures of the global economy.

How America's fine crafts artists will successfully deal with the new global competition has yet to be determined. But, in order to survive, craftspeople will have to consider the possibility that their products, designs,

and intellectual property may, in fact, be copied or otherwise appropriated by the larger world of global commerce, which of course is the same reality that businesses all over the world face.

We strongly believe that the proliferation of imported goods that "look like" American handmade products but that sell for a fraction of the price of U.S.- made work, can be successfully addressed by educating the consumer. We take every opportunity to tell the public that the objects in our gallery are handmade by American artists and that their purchases directly support those artists and the non-profit school that trains them. We strive to instill in them the powerful doctrine and value system at the heart of the American craft movement, which does not exploit labor, material, tools, or the consumer's faith in the durability and functionality of the product.

While there are those who speculate that our handmade culture is disappearing, we do not believe this

171

The rich human connection separates the fine crafts world from the commercial world.

will come to pass. We believe that the highest values of civilization will eventually, prevail. In looking to the future, we must ask, "What do we, as humans, want our planet to become?" Hopefully, not a global consumer culture chasing ever cheaper, ever inferior, mass-produced goods with little lasting value (a shallow and discounted world view), but rather a global culture of diversity which empowers our humanity, individuality, and creativity and produces goods that celebrate the human spirit and the diversity of world cultures. We believe that these values will help our culture to prosper and will enable our artisans to "follow their bliss," as Joseph Campbell would wish for us all.

NURTURING YOUR CREATIVITY

You are different. You were given the ability to express yourself through the creation of beautiful objects. In addition, you have the motivation to develop your creativity. Today you are supporting yourself, or are about to, using your creative abilities backed up by keen business skills. You wouldn't be using this book if you didn't want to compete in the marketplace. Creative people, like businesspeople, often get lost in their work and neglect their body and jeopardize their health. Don't let this happen to you. A strong healthy body is essential to the work you do. Commit yourself to eating well, exercising regularly, and getting enough sleep.

YOUR BODY, YOUR WORK

We all know how important regular exercise is for maintaining a healthy body, but we may not connect exercise to the creative process. But it makes sense, doesn't it? You make your living using your body; it has to be in good

At Penland School of Crafts a healthy body equals a lively mind, so movement classes are part of the regular curriculum.
PHOTO BY DANA MOORE

shape for all the lifting and lugging you do each day. Your brain, the source of your creativity, is going to function best when it is part of a healthy, strong body. Therefore, it's important to your work to devote time each day to body care.

I find it's easier to follow through with an exercise program if I commit to exercising at the same time each day. There are health clubs everywhere these days. However, it isn't necessary to go to a club to do this. Apply as much creativity to this part of your life as you do to the work in your studio. I have a friend who hates exercise classes, but loves to put on a CD and dance around the studio. No membership is necessary to begin a running or walking regime; the only expense is the cost of the correct pair of shoes. You can run or walk anywhere; try to plan a route with some hills for an extra workout. In the winter you can walk indoors at a mall or in the halls if you live or work in a large building. I use the stairs for an extra workout.

I walk nearly every day and find the mindlessness of this a great relief from my otherwise thought-crowded day. I don't take a portable music player, and I try to stay away from thoughts bigger than where to cross the street and whether to go left or right. I find when I get down to work that my head is clear and responsive. Other artists have noted that some of their best ideas, or solutions to problems, come spontaneously when they have cleared the mental board by a simple walk or a swim. Suddenly an elegant solution or a clever new idea will pop into the waiting empty space, an unexpected perk of taking good care of your physical self.

● Feeding the Body

Eating well is essential to success in your creative career. Without good food your body tires more easily, and your creativity may be dulled. I know how hard it is to leave a project to prepare and eat a meal. But you must.

Red Weldon Sandlin, an Atlanta-based ceramic artist, solves this problem by preparing extra large meals when she has time to cook and then freezing the intentional leftovers for easy warm-ups later. A writer friend spent some time at an art colony where lunch was packed and left for you outside your studio door so you could eat without interrupting the flow of work. She replicates this process in her own studio by packing lunch in the morning, before she sits down to work. Then it's ready whenever she finds a natural break in the workday to enjoy it.

Snacking is not intrinsically a bad way to nourish yourself in a long working day, but it needs to be the right snack. Sugary treats or snacks high in salt and fat may provide a sudden burst but will actually deplete your energy over time. Plan ahead and stock your work space with healthy items, like pre-washed and cut fruit and vegetables, hummus or bean dip with healthy chips, or protein-packed treats for a steady supply of energy through the workday.

● To Sleep, Perchance to Dream?

We all know how important it is to get enough sleep. You can't be creative with a tired body and brain. It is also dangerous to operate machinery without proper amounts of rest. But we all get caught up in our work and at times overwhelmed by the number of tasks we need to accomplish. And we are all guilty of cutting sleep short to work under deadline pressure.

Use a calendar to plan for the busy times. When you know you have a large number of orders due on a particular date, plan backwards and allocate enough time so you don't have to work extra long days with no days off, or cut short your sleeping time.

Limit the amount of stimulating drinks or food in the three hours before you go to bed so your nutrition engine won't be revving. Listen to soothing music and

Nature can be a great inpiration. Fabric artist, Sydney Wilson makes the most of it in the sunroom of her Asheville, NC home.
PHOTO COURTESY
FIBERARTS

turn the lights low for an hour before going to bed and put your work aside. Curiously, many creative people who nurture their sleep time discover that great ideas often come to them in dreams, or in the moments just as they are waking in the morning.

CREATIVE ENCOURAGEMENTS

Feed your creative spirit with regular field trips to galleries and museums in search of inspiration.
PHOTO BY
JOHN WIDMAN

Make your studio a live-in sketchbook filled with creative encouragements. Put up postcards of great art, or art you think is great. Tear motivational images from magazines and pin them up with the postcards. Gather fabric swatches and pin them up in combinations that might end up in your product.

If you find inspiration in the natural world, gather bits of it and bring the leaves, stones, shells, feathers, and flowers into your studio. Look at them for clues about color combinations, textures, and forms. You may find

inspiration from other, not so natural, found objects such as crushed soda cans, rusted pieces of metal, broken bits of glass and plastic, or weather-worn wood. Bring them in, too. Think about having a place to make a display using your found inspirational materials. Like a sketch, let it change and evolve as you add to it.

In addition to the living sketchbook, by all means keep an actual sketchbook. Try to have it with you at all times. Use it to record even the tiniest thoughts, either in pictures or words. Be sure not to edit yourself: It's all good. Regularly take a look at your thoughts and develop the ones that continue to have any appeal. I believe that the more sketching activity and idea development you go through, the stronger your designs will be.

FIELD TRIPS

Take a weekly trip to a creativity energizer. This could be the zoo, a walk on a beach, or a hike through the woods. For some of us a trip to an urban center with visits to a museum or commercial gallery or a walk in a busy neighborhood is just what we need. You know what gets you excited about your art; make a plan and go somewhere to nurture this part of you. Use this time to feed your creativity. Take time to appreciate what you are seeing and experiencing. Use your sketchbook to record your thoughts and reactions. Gather something to add to the display in your studio. Work at being in the moment and not letting yourself hurry through this time or be distracted by thoughts of the tasks waiting for you in the studio.

PLAYING WITH PROBLEMS

I think setting design problems for yourself is a very good way to enrich your creativity and your technical skills. Some time ago a Jungian therapist told me that the only way to grow creatively is to give yourself permission to explore ideas as you did in kindergarten. One way to do this would be to focus on one element of your work, and imagine ways that you could do it differently.

For instance, a jeweler could set up a problem related to clasps; a weaver could explore the possibilities of a new color combination; or a potter could explore a new form. In each case I would urge you to play and develop the maximum number of solutions. In addition, you will want to stay tuned to the new materials that appear in your field. A good way to do this is to include using them in your design challenges.

STAY IN TOUCH

Have a plan for regularly connecting with artists in your area, either over coffee or during a morning walk. Keep in touch with your shops or galleries. Make it clear to them that you welcome and expect feedback about your work and information about what kinds of things are selling well for them. Consider asking a more experienced person to function as a mentor to you and think about offering to be a mentor for someone with less experience than you: This is an amazing way to keep your creative side jumping.

While the changing world presents many serious challenges to the American craftsperson, my experiences working daily with both craftspeople and the consumers who buy handcrafted products indicate that it is also a time of great possibility. Using your powerful individual creativity, I am confident that you will be able to adapt to the changes the contemporary scene demands, and in the process create objects that are useful, beautiful and distinctive. Your individual creativity will be part of the collective energy that will carry us forward and allow the handmade movement to continue to flourish in the 21st century.

Spending time with your colleagues is not only fun, but will help you stretch your imagination.
PHOTO BY JOHN WIDMAN

Marketing Costs Inventory

Expense	Jan	Feb	Mar	Apr	May	June	July	Aug	Sept	Oct	Nov	Dec	Total
Booth Rental													
Travel													
Graphic Design													
Photography													
Printing													
Advertising													
Credit Card Fee													
Bad Debts													
Marketing Labor													
Annual Total													

Overhead Costs Inventory

Expense	Jan	Feb	Mar	Apr	May	June	July	Aug	Sept	Oct	Nov	Dec	Total
Rent/Mortgage													
Property Taxes													
Health Insurance													
Business Insurance													
Loan Payments													
Phone													
Gas													
Electric													
Office Supplies													
Payroll*													
Miscellaneous													
												Annual Total	

* not directly related to production

Pricing Sheet

Material Costs (from worksheet) _____ _____
                                  single   annual total

Labor Costs (from worksheet)   _____ _____
                                  single   annual total

Overhead Costs _____ X _____ = _____
                 annual total % of production

Marketing Costs _____ X _____ = _____
                  annual total % of production

Total Annual Production Costs _____ _____ _____

Estimated Number to be Produced _____

_____ ÷ _____ = _____
Annual costs to produce   number to be made   cost per unit

Cost per unit   _____

Profit allowance _____

_____ wholesale cost

Simple Costs Worksheet

Item _____

Date put into production _____

Materials

Material	Amount used	Cost
Total Cost of Materials		

Labor

	Hours	$
Design Time		
Total Labor Costs		

Donald Clark began his career as a teacher, moved on to manage a small shopping center, then planned and opened a retail store. He worked briefly as a sales representative for a major giftware company. Currently he is a partner in P!NCH. a fine crafts store in Northhampton, Massachusetts, where he oversees buying and promotion, and in Ferrin Gallery, where he helps coordinate exhibition calendars and installations. In addition, he has juried numerous regional and national craft competitions. Through it all. he continues to create his own assemblages that have been shown nationally. He lives in Western Massachusetts.

ACKNOWLEDGMENTS

Many artists, photographers, and other sources contributed to this book. In addition to those who are cited in the text, we would like to thank:

Neue Pinakothek, Munich, for permission to reproduce Manet's painting, page 20.

The Smithsonian Institution for the use of excerpts from the oral history interview with Walter Nottingham, 2002 July 14–18 in the Archives of American Art, Smithsonian Institution. Also, Carol Owen, for her thoughtful questions.

DEDICATION

This book is for the women—Clara, Anna, Leslie, Nina, Ronni—who came along, and, as always, Joan.

INDEX